Norfolk Record Society
Volume LXX for 2006

COUNTRY AND CITY

The Wymondham Town Book
1585–1620

JOHN WILSON MA

Ordinances of the Norwich Carpenters' Company
1594 and 1684

PHILIP HOWARD MA, MPhil

John Aldrich of Eaton
Farm Accounts
1663–1667

ANDREW HICKLEY MA

Norfolk Record Society

Volume LXX for 2006

First published in 2006
by the Norfolk Record Society

ISBN 978-0-9538298-9-7

Produced by John Saunders Design & Production
Printed by Biddles Ltd. King's Lynn

Contents

General Introduction   vii

Editorial Practice   viii

Acknowledgments   ix

THE WYMONDHAM TOWN BOOK, 1585–1620

John Wilson editor

Introduction   I

Text   29

Glossary   168

ORDINANCES OF THE NORWICH CARPENTERS' COMPANY
1594 AND 1684

Philip Howard editor

Introduction   179

Text   189

JOHN ALDRICH OF EATON FARM ACCOUNTS

Andrew Hickley editor

Introduction   205

Text   211

Glossary   243

Index   245

MAPS

Parish of Wymondham circa 1600   x

Central Wymondham in the 17th century   157

General Introduction

Contrasting aspects of Norfolk's history in the sixteenth and seventeenth centuries are documented in this volume. Wymondham with its penumbra of rural hamlets was the County's largest unincorporated town. It was governed by the Seventeen, a hybrid body recruited in the mid-sixteenth century from the headboroughs of the manorial leet court and the feoffees of the townlands charity to form a self-perpetuating vestry. Funded by property acquired from the dissolution of Wymondham abbey and its many religious guilds, the Seventeen's responsibilities ranged from maintaining a grammar school, the upkeep of the great parish church and the repair of roads and bridges to the entertainment of visiting dignitaries and the destruction of sparrows. They also undertook poor relief especially by the subsidised sale of firewood, the remitting of rent, medical care, the support of orphans and the clothing of poor apprentices; and they oversaw the town's militiamen and armoury. There is much in their accounts on woodland management and the construction and repair of mostly timber-framed and thatched town property, including the rebuilding of the market cross after the disastrous fire of 1615.

The Norwich Carpenters' Company was a survivor from the medieval trade guild system. It is seen in ordinances agreed in 1594 and 1684 attempting to control the industry, maintain the apprenticeship system and by careful inspection to discover and punish defective workmanship. However, alien (that is, non-Norwich) carpenters with skills not available locally were permitted to practise, the immigrant communities were allowed their own separate company, and country carpenters could, for a fee, set up timber-framed buildings prefabricated outside the city. The company finally disbanded about 1740.

John Aldrich of Eaton, then a rural hamlet of Norwich, is a shadowy figure except in his precocious farming practices. His account book of 1663-7 shows him anticipating many of the innovations of the next century in an operation that included a sophisticated credit system. It involved the purchase at local fairs of Scotch, Irish and Cumberland cattle, their fattening over winter and sale, and the large-scale cultivation of turnips and other innovative crops in a mainly enclosed landscape. He diversified into sheep and cereals, especially barley, on his partly light-soil farm.

Editorial Practice

Original spelling is retained, but capitalisation has been modernised and abbreviations expanded. Insertions and interlineations are indicated by asterisks, * *, and deletions by angle brackets, < >. Marginalia are brought into the text and shown thus /....../. Missing words supplied by the editors are placed between square brackets and editorial comments and additions between square brackets and in italic.

Acknowledgments

All three documents are published by kind permission of the County Archivist, Dr John Alban, in whose custody they are. The Dean of Norwich, the Very Reverend Graham Smith, gave his consent, on behalf of the Chapter of Norwich Cathedral, to the publication of John Aldrich's account book.

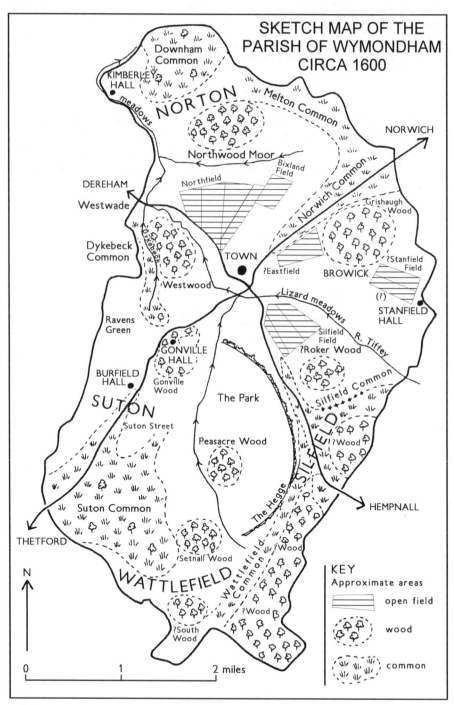

SKETCH MAP OF THE
PARISH OF WYMONDHAM
CIRCA 1600

Downham
Common

KIMBERLEY
HALL

meadows

NORTON

Melton Common

NORWICH

Northwood Moor

Bixland
Field

DEREHAM

Northfield

Norwich Common

Westwade

Grishaugh
Wood

Dykebeck
Common

TOWN

?Eastfield

BROWICK

?Stanfield
Field

Westwood

(?)

STANFIELD
HALL

Lizard meadows

R. Tiffey

Ravens
Green

Silfield
Field

GONVILLE
HALL

?Roker Wood

BURFIELD
HALL

Gonville
Wood

The Park

Silfield Common

SUTON

SILFIELD

?Wood

Suton Street

Peasacre Wood

Suton Common

The Hegge

HEMPNALL

THETFORD

?Wood

WATTLEFIELD

?Setnall Wood

Wattlefield Common

N

?Wood

?South
Wood

KEY
Approximate areas

open field

wood

common

0   1   2 miles

Map 1

The Wymondham Town Book 1585–1620

EDITED BY JOHN WILSON

Introduction

Setting the scene

The Town Book[1] contains the accounts of the Wymondham select vestry which was known in the early seventeenth century as 'The Seventeen'.[2] This body was dominated by a group of feoffees which took responsibility for the property of the religious guilds confiscated by the Crown in 1547[3] and largely returned to the town early in Elizabeth I's reign.[4] These houses and pieces of land formed the town 'stock'. Its income was meant to maintain a free grammar school and to be put to 'other godly uses in the town', for example repairing the parish church and helping relieve the poor. To these ends it recorded its income from the town lands and property and the ways in which it spent that money in its Town Book. This volume contains the text of the first extant volume from 1585 to 1620.

In 1600 Wymondham was the fourth largest town in Norfolk after Norwich, Yarmouth and King's Lynn with a population estimated at about 2,250, approximately half of which lived in the town proper.[5] With an area of 10,484 acres, the parish or township was the second largest in the

---

[1] Norfolk Record Office, MC 2379/3. It was presumably taken to Blickling by one of Hobart family, lords of the principal manor in Wymondham, and it now forms part of the Hobart of Blickling Collection in the Record Office.

[2] Much general background material is to be found in C.Barringer, R.Fowle and S.Spicer, eds, *Wymondham in the Seventeenth Century*, (Wymondham, 1993) and F.Blomefield, *An Essay Towards a Topographical History of the County of Norfolk* (1805–10), vol. ii, pp. 498–534. These will not be cited again in the notes. The following abbreviations will be used: Norfolk Record Office (NRO); The National Archives, Public Record Office (TNA, PRO); Wymondham Parish Records, in Wymondham Abbey (WPR); Wymondham Town Archive, in Wymondham Council Offices (WTA).

[3] The Act for the Dissolution of the Chantries of 1547 (1 Edward VI, c. 14) ordered the confiscation of the funds and sale of the lands of the religious guilds.

[4] WPR, Court of Chancery, state of facts and scheme of the Right Honorable Lord John Wodehouse and others concerning the Wymondham charities, 11/2/42. This document relates to a grant with origins dating back to 1559 which was enrolled among the records of the court of the Queen's manor at Wymondham in 1561.

[5] This estimate is based on the Communicant Returns of 1603 compiled by Simon Wells, vicar of Wymondham. See Blomefield vol. 11, p. 508.

county after Methwold (12,958 acres).[6] The town centre sits astride the main route from London to Norwich on the eastern side of the valley of the River Tiffey. The origins of the parish probably lay in a pre-Conquest estate and of the town in a Saxon settlement.[7] The original Domesday manor had been divided and sub-divided until by the sixteenth century there were thirteen manors, including eight principal ones, with their lands scattered between the four medieval divisions or shifts of Norton (virtually coterminous with Downham), Suton, Silfield and Wattlefield. Around the periphery of the parish were scattered hamlets such as Spooner Row and Stanfield.

The parish lies in the central clayland area of the boulder clay region of East Anglia. The soils varied from the heavy clays of the plateau to the lighter and sandier ones of the valleys of the Tiffey and its tributaries.[8] By about 1600 Wymondham still had as many as nine open fields which seem to have retained areas of strip cultivation among the increasing number of enclosures, some put down to grass. There were probably as many as 5,000 acres of field land, 3,000 acres of common and hundreds of acres of meadow and woodland. The farming activities within the region were described in 1596 as 'sustayned cheefelye by graseways, by Dayries and rearinge cattell . . .' in an area '. . . able to maintayne itself with Corne and to afforde an overplus to their neyboures of Suffolk'.[9] Thus about half the area was devoted to arable farming and the other half to meadows and pasture. One of the earliest complete Wymondham tithe books reveals that in 1647 by acreage of great tithes 34 per cent was devoted to mixed crops, 22 per cent to barley, 15 per cent to wheat and 2 per cent to summer ley. The small tithes show that cattle fattening, dairying and the production of wool were also important.[10] In addition there were over 3,000 acres of common land for grazing and still plentiful supplies of timber as was shown by the rebuilding of houses after the fire of 1615. Much of the timber was growing on meadow land and in at least seven woods mentioned by name not only in the Town Book but also in contemporary probate inventories, wills and leases.

[6] Contemporary documents refer more frequently to the whole area of Wymondham parish as 'the township' and the terms can be taken as synonymous.

[7] For a discussion of Wymondham's early development see T.Williamson, *The Origins of Norfolk* (Manchester, 1993), pp. 96–99.

[8] Wymondham's farming 'country' is explored in S. Wade Martins and T.Williamson, eds, *The Farming Journal of Randall Burroughes, 1794–1799* (Norfolk Record Society, lviii, 1995), pp. 3–5.

[9] W.Rye, *State Papers Relating to Musters, Beacons and Ship Money etc. in Norfolk* (Norwich, 1906), pp. 181–2.

[10] The number of animals tithed were calves 756, lambs 1045, ewes (estimated) 1308, sheep (estimated) 2645. 968_ acres of grass and herbage worth £27 were also included (see WPR, Wymondham tithe books 1647C and 1647D, 4/1/3, accn. 132 and 4/1/4, accn. 132).

The first surviving volume of the Wymondham Town Book is incomplete. In its original state it covered the years 1577 to 1626. The unbound manuscript now contains one hundred folio pages measuring approximately 8½ × 11 inches (20 × 29 centimetres) out of an estimated original total of 141.[11] The edited version is concerned with the thirty-one complete years in the manuscript, i.e. 1585–90 and 1594–1620 and one of the three incomplete years, i.e. 1590–91. The other very incomplete years are 1584–85 and 1620–21. The first nineteen folios covering approximately the years 1577–78 to 1583–84, three folios covering 1591–92 to 1593–94, part of 1620–21 and the years from 1621–22 to 1626–27 are missing.[12] The general condition of surviving pages is good and mostly written in legible hands. Some items of importance to the accountant are marked with a pointing hand or a cross. These refer especially to church and legal matters and to poor relief.

The series of Town Books, which runs almost without interruption from the sixteenth to the twentieth centuries, is a prime source for the study of Wymondham from the 1580s through to the early eighteenth century. The first two volumes are particularly rich in the details they reveal of life in a non-corporate town.[13] The township was adjusting to the changed religious scene after the Reformation and attempting to make use of some of the material resources it released for the benefit of its inhabitants. It was also developing new means of self-government by combining powers derived from the vestry, the townlands feoffees and the ancient court leet in a new body, the Seventeen, whose accounts these are. The devastating fire of 1615 marks a watershed in the development of the town as large areas had to be rebuilt and the lives of many people must have been seriously affected for several decades. Reference to the succeeding volume covering 1627–62 gives a clearer picture of how Wymondham was governed. Similarly, given the limitations of accounts as a source, some reference will be made to events before the mid-1580s.[14]

The accounts for each year are laid out in a fairly consistent pattern, beginning with an opening statement which indicates the name of the collector of the rents for all the lands and buildings belonging to the township and the year to which they refer. This is usually from Michaelmas

[11] That the Town Book began in 1577 is an estimate based on the number of folios, twenty-three, lacking or fragmentary at the front and the assumption that each year's accounts occupied an average of three folio pages.

[12] As the second volume of the accounts (NRO, ACC 200/156) begins in 1627 it is reasonable to suppose that the missing end pages covered 1621 to 1626 inclusive.

[13] From about 1648 the Town Book (NRO, ACC 1997/240) becomes increasingly formulaic and more narrowly focused on charitable purposes.

[14] WPR, the Wymondham Churchwardens' Accounts 1544–61, 7/1 and the reference in n. 4 (WPR, 11/2/42), are the principal sources for the mid-sixteenth century and the foundation of the grammar school.

(29 September) to Michaelmas, although the accounts are sometimes 'rendered up' several months later (p. 84). The entries begin with the balance brought forward from the previous year's accounts; only four years saw a deficit: 1590–91, 1598–99, 1603–04 and 1610–11 (pp. 50–1, 70, 92, 131). This is followed by other sources of income: 'free rents' for town property provided at a nominal rent to poor people who were, perhaps, mostly not expected to pay, rent for land and buildings from those who were expected to pay and interest on loans (usually at $7\frac{1}{2}$ per cent) made to individuals (p. 102). The expenditure section opened by 'respiting' the unpaid rent – thus counting it as expenditure – and then dealt with 'payments'. The account was completed by stating the size of the surplus or deficit to be taken forward into the following year. In addition, memoranda, often in the form of orders or resolutions, were recorded which determined the rules for future expenditure or the letting of town property.[15]

The regularity of practice outlined above was not often matched in the accounts. At a late stage, after the expenditure had been calculated, fresh income could suddenly be recorded, loans made, or a surplus taken out of the main account to top up the kitty for buying firewood which was sold at a subsidised rate to the poor.[16] The amount in this kitty was not referred to in every year's accounts but disappeared from view for a while only to reappear for a few years before fading from view yet again. There are many other seeming irregularities. On occasion money was taken from the wood fund to clear a deficit in the annual accounts and a substantial legal bill (p. 131). The unpaid rents were not respited but just not 'allowed' in a particular year. On one occasion free rents were counted twice as income (pp. 60–2). In 56 per cent of years (18) the arithmetic of the calculations is incorrect, in 44 per cent (14) correct. Faulty addition of one or more sections may be followed by an accurate final sum, suggesting that some of the calculations were incorrectly transcribed from scrap paper into the formal accounts. It may be that the continued use of Roman numerals for nearly all of the entries contributed to inaccuracy. On a few pages dot calculations were made in the left-hand margin with vertical or oblique lines used to separate pounds, shillings and pence, a method which may have overcome some of the difficulty of using Roman numerals.[17] In places there is evidence of attempts to audit the accounts by making alterations to correct mistakes. In a few years it is very difficult to determine what was

[15] See NRO, Wymondham Town Book 1627–62, ACC 2002/156, ff. 215v.-f. 217r. for a copy of a bye-law passed in 1635 by the Grishaugh leet. This indicates how business and personnel overlapped between different bodies in the township.

[16] It would seem that on p. 141 £6 8s 2d had been taken from the year's surplus of £17 0s 9d and may have been added to the wood fund, for by the end of the next year's accounts the wood fund had increased to £20 16s 1d.

[17] See C.T.Martin, *The Record Interpreter* (Dorking, 1976), pp. xii-xiii for a full explanation of dot calculations.

happening, for example in 1602–03. Occasionally, too, the townsmen's meeting refused to accept an element in the accounts, as in 1613–14, but this action is very unusual in this volume (p. 147). Arabic numerals were used only occasionally and sometimes to repeat totals already given in Roman form (p. 67, here £9 11s 8d). There is no apparent reason why fractions of a penny appear in only four years' accounts.[18] Latin words, phrases and complete sentences are used regularly but sparingly. There is evidence to suggest that the accounts were written up at times by a professional scrivener, or possibly by the parish clerk.[19]

How frequently the vestry met is unclear. It seems likely that it would have met once a year to pass the accounts, although such a meeting is only mentioned in thirteen of the years after 1604–05. Sometimes this is when payments for food and drink consumed in the course of business are recorded.[20] In 1606–07 it met four times, when exceptional circumstances demanded an all-day session, from breakfast to supper, 'fynishinge the accountes for the towne'. However, it may have met more frequently to transact business which did not give rise to accounting items. Just how the accounts were drawn up is unclear. Sometimes payments were made to reimburse members of the Seventeen for payments made or work done on behalf of the town. At other times bills seem to have been submitted to the vestry for payment, no doubt to be filed until the accounts were written up before the annual adoption meeting.

Even less certainly known is who attended these meetings. Usually the reference is to the 'Seventeen' or the 'townsmen' or the 'headboroughs', terms which can probably be taken as synonymous, but in 1608–09 not only the headboroughs but also 'the rest of the inhabitantes of the towne' met to take the accounts.[21] This raises the question of where the Seventeen met. Specific places are mentioned only twice in the accounts: the guildhouse in 1606–07 and the schoolhouse in 1619–20. Since at least 1561 the town had been in possession of two guildhouses, formerly property of religious guilds, namely the old guildhouse part of a messuage called Boystes and the new one part of a messuage called Pulleyns. A rental of c. 1560 relates: 'The inhabitants of Wymondham do hold freelie one messuage called Holie Roode guild howse . . .', seemingly a third one in the town's hands.[22] One of these was let by the township to William Daynes from

[18] 1588–89, 1589–90, 1590–91 and 1597–98.

[19] See p. 39. Peter Harvy was paid 2s as his fee, quite possibly for writing up the accounts, while John Symonds received his payment of 13s 4d for his work as collector.

[20] Bread, cakes, cheese and beer are mentioned at different times, firing on two occasions, presumably indicating a meeting delayed beyond Michaelmas. Evidence from after 1627 suggests that the accounts were often taken at Christmas.

[21] It may well be that in practice a few of the 'chief' inhabitants attended on behalf of the whole township.

[22] NRO, rental of Wymondham Grishaugh, MS 21046, 39 D 4.

1585 (p. 30) until 1599 and thereafter (p. 72), until it was burned down in
June 1615, to Alexander Foulsham.[23] These two men seem to have acted
not only as tenants but also as caretakers of the building for the town,
possibly letting out the hall for functions when the town's pewter, brass and
other 'implements' could be hired for a fee.[24] Foulsham was paid on
several occasions for food and drink consumed at meetings of the vestry,
further strengthening the idea that he acted as more than a mere tenant
(p. 122). Other evidence suggests that this building was used for official
business. Much money was spent on it from the 1590s onwards, far more
than would have been justified for other houses on the town's rental. An
extensive rolling programme of repairs to the fabric was carried out.[25]
Over £14 was spent on reed thatching in 1610–11, over 25 per cent of the
township's expenditure in a year of near average income (pp. 129–30).
Actions such as putting up the king's arms in the hall were as much expres-
sions of local pride as demonstrations of loyalty to the Crown (p. 113).
Much furniture was bought, possibly to make the hall of the guildhouse
suitable for public meetings and for hiring out.

Town government

Given the size of Wymondham and the prosperity which it enjoyed,
perhaps most notably in the fifteenth century, it is surprising that it did not
become a borough.[26] The reasons remain elusive but may have origins
buried in the early medieval period. The twelfth century began the process
of sub-dividing the manor of Wymondham, which may have inhibited the
grant of a borough charter. In 1107 the d'Albinis, lords of Wymondham,
founded the Benedictine Priory, combining monastery and parish church,
and in 1174 they founded a chapel dedicated to St Thomas Becket. A third
of the original manor was granted to the priory (which was later given
abbey status). Its dominance may have discouraged the establishment of a
borough, and the d'Albinis may have preferred to secure borough status
for their planned towns at Castle Rising and New Buckenham. Equally,
the township contained no leading gentry and no single wealthy family
dominated its affairs. Important gentry lived just outside the bounds of the
parish – the Wodehouses at Kimberley, the Knyvetts at Ashwellthorpe and
the Drurys at Besthorpe – or well beyond it in the case of the Cleres and

[23] This building is also referred to as 'the town house(s)' and the 'town hall'. 'Houses' in
Norfolk was sometimes used to describe a multi-roomed building.
[24] P. 59 contains entries showing that the town 'changed' its pewter, i.e. traded the old ware in
for new, and that it had a stamp made to mark it. On p. 57 hiring out the pewter is mentioned.
[25] See section on maintaining town property below for more details.
[26] For a fuller discussion of this topic see J.H.Wilson, 'Keeping Wymondham Working; the
Wymondham Town Book c.1585–c.1662', The Annual (Norfolk Archaeological and Historical
Research Group, 13, 2004), pp. 27–43.

then, from 1616, the Hobarts at Blickling. Local JPs had a statutory obligation to maintain law and order and to attend to matters concerning roads, bridges, poor relief, binding apprentices and granting begging licences. From time to time they intervened in Wymondham's affairs and liked to be seen doing their duty by local people, especially when pressed to do so by privy councillors from London or by a major county figure such as Sir Henry Hobart of Blickling, Lord Chief Justice of the Common Pleas, lord of the manors of Grishaugh, Cromwells and Rustens, who controlled the market and the leet which served the whole township.[27] Sir Henry can be found writing to a group of his fellow Norfolk justices in 1622 asserting his seniority, both as a national figure and the most powerful lord of the manor in Wymondham, over the matter of the impoverished bridewell keeper in the following terms:

> I as haveing more then ordinarie interrest in this towne and Countie doe earnestlie recommend the care of it unto you and shall be readie to acknowledge a particular obligacion unto you if at my request you take extraordinarie paines in it.[28]

He had made his commitment to Wymondham clear at the time of the fire of 1615. Not only did he set up the team which investigated and listed the losses suffered by individuals but he also urged the inhabitants to rebuild the market cross.[29]

A relatively small group of professional men, including a few lawyers, the vicar and the schoolmaster, were joined by a larger number of prosperous yeoman farmers and successful merchants to provide leadership within a centralised parochial organisation in the town. Long-term clashes between the monastery and the townsmen over which areas of the church should be used by parishioners had helped to intensify a shared and combative community feeling. The widespread involvement of many inhabitants in the running of the twelve religious guilds gave them an experience of responsibility and serving their community, not least by defending their parish church against the monks. These circumstances seem to have fostered a degree of self-reliance, even of independence, among the people of Wymondham. The townsmen were certainly very

[27] See three letters concerning various troubles in Wymondham in 1622 (Bodleian Library, Tanner Collection 243, 40v and 243, 41v) for an indication of how central government could affect life in Wymondham through the agency of Norfolk's leading gentry.

[28] Bodleian Library, Tanner Collection 243.

[29] See WPR, The Booke of the Losses by the Fire, 11th June, 1615, Class 23/1, for the setting up of the claim-collecting team and WPR, The humble petition of your Lordshipps pore tennanntes the inhabitantes of Wymondham, Class 23/8, no date but probably 1618, for Hobart's encouragement of the rebuilding of the market cross.

quick to resort to the law.[30] Sir Thomas Wilson in his *The State of England*
(1600) commented on the land-based wealth displayed by the leading
inhabitants of smaller towns such as Wymondham. This view was substan-
tiated in a survey of 1621 by means of which James I sought to determine
who could afford free gifts towards the cost of his military activities
abroad.[31] The town's wealth was such that in the fifteen Forehoe parishes
thirteen of the thirty-two people listed as eligible were from Wymondham.
These included:

> John Moore a mercer in very great tradinge, in lands £120 per annum & still
> purchaseth & buildethe muche   £30
>
> Thomas Weld an attorney at the common lawe: in great practise: £400 a yere
> in lands purchased: £300 a yere in lands by his wyfe at this instaunt offerethe
> £1800 for an other purchase & lyvethe at a meane rate: he may well lend
> above a £100 yett hee is sett downe butt at a hundred   £100
>
> Philipp Cullyer cheefe cunstable a yeoman, a hundred pounds per annum:
> riche besides, never a childe: but good to the pore   £30
>
> John Ballyston yeoman, an usurer a good estate of lands in reversion, very
> riche in stocke & offereth to buy the farme he useth valued at £2050   £20

Men of similar standing in Wymondham society formed the body of
feoffees which took charge of the townlands charity created by Elizabeth I.
This foundation was confirmed at a meeting of the court of the Queen's
manor in 1561.[32] What seems to have happened by the 1580s is that this
group had merged with the earlier members of what may have been originally an open vestry to become a select one called the Seventeen
Headboroughs or the Seventeen. This earlier vestry implemented the work
of the four, annually elected, churchwardens and that of other parish officials. The incomplete set of churchwardens' accounts surviving from 1544
to 1561 shows that it was both serving the church and carrying out the
civil, secular, duties which the Tudors were imposing upon it.[33] It was also
adjusting to a new future following the dissolution of Wymondham Abbey.
For example, in 1539 and 1540 it used donations from religious guilds to
purchase land and disused Abbey buildings, including their roof lead, from
the Crown.[34] In 1550–2, as the churchwardens' accounts show, the 'hoole

---

[30] See NRO, KNY 471, 372 x1, the copy of a letter from Sir Thomas Knyvett to Sir
Nathaniel Bacon in 1607 in which he mentions a suit between himself and the 'unruly' people
of Wymondham.

[31] W.Hudson, ed., 'Assessment of the Hundred of Forehoe, Norfolk, in 1621', *Norfolk
Archaeology* xxii (1923), pp, 258–309.

[32] WPR, Court of Chancery state facts concerning the Wymondham charities, 11/2/42.

[33] WPR, Wymondham Churchwardens' Accounts 1544–61, 7/1.

[34] WPR, The Account Book of the Gild of the Nativity of the Blessed Virgin, 1458–1544,

inhabitantes' sold to an Ipswich merchant Thomas Cowper six bells and lead to fund the purchase of a house and land that formerly belonged to the guild of St Thomas Becket, thus forming the basis for an enlarged town 'stock'.[35] From 1561 the new townlands feoffees were in a material sense legatees of the abbey and religious guilds. In providing a grammar school they were replacing the school which had been maintained by the monastery with a more limited clientele and purpose.[36] John Flowerdew, a sergeant at law from Hethersett, enraged the parishioners by carrying out the demolition of the abbey buildings in such an insensitive manner that he left the south side of the nave exposed to the weather. This led to their purchase of some of the remaining monastic buildings and Becket's Chapel. They then set about repairing the south aisle of the building they had long used as the parish church.

Sparse surviving evidence makes it difficult to trace developments in the town's affairs between 1561 and 1585. What can be gleaned, principally from Blomefield, is that because of a period of negligence by the feoffees the roof of Becket's Chapel was stripped of lead and thus, for a time, the school did not operate. Following complaints the Privy Council intervened in 1570 to ensure that the chapel was repaired and a master installed to teach pupils in the grammar school. The school, by 1585 operating with Master Leverington at the helm (p. 31), significantly increased the vestry's responsibilities. As stated above, after 1561 the churchwardens were joined in the vestry by the feoffees of the townlands charity. There was a marked overlap in personnel between the charity and the mid-sixteenth century vestry. Five of the thirteen feoffees named in 1561 had served as churchwardens in the previous four years.[37] From 1585 onwards the churchwardens were presenting their accounts to the vestry meeting for approval and major items from their work were detailed in the Town Book (p. 35). The only full churchwardens' accounts for the sixteenth century are for 1544–1561; those scraps which survive, for the late seventeenth century, were perhaps ephemeral notes to be discarded after their approval by the town meeting.

Details of expenditure on many items required by the parish church, present in the churchwardens' accounts, are not found in the Town Book, but there is a strong similarity between the structure of the last full church-

---

10/1/1, cited in B. Garrard, *Wymondham Parish Gilds in the Early Sixteenth Century* (Wymondham, 2003), p.31.

[35] WPR, Wymondham Churchwardens' Accounts 1544–61, 7/1.

[36] There seems to have been a school in operation for at least part of the time between the dissolution in 1536 and 1561. See WPR, Churchwardens' Accounts 1544–61, 7/1, entries for payment of schoolmaster in 1550–52 and 1552–54.

[37] John Foster, John Cooper, Valentine Knight alias Kett, John Mitchell and James Colman.

wardens' accounts and those in the Town Book from 1585 onwards. What is markedly different is the scale of income and expenditure, and upon what money is being spent. In the seven years down to 1561 the income of the vestry averaged £10 8s per annum; for the seven years from 1585 the average income recorded in the Town Book was £37 5s 1d. Expenditure for the two periods averaged £9 13s 7½d and £34 10s 8d respectively. This difference can be explained by the acquisition by the town in the intervening years of a sizeable stock of land and properties, much of it coming originally from the dissolved monastery and religious guilds. A significant part of this stock had been granted by the Crown to the feoffees of the townlands charity in 1561. Before 1561 there was an understandable preoccupation with the effects of the changes in religious practice which accompanied the Reformation.[38] The Town Book is concerned with a much wider and more secular range of business.

The select vestry

The only specific reference to membership of the select vestry is in an entry dated 3rd January 1604 (pp. 86–7; new style 1605). This takes the form of a list which confirms that it is safe to refer to the membership of the Seventeen as headboroughs. It was altered to include replacements for those who moved out of their division or died. Apart from Robert Cullyer who 'removed into Brathewaighte' (Browick) in 1606, the timing of these changes is unclear. It is a little difficult to arrive at a body of exactly seventeen headboroughs from this list. However, the areas which these men 'represented' are clear and include not only the four anciently established divisions or shifts but also peripheral hamlets like Browick and divisions of the town proper.

It is also difficult to relate the seventeen headboroughs of the Town Book to the much larger body of headboroughs appointed annually at the leet court. Headboroughs were the leading members of tithings, groups of ten or sometimes twelve men sworn at the leet court for mutual good behaviour. There were about seventy headboroughs in the whole township and it must be that it was from this body that some of the Seventeen came.[39] There are indications from the 1604/5 list that they formed in effect a select vestry. Five vestry members stayed in office until they died. Nepotism was possibly the reason Steven Agas took his father's place when Thomas Agas died in 1604. The collectors stayed in office for long periods

[38] The churchwardens' accounts provide evidence of land acquisition and of the practical effects of changes in religious practice. For a detailed examination of religious change in the mid-sixteenth century, see E.Duffy, *The Stripping of the Altars; Traditional Religion in England 1400–1580* (1992), pt. II.

[39] NRO, STA 219, manor of Wymondham Grishaugh court leet book 19 August 1657.

and may well have been generally honest but the opportunity for pecula-tion existed.[40] In 1613–14 John Reynolds had part of his accounts rejected by the headboroughs. When in 1622 five Norfolk J.P.s were asked by central government 'to take amongst other thinges the examinacion of the misimployeinge of the profittes of the towne landes of Wymondham' they found that

> . . . there is in Arthur Earle his hand collector of the same profittes £12 8s ld bysides £21 8s 6d with other moneyes which is still oweing from divers of the fermers of the said towne landes amounting in the whole to £50 12s 9d as appeareth upon an account delivered in by the said Arthur Earle whoe hath bine collector for seaven yeares [*correct figure nine*] ended at Michaelmas 1622.[41]

Had collectors' accounts been subject to more effective annual scrutiny, which would have been more likely with an open vestry, then in all proba-bility terms of office would have been shorter and malpractices more readily uncovered. Much of the evidence for the existence of a select vestry is to be found in the decades after 1620. In 1650 the Town Book records a meeting of fourteen headboroughs at which it was decided to solve the problem of how best to find a new collector[42]. That they were doing this by drawing lots between themselves tends to confirm the close nature of the vestry. Whatever its precise origins, the select vestry principle seems to have been accepted by the inhabitants of Wymondham in the seventeenth century. The geographical spread of the Seventeen would have made sense, enabling them to keep an eye on each sector of the parish as well as giving some show of representation.

Ultimately, the first volume of the Town Book does little to help explain how the headboroughs of the Seventeen were chosen. Members were among the more prosperous inhabitants of Wymondham and there is evidence, both before 1620 and after 1627, of membership running in families. The headboroughs listed in 1604/5 provide a useful starting-point. Some were linked by family. Thomas and Steven Agas were father and son and Steven was the cousin of Edward Agas, vicar from 1607. Status united Phillip Cullyer and Stephen Wiseman; they were yeomen and were much concerned with advancing their fortunes by shrewd prop-erty deals including doing business with each other. Six of the Seventeen were gentlemen, including the schoolmaster, Thomas Leverington. Education may have been a further bond because some of these men went to both the grammar school and to Cambridge. In 1574 Archbishop

[40] Nicholas Dickerson for eight, Arthur Earle for at least nine and John Reynolds for eleven years.
[41] Bodleian Library, Tanner Collection 243, f. 40v.
[42] NRO, Wymondham Town Book 1627–62, ACC 2002/156, f. 129r.

Matthew Parker had established a scholarship worth £20 p.a. to support a pupil from the Wymondham grammar school at Corpus Christi, his old college at Cambridge. Thomas Weld, a lawyer, acted as personal legal adviser to a number of the headboroughs and as a public one to the town. What appears to have happened in Wymondham is that after 1561 there was a shift in power from the churchwardens to the feoffees as the two bodies merged. This was not a difficult task given the degree of overlap in personnel and the considerable growth in income the feoffees brought to the vestry. At the same time the increasing secular demands made of the parish by Elizabeth I's government fell on, and helped shape, this emerging body.

The old network of manor courts was in operation at Wymondham and in good health at least until the Restoration. Each manor held its court baron, whose main business included land tenure and the orderly use of the common fields. Leet jurisdiction, concerned with petty delinquencies and neighbourhood offences, was attached to the senior manor of Grishaugh and extended over the whole township. The fines it exacted were frequently paid by the vestry on behalf of its members and the tenants of town properties. It also appointed the parish constables who in a sense spanned both the old manorial system of local control and the increasingly powerful vestry.[43] The other officials elected annually were ale tasters, searchers of fish and flesh and leather searchers, sealers and registers. Occasionally, the shared interests between the court leet of Grishaugh and the vestry led to a copy of proceedings in the leet being made in the Town Book. For example, in 1635 a bye-law passed in the Grishaugh leet to prevent incomers to the town becoming a burden on the poor rates was copied in.[44]

How long the select vestry held sway is difficult to determine with precision. However, the disputed appointment of a new schoolmaster, Mark Pert, in 1709 suggests that it could no longer count on automatic approval of its actions. This choice seems to have been unpopular with local people and a 'public town meeting of the chief inhabitants' overturned the vestry's decision, appointing the vicar, George Taylor, schoolmaster instead.[45] Eighty-three people put their names to this decision, seventeen by signing their names, the remainder by making their marks. This is the first event of this nature recorded in the Town Book, showing that the vestry could not always depend upon public agreement with its decisions.

---

[43] Constables worked directly under the half-hundred chief constable and in many of their duties responded to statutory demands channelled through the local JPs.

[44] NRO, Wymondham Town Book 1627–62, ACC 2002/156, ff. 215v.-217r.

[45] NRO, Wymondham Town Book 1663–1772 ACC 1997/240.

Church work

Many features of the vestry's work date from the time before the Tudors made the parish the unit of local civil administration. Of the parson – the vicar in Wymondham's case as the rectory had passed to the Crown at the dissolution of Wymondham Abbey – there is little mention in the accounts. He was not counted a member of the select vestry, but the vestry paid attention to his needs when they occurred. Some of his problems arose from his relatively impoverished living so money was lent and sometimes given to the vicar (pp. 47, 69).[46] Simon Wells, who combined the posts of vicar and schoolmaster for eight years of the seventeen he spent in the living, was treated with special consideration. Not only did the town pay £4 3s 2d towards searches and legal actions related to his rights as vicar but in 1590–91 he was given £6 without explanation (pp. 50-1, 84). His courage led to extra payments being made to him 'in consideracion of burying the people in the time of the visitacion' (of the plague) in 1602–03. The only mention of Edward Agas, vicar 1607–29, is in the remnant of the torn out accounts for 1620–21 when he was paid £10 'for the buildinge of him a studdye att the vickaridge' after its destruction in the fire of 1615.

While the vicar was seemingly seldom involved, the churchwardens feature more prominently in the town's accounts, but only when dealing with major matters seen as directly relevant to their traditional role. As suggested earlier (p. 9), the minutiae of their work were probably too transient in nature to warrant inclusion in the main accounts. They are to be found, after their year in office, in some cases paying in money still in their hands and in others receiving reimbursement for payments made then (p. 46). This seems to prove that the town chest was controlled by the headboroughs and not the churchwardens by the 1580s. However, within the accounts, the churchwardens can be seen exercising their long-standing responsibilities. One of these was to keep the parish church in good repair. Thus we find them paying for extensive work in the nave by Thomas Goodwin, the Norwich master mason, in 1584–85,[47] for work on nave pillars by William Ebbes in 1585–86, and on the west tower by Goodwin again in 1599–1600. In the latter case the churchwardens negotiated the contract in June 1599. It was agreed that Goodwin would repair the south side of the west tower from the bell soller to the top of the 'steaple'.[48]

On 5 January 1601 a special payment of £5 was made to the church-wardens to offset the considerable cost of repairing the bells. Other forms

---

[46] After the fire in 1615 an appeal was made to the clergy of Norfolk to give money for the relief of Edward Agas, vicar of Wymondham, ' . . . his living (though a veary great chardge) yet verie small mayntenance, having but half the small tithes and none of the offerings . . . ' (Bodleian Library, Tanner, 137)

[47] Indicated by a fragmentary page at the beginning of the book, not printed here.

[48] WPR 7/4/32 (Welch 3/5).

of maintenance included retaining the services of John Clere, a glazier, and providing him with a town house at a reduced rent to keep the windows of the church in good repair. The entries in 1585–86 under the heading 'Chirche' give some indication of the materials which had to be bought for repair work (pp. 32–3). In 1607–08 Knightes and Clayborne were paid 5s for 'mendinge the organs'. A variety of minor items included making a lectern, a vestry door key, and the church bier. Payments were received for burials within the parish church (p. 76). One of the duties of churchwardens was to present crimes relating to the church, clergy and parishioners to the bishop's and archdeacon's courts when visitations occurred. This involved the often very considerable expense of entertaining ecclesiastical officials, sometimes including the bishop himself. In 1603–04 the bishop's 'charges' at the visitation cost £8 and again in 1619–20 a visit by his lordship cost £6 10s 9d. Even when a lesser diocesan official, the chancellor John Overall, came in 1617–18 he brought with him a retinue consisting of 'Mr Doctor Norrys a commyssioner . . . the preacher the register servauntes & clarkes dyvers'. These all had to be wined and dined; their horses alone cost 5s for hay and oats.

One religious celebration which survived the Reformation was that of Rogationtide. In 1567 Archbishop Matthew Parker provided 6s 8d a year for a sermon to be preached on Rogation Monday either by the master or one of the fellows of Corpus Christi, Cambridge. In 1574 the links with Corpus had been increased through the Matthew Parker scholarship for Wymondham grammar school pupils. Thus upon 'Gang' Monday the grammar school pupils joined a procession and a 'scholar' from Cambridge preached a sermon (pp. 95, 155).[49] There is no direct reference to the pupils taking part before 1629–30, but it is reasonable to suppose that they did. A Town Book entry in that year reads, 'Paide for beere & cakes for the gramer schollers when they went the pressession 2s 6d'.

There is good evidence for the existence of a parish clerk in the churchwardens' accounts prior to 1561 and, quite separately, of two sextons. By contrast there are no references in the Town Book to a clerk until 1607–08. Entries then make it clear that the clerk was hired for a quarterly wage of 15s, and work was done on a house for him to live in before he was installed (p. 111 to p. 113 inclusive). Wages were regularly paid to a clerk until the end of 1609–10 but not thereafter. It appears that, apart from the exceptional years, the churchwardens were paying a clerk from within their own budget and thus no mention of him was made in the Town Book. It seems unlikely that Wymondham had no clerk before 1607 and it is well established that in 1615 Thomas King became clerk and

---

[49] If this procession was a true beating of the bounds, the event must have been spread over several days for some parts of the parish were over six miles apart.

sexton at the age of fifteen and served until he died in 1680.[50] No mention at all is made of sextons in the Town Book down to 1620, but bell ringing, often a duty of sextons, was paid for on two occasions (pp. 135, 146).

Relieving poverty

Even before the formation of the townlands charity it had been a statutory duty of churchwardens to help relieve the poor.[51] By 1563 the idea of appealing to parishioners to give alms had been found wanting and JPs were empowered to use compulsion to extract money.[52] From 1576 the able-bodied poor were to be provided by the town with the basic tools and raw materials (wool, hemp, flax and iron) needed to produce goods which could then be sold to buy further materials.[53] The Elizabethan system reached its maturity in the Poor Relief Act of 1598.[54] This confirmed that relief was organised by the churchwardens with the newly-created over-seers of the poor and paid for by poor rates. Four overseers were to be elected annually and approved by local justices. Apart from maintaining a free grammar school, the feoffees were expected, according to Blomefield, to devote their remaining funds to other charitable purposes, one of which was poor relief. Thus part of the townlands charity's money supplemented the poor rates in a variety of ways, but the statutory system of poor relief operated separately and there are few direct references to it in the first Town Book. In the years between 1585 and the late seventeenth century the 'collector', who was appointed annually, distributed additional moneys in support of the poor.[55]

Until the late 1640s the vestry provided only two types of relief to all poor people; bread or corn and firewood were sold to the poor at a subsidised price (pp. 70, 100). One source of wood was the enclosed pasture land known as Teddes Close in Silfield. The vestry treated this asset with great care and ensured that the gates, hedges and ditches were kept in good repair (pp. 91, 150). Additional costs were incurred for carting and stacking wood and hiring barn space in which to store it. Wood was in continuous and strong demand so it was easy for the vestry to raise income by selling it at its full market price. This meant it was always likely to be

[50] Clerks were commonly appointed for life. A memorial in Wymondham Abbey records that he was clerk and sexton for 65 years and died in 1680.

[51] An Act for the punishment of sturdy vagabonds and beggars, 22 Henry VIII, c. 12.

[52] 5 Eliz. I, c. 3.

[53] 18 Eliz. I, c. 3.

[54] 39 Eliz. I, c. 3.

[55] The only exception was around 1660 when, for a brief spell, lump sums were handed by the vestry to the four overseers and no other money was distributed to the poor by the collector.

stolen (pp. 31, 95, 161). Otherwise relief from charity funds tended to be directed to the particular needs of individual paupers.[56]

One major preoccupation was the support of orphans and illegitimate or 'town' children. The Town Book reveals that the vestry was paying families for the upkeep of such children: in 1586 Thomas Sporle was paid 1s 8d 'for kepyng of a towne chylde' and in 1587 Jone Lenard received 6s 8d for keeping 'one of John Frances chyldren'. Some were fostered by local women before being bound apprentice. Arranging apprenticeships for poor children was a task that belonged to the parish or petty constables. While there is no indication that the vestry was inspecting their accounts, it was paying fairly frequently for the clothing of apprentices and their indentures and yet constables are not mentioned as the agents in these transactions (pp. 117–18, 144–5). The boys were usually consigned to a trade apprenticeship and a smaller number of girls probably to domestic service (p. 145). Often details were given of 'apparelinge', as in 1610–11 when Gibbes went to Thomas Kett and £1 0s 9d was spent on his clothing (p. 129).

Sometimes it is clear that the town wished to rid itself of responsibility for an illegitimate child or perhaps a child born to an incomer who threatened to stay and become a charge on the rates (p. 159). By contrast the town paid for many types of medical attention for its own poor. It could show considerable compassion and dig deep into its funds, including paying for the treatment of serious complaints such as 'fallinge sickenes' (epilepsy) (p. 155) at one of the five lazar houses outside the gates of Norwich. This sometimes necessitated paying for a visit by a proctor to consider the merits of a case, as in 1589–90 (pp. 47). On this occasion the sick person was accepted and the town made a payment of £1 10s to 'John Gyllyngforde for & towardes the helyng of . . . Chambelen'. Sometimes, the outcome was less happy and determined by necessity. When the plague struck in 1602–03 £3 6s 6d was given to those confined to their houses. Between October 1603 and January 1604 the town paid Henry Kett, the plague watchman, £18 8s 4d 'to kepe in those where the syckenes was'. A surgeon's work was expensive as was demonstrated in 1617–18 when £3 6s 8d was paid to 'Mr Wylliam Wells for the cuttinge of Lemondes legg which the surgeons had'. In 1605–06 £1 was given to a poor apprentice, Christian Smythe, 'being lame & diseased, towardes his going to the bathe' (p.101). Money was also given to 'releeve poore women to laye in'. Finally, when a pauper died the town often paid for a winding sheet.

---

[56] From the late 1640s onwards small payments were made regularly to a relatively large number of the poor.

Controlling the poor

The Elizabethan Poor Law of 1576 had first required that JPs set up houses of correction in their local areas, but it was not until 1598, a time when poverty and unemployment in Wymondham were mounting concerns for local JPs, that the building of a bridewell at Wymondham was ordered.[57] This was intended in part to punish those who would not work freely in return for relief. The Town Book only provides confirmation that a bridewell existed in the town by 1618–19. In that year reference is made to an area of the town as 'nere the Game Place nowe Bridewell'. Local justices had obtained the use of a medieval merchant's house as a bridewell which in turn had led to the name for the area being changed (p. 161). Furthermore, it is possible to trace the background to this development in the accounts. In October 1603 a booth was built in Wymondham for the justices to sit in at the Sessions (p. 83). These were probably one of the first divisional or 'petty' sessions which had grown out of the so-called 'bridewell sessions' held between quarter sessions to supervise the running of the new bridewells.[58] In 1613–14 the JPs were in Wymondham 'in the case for the releife of the poore'. The following year the town paid charges for a meeting of the justices 'concerning the relief of the poore at Wymondham' and in 1619–20 they met in the town again (pp. 144, 149, 167). In 1622, as we have seen, a crisis in the management of the town's funds led to active intervention by two judges of Assize directing that the running of the bridewell should be improved.[59] The letter from the judges reveals just how bad conditions were for the poor in Wymondham.

> . . . there are at this instant some Sabboath dayes twelve or more prayed for in the church and readie to perish for want of foode, the number of the severall persons of poore being in the same towne about 400. . . . that the keeper of the house of correccion hath noe stocke in his handes to sett the idle & obstinate people on worke, but onelie interrest of some moneyes, and the keeper not fittinge to be there partlie by reason of his povertie, but principallie by reason of the misdemeanors of him & his people. And lastlie . . . there are 33 alehouses within the said towne which suckes the thrifte from a nomber of those poore people . . .

The sequel to these developments, again strictly outside the time-frame of the first Town Book, was the order by local JPs in 1631 that the vestry set up a workhouse. This was again done as cheaply as possible. Richard

---

[57] A.Hassell Smith, *County and Court: Government and Politics in Norfolk, 1558–1603* (Oxford, 1974), p. 104.

[58] *County and Court*, pp. 104–5.

[59] Bodleian Library, Tanner 234 f. 40v. and 243, f. 41v.

Male and John Inglishe were cleared out of their town houses in Town Green so that the headboroughs could obey their statutory duty to 'set the poor on work'.[60]

Maintaining town property

From 1561 onwards the town stock of land and property increased considerably as did the income it produced. By 1600 the township maintained approximately thirteen town houses, two town shops, the parish church and the schoolhouse (Becket's Chapel and perhaps a second building), the guildhouse and the market cross. It was also responsible for the town wells, pumps, gates, fences, bridges, stocks, pillory and cuckstool. The town lands had increased to about forty-five acres. The proportion of the town's expenditure devoted to building activity between 1585 and 1620 varied from 0.7 per cent to 53.4 per cent, the maximum sum spent in one year being £35 6s 1d immediately after the great fire of 1615. This was the period of maximum expenditure: by comparison, a maximum of only 28.6 per cent of expenditure was building-related between 1627 and the outbreak of the Civil War. On average over the years fully recorded in the first volume of the Town Book 22.6 per cent of expenditure was on buildings; for the period to 1642 it averaged 10.9 per cent. Figures for the later stages of the seventeenth century were generally lower still.

Payment for the repair of town houses occurred in the most years (22 out of 32), followed by the guildhouse (17), church (16), schoolhouse (11), wells (9), bridges (8), shops (5), fences (5), cuckstool (3) and pumps (2), although the latter were only installed about 1616.

Town houses were timber-framed buildings whose main need was protection against the weather; rethatching and wall repairs were frequently required (pp. 59, 91, 152). The most popular 'thacking' materials were rye, barley and winter corn straw, the last two often being weakened by threshing. The frequency with which some roofs had to be repaired suggests that, while many were willing to turn their hands to thatching, for a lasting result you needed the expertise of thatchers (pp. 135–6). Thus, in 1595–96, Benton was engaged to thatch houses in Town Green and paid 7s 6d for seven and a half days work, with his board (p. 59). For a quality result reed was used and it seems that both the raw material and expert craftsmen had to be brought in from outside. When part of the guildhouse roof was rethatched in 1610–11 reeders were hired from Norwich with all the attendant expense for their travel, board and lodging. Due to an apparent shortage of skilled reeders they were paid 3s 4d 'more then theire wages' (p. 130). In all £14 13s was spent on reed thatching, 23.3 per cent of

[60] Town Book 1627–42, NRO ACC 2002/156, f. 19v.

the town's expenditure for that year, but the remainder of the roof was tiled. This was a much cheaper operation than reed thatching; local pin tiles cost about 15s per thousand, reed £3 15s per hundred bundles. Nevertheless, money was lavished by the vestry on its guildhouse meeting-place. Between 1594 and its destruction by fire in 1615 much was done. Its walls were repinned, daubed for two days by five men and whitewashed. Its ground sills, brick and wooden floors, windows, doors, locks and fireplaces all received attention. In 1594–95 a new manteltree was installed in the kitchen and a new chimney, perhaps its first, in brick. Between 1606 and 1608 its interior was embellished with a royal coat of arms and furnished with new trestles, forms, stools, a dresser and a large table constructed from a thirty-seven foot tree (pp. 106–7, 111–13). It is quite clear that this building, like the market cross, was seen as an important symbol of Wymondham's pride in itself as an independent town.

The Town Book is a mine of detail about building materials and techniques used for the preparation of those materials. By about 1600 the timber frame of most houses rested on a plinth of brick or brick and flint (rather than flint alone) but it is difficult to be certain that references to the simultaneous purchase of brick and 'stone' do refer to dug flint and not freestone or indeed ordinary field stones (pp. 134–5). Much depends on the context. Bricks used for a variety of purposes, such as chimneys, hearths and bread ovens, came from kilns of brickmakers in the town or masons like Henry Wade or from the estates of enterprising gentry (pp. 106,123). Wattle and daub was used to fill the gaps between studs with 'splentes' often of oak or hazel used to form the vertical framework. Spills of split hazel, oak and ash were commonly used as horizontals woven between these splints. Splint yarn of hemp was often employed in walls and internal partitions, in the place of spills, to form a crude grid with splints. A clay daub mixture was slapped onto the wattling and in Wymondham the outside walls were covered with lime plaster containing hair from the glover or tanner and then lime washed (p. 106). References abound to digging sand, to large quantities of lime and to their delivery, the raw materials of mortar (p. 111). Oak was used for most building purposes with ash and other timber occasional alternatives (p. 135). The steps by which timber was prepared can be traced in detail. After trees were cut down, often in Teddes Close, the smaller branches were cut off ('shredded') and the trunk hewn into board stocks. A variety of items was then produced, either by pit-sawing for boards and planks or by riving for heart and sap laths or paling to erect round yards. While green oak was generally used, some boards were water seasoned and then 'perked' or stacked wigwam fashion to dry out. Transporting timber to the building site was expensive. The 1920 boards for work at the schoolhouse in 1615–16 cost £2 4s. 4d. to cut and season. Transport, including the cost of rope and stays used in loading and dinners and beer for the carters, was 21s 6d (pp. 152).

Iron was used in a variety of ways. Nails are often mentioned; the names of some explain their function, e.g. lath, lead, plank and board nails. Pale nails were for fencing but threepenny, fourpenny and great nails tell us more about cost and size than function. Brads – headless nails – were also used. Local smiths made and supplied nails. Hinges of the hook and hingle or gemowe type were common, as were iron rings to operate snecks or latches. Door locks and keys needed frequent attention. Crampets or crampons and anchors were employed to hold together blocks of stone or timbers; manteltrees were anchored to the brick or stonework of fireplaces. Old ironwork was too valuable to discard and was reworked (p. 31).[61] Iron bars were employed to carry glazing, iron wedges being driven in between the horizontal and vertical bars used to support lattices of glazing to tighten them (p. 118). Lead sheets laid over boards covered the church roof. The resident glazier, John Clere, used the reliable high temperature of ash billets to melt lead when casting cames for the diamond lattices and pouring it into sockets to hold iron bars in place (p. 130). Lead was supplied by Norwich ironmongers, e.g. Henry Davy in 1586–87 (p. 36).

In 1588–89 a sequence of entries appears to relate to the building of a house in the churchyard (pp. 42–3). This is interesting because it not only brings together many of the building elements discussed above but also because it mentions raising the framework of the house and hinting that extra hands had to be called upon for this heavy task. In this pre-fire period, when the township had more money available for individual projects and there was less competition for timber, the quality of building materials was noticeably higher than after 1615. Not only was reed thatch used but the construction of two fireplaces was not skimped. Two manteltrees were purchased, at least one of which was supported on timber hearth trees rather than brick.

Some town houses seemed to need endless repairs, e.g. a nine-year series (1605–13) relating to the Widow Tooley's house on Norwood Common. So much attention was paid to the lady's house that it is tempting to suspect the Seventeen's motives in approving such a continuous programme of work. The reasons were probably the house's exposed position on the edge of a common and, more speculatively, her influence as the aunt of Philip Cullyer, a leading figure in the town's affairs. Changes of use could also occur. In 1613–14 a house belonging to the town was fitted with shop windows (p. 145).

Not surprisingly, the schoolhouse required frequent repairs to its windows and furniture, as did its locks and keys. The pupils who boarded also played their part for in 1615–16 the vestry had to pay a shilling 'for mattes for Mr Serjont Richardsons sones which were decayed by the

---

[61] John Palmer supplied crampets for work on the pillars in the nave of the parish church and also reworked some of them.

schollers'. The details of major expenditure on the school following the fire of 1615 leave some doubt about the identitiy of the schoolhouse. Presumably this was the timber-framed building mentioned on p. 152, not Becket's Chapel which does not seem to have been affected by the fire.[62] However, there is no direct evidence to prove the existence of a second building. Reference has already been made to work on the parish church, both major structural projects and the near-continuous round of less costly tasks (pp. 32–3).

The great fire of 1615

A major crisis in the history of Wymondham was the great fire which was started quite deliberately on 11 June 1615 'through the malicious & wicked practise of evill disposed persons'.[63] This affected 327 people and their families by causing damage estimated at £14,944 19s 0d. As many as 55 per cent of the *c.* 1125 people living in the town proper may have been affected by loss of housing and/or goods and this in a year when poverty in Wymondham was causing concern among local justices. The Book of Losses, drawn up in 1616, contains a claim for losses by 'the towneshipp of Wymondham in the schoolehouse & dyvers other houses, the markets crosse and dyvers goodes burnt in the guildhouse' amounting to £1000.[64] A detailed account of the fire depends in large measure upon documents other than the Town Book, but the scene is partly set within the accounts. From this limited evidence it appears that two things happened.

Firstly, the town set out with urgency to rebuild the schoolhouse and the market cross.[65] Both buildings were symbols of local pride and both had a pressing practical purpose. It seems possible that the visit by Sir Henry Hobart recorded in 1614–15 was to survey the damage and to urge the townsmen to rebuild as soon as possible. The market cross came under his ultimate authority. In the same accounts money was paid for the carriage of riven timber to the schoolhouse, probably to begin repairs, and in 1615–16 a large number of boards were cut for this rebuilding work (p. 152). Within the vestry there were individuals devoted to the town; Philip Cullyer (d. 1625), a prosperous yeoman, lent a total of £55 7s towards the rebuilding of the schoolhouse and the market cross (pp. 156, 163). He

[62] For a list of claims for losses in the fire, see WPR, Booke of the Losses by the Fire, 1615, 23/1.

[63] For a full discussion of the fire and its aftermath, see J.H.Wilson, 'The Great Fire of Wymondham 1615', *The Annual* (Norfolk Archaeological and Historical Research Group 10, 2001), pp. 29–42.

[64] WPR, Booke of the Losses by the Fire, class 23/1.

[65] By contrast the guildhouse was only mentioned when a 'platt' for a new one was paid for in 1620–21. No further reference to the guildhouse has been found. The Seventeen met in the schoolhouse from 1619–20 onwards.

further demonstrated his compassionate and charitable nature by building six almshouses at his own cost to relieve poor people who had suffered in the fire (pp. 154, 161–2). By 1618 the market cross was completed[66] and in 1618–19 Sir Henry Hobart was back in town to congratulate the headboroughs on their achievements.

Secondly, the headboroughs presented a brave face to the outside world almost seeming to deny the crisis that was upon them. They continued to entertain visiting dignitaries at considerable expense. Sir Henry cost £6 11s in 1614–15 alone. And yet, while they spent the best part of an average year's income on replacing the school and the cross, the collector, Arthur Earle, retained an average of £30 16s 3¾d between 1614–15 and 1619–20. It was this kind of behaviour, as we have already seen, that led to complaints reaching the Privy council from Wymondham in 1622. It may be that one reason for the apparent lack of reference to the fire in the Town Book is that Sir Henry and his fellow justices had set in motion the collection of claims arising from the fire and secured a royal brief under which claimants could expect some compensation.[67] It would be wrong to assume that all was rebuilt within a very few years of 1615. A document dated 1621 contains a list of sixteen tenements including the guildhouse that had not yet been rebuilt.[68] The bye-law of 1635[69] relating to the letting of town property excepted any cottage or dwelling house that was 'standinge & erected on the eleaventh day of June Anno Domini 1615 and then was wasted and consumed by fyer'. Some plots were still derelict twenty years after the fire.

Roads and bridges

Acts passed in 1531 (Statute of Bridges) and in 1555 (First Statute of Highways) had made justices responsible for the repair of bridges and roads. At parish level the work was to be organised by two surveyors of the highway on penalty of indictment by Quarter Sessions and the imposition of appropriate fines.[70] The main concern reflected in the Town Book is for

[66] Evidence for this survives in the form of a petition of the inhabitants to Sir Henry complaining that his 'officers' had erected shops around the new market cross. See Bodleian Library, Tanner Collection 243.

[67] See Bodleian Library, Tanner 242, 40v. and 243, 41v. No copy of the brief has been found but the distribution list has survived (WTA unlisted, A booke of the severall distributons made to every particlar person of the mony which came to the handes of the distributors toward their losses susteyned by the fire in Wymondham 11 *Junii* 1615) This shows that the brief raised £2,171 8s 5d and that on average the victims of the fire received a seventh of their claimed losses from this fund.

[68] TNA, PRO Survey of Wymondham and Aylsham 1621, E 317/360.

[69] NRO, Wymondham Town Book 1627–62, NRO ACC 2002/156, ff. 215v.-217r.

[70] 22 Henry VIII, c. 5 and 2 & 3 Philip and Mary, c. 11 respectively.

bridges to which there are about a dozen references. Those mentioned are Westwade, Tifford, Damgate, Half Mile, Mile and Bartlett's.[71] Of these the bridges at Westwade seemed the least reliable. Repairs to them were paid for in 1590–91, 1595–96, 1603–04 and 1615–16 (pp. 50, 58, 90, 152). The repair of bridges must have been the responsibility of the parish constables as in 1603–04 Richard Wytherley was amerced for Westwade bridges and in 1604–05 he is stated to be a constable when he was amerced for the butts. There were two patterns of action: to carry out repairs only when fined for default of bridges or when a crisis loomed.[72]

Sometimes the town was able to use legal arguments to avoid repairs and save money, as in 1612–13 when Francis Plomer appeared to an indictment found at the Sessions for Bartlett's Bridge which was discharged 'by reason yt was no common bridge for the passage of the Kinges leadge people'.[73]

Defending the town's legal interests

Throughout the period of the first volume of the Town Book the vestry showed a marked willingness to defend the town's interests in court. Officials were reimbursed for costs arising from their involvement in legal actions on behalf of the town. Small sums were paid in cases like that of Francis Plomer (p. 112). However, when Stephen Wiseman and Thomas Agas went to London to defend the suit against Sir Henry Woodhouse of Waxham for the town land in January 1599 their expenses amounted to £15 4s 4d, including 10s to hire a horse for Thomas (p. 70).

One charge on the town that continued to be paid needs to be explained. Each year at a cost varying between 5s and 11s the sheriff was paid for the allowance of the 'charter'. The nature of this charter is not made clear but it probably related to Wymondham's claim to the privilege of ancient demesne. Ancient demesne, land vested in the Crown in 1066, conferred on its tenants privileges including freedom from tolls at markets and fairs and exemption from serving on juries outside the parish. An attested extract from Domesday Book requested in 1582 by tenants of the manor of Wymondham[74] and further requests for official extracts in 1582 and 1583 show Wymondham claiming these privileges,[75] which were still remembered, and perhaps asserted, in the 19th century.[76] Significant especially for the operation of the market, it was crucial to ensure that the

---

[71] Where the last three were is unknown.

[72] As in 1616–17 (p. 156) when a gang of workmen was put to work on Damgate Bridge because some judges were expected to come over it.

[73] The Statute of Bridges of 1531 referred to bridges broken 'to the damage of the King's liege people'.

[74] WPR 11/2/3.

[75] TNA, PRO, Chancery File, Tower and Rolls C 260/171, October 1582 and May 1583.

[76] W.White, *History, Gazetteer, and Directory of Norfolk* (Sheffield, 1845), p. 444.

charter thus obtained was capable of resisting challenges.This need explains the sums expended for lawyers' advice about the charter, its renewal, and its recording in the Exchequer (pp. 39, 90, 96).

Some of the legal personnel acting for the town were Wymondham residents such as Thomas Funston, an attorney 'on the make', with close links with the Exchequer and with Lord Hunsdon at court, who in 1587–88 was paid for discharging men at the Michaelmas Sessions and recording the 'charter' in the Exchequer.[77] Most frequently mentioned was Thomas Weld senior, a much trusted lawyer, tackling issues varying from the renewal of the charter to the defence of Tedds Close in the Exchequer (p. 131). One particular case touched on in the accounts was the attempt to secure reduced entry fines in the King's (later the Prince's) manor. As early as 1609–10 Henry Gay was paid expenses of £5 for pursuing this cause. The problem was still not resolved by 1619–20 (p. 167). In 1620–21 Phillip Cullyer showed himself sufficiently public-spirited to travel, at the age of sixty-three, on several occasions to plead for a reduction on behalf of his less fortunate fellow citizens.[78] By the Restoration, the vestry was tending to concentrate on its central charitable purposes and shrug off matters which might bring costly legal actions in their wake.[79]

Spiritual privileges were not forgotten after the Reformation. Blomefield relates that when all the inhabitants of Wymondham tried to claim exemptions from the jurisdiction of the Bishop of Norwich in 1450, because the Abbey's tenants had them, their case was shown to be untenable. However, they managed to ensure that henceforth none should be compelled to attend the bishop's court at Norwich. In the churchwardens' accounts for 1550–52 there is an item for the expenses incurred when 'the Busshop of Canterbury visited for the establysshing of the libertie of the town of Wymondham'. This could well be a renewal of the privilege established about 1450 following the initial disruption caused by the Reformation. It is likely that 'pledyng of the lybertye for the spirituall courte' for which Dr Prethro was retained and which Mr Griggs registered in 1585–86 related to this old right as did a later payment to the bishop's secretary 'for the alowance of the pryvlledge' (pp. 31, 100).

[77] A.Hassell Smith and G.M.Baker, eds, *The Papers of Nathaniel Bacon of Stiffkey III, 1586–1595* (Norfolk Record Society, liii, 1987 and 1988), p. 340, n. 191.

[78] Philip Cullyer was paid £1 12s 'att his goeinge to London aboute the fynes for the Prince his Highnes mannor'.

[79] In the Town Book 1663–1772 (NRO, ACC 1997/240, f. 35) in a memorandum dated 31st May 1670 the vestry agreed that henceforth no money intended by donors to be given to 'the maynetenance of the schoole & other pious & charitable uses' should be spent on any bridges or 'causeies' belonging to the town.

Law and order

The local Justices had two officers helping them to enforce law and order: the chief constable and, responsible to him, the petty or parish constable. Wymondham had one of the two chief constables in the Forehoe hundred, the other being based at Hingham. Petty constables had their origins in the manorial system and in Wymondham they were appointed annually by the headboroughs within the Grishaugh leet .[80] In 1653 three were chosen by the headboroughs for Norton division including two for the town (Marketstead and Damgate, Vicar Street and Chapelgate) and one for the hamlets of Downham, Browick and Stanfield. Three further constables were appointed, one each for the remaining traditional divisions of Suton, Silfield and Wattlefield.[81] The petty constables formed the 'sharp end' of law enforcement and were directly answerable to the chief constable but on these duties, which included collecting county rates, returning the poor to their parish of birth and carrying out punishments such as whipping, the first Town Book is silent. However, repairs are mentioned to some of the instruments of punishment: the pillory, the cuckstool and the stocks (pp. 96, 134, 152).

The constables also had military duties. From Henry VIII's reign the increased fear of invasion had caused the lord lieutenants of Norfolk to hold frequent musters of the county militia. The Wymondham constables normally sent two men, occasionally four, to train with the hundred militia for between one and two days every two and a half years on average between 1585 and 1620. Norfolk was divided into seven divisions and the contingents from the thirty-three hundreds were shared between these divisions. Thus, in 1584, Wymondham sent its two men to join the Forehoe contingent of the divisional company, which included the hundreds of Depwade and Mitford, to train under its captain, Thomas Gawdy. They met at Carleton Rode on 6 July and again on 12 August to remedy any defects. In all Forehoe Hundred sent thirty-four to train with pikes, seventy-one with calivers (light muskets) and fifteen with longbows.[82] Constables had to maintain the parish butts for longbow practice but as the figures show these weapons were waning in importance during Elizabeth's reign. The last Town book reference to butts occurs in 1604–05 (p. 95). However, it was the constables' responsibility to keep the parish's arms and

[80] NRO, Wymondham Grishaugh, Court Leet of Lady Hobart, August 1653, STA 219

[81] An entry in the second Town Book (NRO ACC 2002/156, f. 77r.) states 'Paid Arthure Plowman, Jacob, Edward Parke, John Moore and Raph Jesopp by order from the townsmen £4 8s 6d which they beinge constables had laid out for pressinge & apparilinge of souldiors'. In a later entry John Reynolds, 'constable of Suton', was reimbursed for paying the coroner to register a suicide (f. 199v). These items would appear to incline the argument in favour of there being six petty constables of equal importance.

[82] NRO, NNAS C 3/1/9.

armour clean and in working order. There are numerous references to
pikes, swords, daggers, muskets, powder flasks, bandoliers, corselets and
helmets. Gunpowder, match and shot were also supplied to the trained
men (e.g. pp. 80, 95–6). Pay was one shilling per day; extra money for beer
was a short-lived experiment in the 1630s. Of the constables' duty to
impress men for military service there is but one fleeting reference in
1598–99 when conduct money is mentioned in a somewhat ambiguous
reference (p. 69).[83] This was a time of crisis in Ireland when extra soldiers
were needed to combat the successes of the Earl of Tyrone.

Conclusion

The first extant volume of the Town Book shows a non-borough town
conducting its affairs at a crucial time of adjustment to the effects of the
Reformation and the ever-extending control of statute on the local government of parishes. In many ways it is a rich resource – not least in what it
reveals about the variety of work which came within the vestry's ambit and
the very detailed information yielded up about the maintenance of timber-
framed buildings – and yet the document has to be related to a wider time
frame for its full significance to be revealed. The intimacy of early seventeenth-century life in a market town provides a major obstacle; everyone
knew each other in a relatively small community and so often we are not
told what office or status people held. Much has to be inferred from the
particular tasks they carried out. Further, it is possible to exaggerate the
significance for contemporaries of the growing importance of the vestry by
comparison with the role of the manor courts and their officers. The
administrative changes which were under way in Wymondham late in
Elizabeth I's reign were slow-acting in some respects. The bridewell only
found a permanent home twenty years after the great Poor Law had been
passed. A workhouse did not appear until 1631. It took the period of the
Civil Wars and the Interregnum to refocus the vestry upon its charitable
commitments. Poverty, fluctuations in trade and plague were all to have
significant effects upon Wymondham after 1620, as did the fire of 1615,
but these hardly impinge upon the first set of Town Book accounts. Such
limitations as there are do not prevent much that is warmly human from
showing through, whether it be the compassion shown for the sick and
needy or two joyful days of 'tryumfe', abetted by gunpowder and beer, to
mark the coronation of James I (p. 84).

---

[83] Conduct money met the costs of escorting recruited soldiers to their fighting unit.

Acknowledgements

The research for this study could not have been carried out without the support and approval of the Norfolk Record Office, Wymondham Town Archive and Wymondham Parish Records. The author is especially grateful for the kind encouragement, help and advice given him over many years by Janet Smith, Chris Barringer, Paul Cattermole and Hassell Smith.

The Wymondham Town Book 1585–1620

[1585-86]

The acompte of John Symondes junior collector for the rentes & fermes of & for all & syngler the landes and tenementes belongyn to the towneshepe of Wymondham acomptyng from the Feaste of Saynt Mychaell Tharchangell in the yere of our Lord 1585 ontyll the *sayd feaste in the* yere of our Lorde 1586 for one hoole yere then ended

	£	s	d
Firste he doth acompte for the arerage of his laste acompte	3	18	3
Item of Edwarde Crane		3	0
Item of Agnes Wyseman wedowe		1	10
Of Ales Frostyn *wedowe*		2	0
Of Robert Porter *for fre rent*			4
Of Peter Neve for fre rent			10
Of Wylliam Grene for fre rent			10
Of Edmund Culliour for fre rent			1
Of Wylliam Luce for ferme	2	0	0
Of Jefferye Stewarde for Teddes Cloose[1]	6	0	0
Of Thomas Amyas gent for a cloose at Bettes Lane		16	0
Of hym for halffe an acre of medow nere Kyddes Wyllowes		6	0
Of Robert Ryngwoode for a medow nere Salters Forde	1	0	0
Of hym for 4 acres of lande in the North Fylde		16	0
Of him for one acre in the Parkefylde		3	0
Of Thomas Grene for a medow nere Wyndams Cloase		10	0
Of hym for a nother parcell of medowe there nere Salters Forde		6	8
Of Robert Norton for a parcell of medowe nere Hockehams Carre		3	4
Of John Symondes junior for 8 acres *one roode* of land in dyverse peces	1	12	4

Summa   £18 6d

[f. 24v] Of Wylliam Sparham for one acre and a halffe of lande		6	0
Of Thomas Agas for halfe an acre of lande		2	0
Of Wylliam Kett for 2 acres & halfe of lande in Holme Fylde		8	4
Of Robert Hobbes for 2 acres of lande there and a parcell of medowe nere Wade Brygge		7	0

---

[1] Town meadowland in Silfield, also known as tenement Brixy, which provided a regular supply of timber and the largest rental income of the town's properties.

	£	s	d
Of Abbacooke Lawrence for a cloase nere Ryvaldes & 3 roodes of lande there	1	0	0
Of John Venyour gent for one acre of land in Claxwell furlong		4	0
Of Peter Pyttcher for a cloose cauled Howlyns in Howngate		14	0
Of Richard Rawlyn for 2 acres of land in the Northe Fylde & one acre in Byxelondfylde		10	0
Of Robert Wyseman for 2 acres 3 roodes of lande in the North Fylde		11	0
Of Loye Agas for 7 acres of lande there	1	8	0
Of Richard Apleton for 2 acres of land at Hellanes Ende in Stanbridge Fylde		6	8
Of John Sayer for 3 acres of lande in the Northe Fylde		9	0
Of John Symondes senior for an orteyarde		1	0
Of Henry Norton for 2 acres 3 roodes of land in the Northe Fylde		10	0
Of Thomas Woodcoke senior for 3 roodes of lande in Well Crofte		2	0
Of John Kensey gent for one cloase and 2 acres of lande		16	0
Of Master Thorneton for a parcell of medowe at Wade Brigge		4	0
Of John Busshe for 2 acres of lande in the Northe Fylde		6	0
Of Stephen Wade for 2 acres nere Teddes		9	0
Of John Kett for 3 roodes of lande nere Bettes Lane		3	0

Summa £8 17s

	£	s	d
[*f. 25r*] /x/ Of Thomas Talbotte[2] for one acre of lande lyeng in his cloose nere the Game Place		4	0
Of Antony Caryngton[3] clarke for a cloase at Norwood Grene	1	0	0
Of Cristopher Foxe for a cloase nere Hockhames	1	0	0
Of Wylliam Daynes for the towne howses and the pewter & all other thynges belongyng to the howse fyndyng reparacions	3	0	0
Of Raygnolde Kene for his howse	1	10	0
Of Antonye Englyshe for a tenement		16	8
Of John Tayler for the towne shoppe[4]		8	6
Of Edmund Fedymont for his howse		6	8
Of Robert Bettes for a tenement		6	8
Of Jone Symondes wedowe for a tenement		6	8
Of Wylliam Cooke for a tenement		6	8
Of Richard Elder for a tenement by yere		6	8

[2] Dr. Thomas Talbot (*c.* 1561–*c.* 1628) of Gonville Hall, judge in the vice-admiral's court 1592, J.P. 1600.

[3] Anthony Carrington, vicar of Wymondham *c.* 1581–89.

[4] The town shop was built against the east end of Becket's Chapel. By 1627–28 at the latest there was a second town shop at Bridewell rented out for 3s a year to William Thurston, a blacksmith.

	£	s	d
Of Maryon Meyere for a tenement by yere		6	8
Of the wedowe Ferme for a tenement by yere		6	8
Of Richard Cotton for a tenement by yere		6	8
Of John Palmer for 38 pownde of weight of the oulde iron crampettes wich came out of the pyllor in the chirche		3	1
Of Mr Caryngton for fyve score fagottes		9	0
Of Wylliam Sparham of one hundered wood		12	0
Of Artur Cossey for stone & coulder that came out of the chirche		1	3
Of Abbacooke Lawrence for one loade of woode		5	0
Item receyvyd of the wedowe Byrdde for buryeng her husbonde in the chirche		6	8

Summa   £12 9s 6d

The hoale some charged in this accompte is   £39 7s
Whereof he aske to be alowyde of fre rent on payd   9s 11d

And so the hoale some receyvyd is   £38 17s 1d

Where of

[f. 25v] /Paymentes/

	£	s	d
Firste payd to the Quenes Majesties balye for one hoole yeres rent	1	7	11
Item payd to the balye for the maner of Cromwells for the same tyme		4	1
Item payd the balye for the maner of Hethersetes			6
Item payd to Master Leveryngton[5] scolemaster for his yeres wages	15	0	0
Payd to Robert Bettes of an oulde dett for kepyng of a chyelde		9	0
Payd to Bartylmew Reade the therde of Febrewararye for makyng of a dore and for <layeng on> *settyng up* of a spondell and a sparre at Fedemontes howse			6
Payd to Wylliam Bucke for a pece to make a barfraye for Fedem[on]tes howse			4
/☞/ Payd for the prechars charges the 9 of Maye		3	4
Payd to John Gedneye[6] for a pottell of wynne geven to the comysaryes		2	0
Payd to Wylliam Ovyngton for syxe planckes for tables for the towne howse	1	0	0
/☞/ Payd to Doctor Prethro for pledyng of the lybertye for the spirituall courte		6	0

[5] Mr Thomas Leverington senior gent. was schoolmaster from *c.* 1584 until 1589 See N.H.Williams, *The History of Wymondham Grammar School, 1559–1903* (typescript in WTA). See n. 24 for details of his son.
[6] John Gedney seem likely to have owned an inn or a shop. He regularly supplied wine for important visitors to the town until 1595–96. Thereafter, until 1615–16, his widow Agnes continued to provide church wine, dinners for the Rogationtide preachers and refreshments when the town accounts were taken by the townsmen.

	£	s	d
Payd to Mr Griggs for regestring of it		3	4
Payd for my owen charges at Norwitche		1	0
Payd to Thomas Austen for fellyng and makyng of 2 hundered fyve skore & fyften fagottes of woode		4	2
Payd for caryng of the same woode		6	0

/ *Chirche*/

	£	s	d
Item payd to Wylliam Ebbes when he take the pyllor to make		1	0
Payd to Wylliam Berte for pykyng downe of stones for the chirche		2	10

Summa £19 1s

	£	s	d
[*f. 26r*] Payd to John Ferme for pickyng downe of stones for the chirche		2	10
Payd to Nykson for one chalder of lyme		4	8
Payd to John Kett for bryngyng home of syxe combes of lyme for the chirche		1	8
Payd to Wylliam Clarke for 2 dayes worke of hym & his man & a nother dayes worke of his man		4	6
Payd to Nykeson for halfe a chalder of lyme		2	4
Payd to Wylliam Buckenham for a payle			8
Payd to Thomas Stubbes for bringyng home of syxe combes of lyme and nyne stone of leade		1	10
Payd for one pownd & halfe of rosen			3
Payd for one pownde of waxe			10
Payd to Wylliam for workyng the newe pyllor	7	0	0
Payd to hym for a dayes worke whigtyng of the arches & for a dayes worke for mendyng of the buttresses agaynste the vestorye		2	0
Item geven to them to drynke			6
Payd to Henry Davy irone monger for nyne stone of leade		13	0
Payd to John Palmer for 4 score pownd and seven of irone crampettes		18	1
Payd to hym for one hundered nayles			6
Payd to John Dorant for one loade of sande			8
Payd to the mason & his man makeng up of the dore goyng in to Abye steple *2 dayes*		3	10
Payd Wylliam Ebbes in parte of payment for the newe pyllor		10	0
Payd to Thomas Combes the masone for whightyng of the oulde pyllor			10
Payd Wylliam Clarke & his man for dayes worke done at the chirche		2	9

Summa £10 11s 9d

	£	s	d
[f. 26v] Payd to Nyckeson for 2 chalder of lyme		9	4
Payd to John Palmer for newe workyng of thirtye pownde of the ould crampetes		2	6
Payd to hym for one hundered nayles			8
Payd to hym for halffe a hundered nayles			3
Payd to hym for 2 plates for the chirche ladder			4
Payd to Wylliam Rednalle for halffe a dayes worke done at the chirche			3
Payd to Wylliam Ebbes for workyng of the last pyllor	4	10	0
Payd to Wylliam Daynes for drynke when theye hadde done			3
Payd to Richard Coolye for 4 dayes worke for trymyng & whightyng of the wyndowes and arches		4	9
Payd to Wylliam Ebbes <& his boye> *for 4 dayes* worke of his boye & one dayes worke of hym selffe done at the chirche		4	6
Payd to Thomas Stubbes for bryngyng home of one chalder of lyme		2	8
Payd to Henry Norton for bryngyng home of a chalder of lyme		2	6
Payd to John Ferme for certen dayes worke done at the chirche		3	0
/☞/ Item payd to Thomas Agas when he went twyse to Norwitche to Sir Edward Clere[7] <who> for the gylde howses[8] & the landes to shewe the dedes		3	2
Item alowyd to hym for his fee		13	4

Summa £6 17s 6d

The hoole of the paymentes is £37 1s 3d

And so the recytes excede the paymentes £1 15s 10d

Memorandum that he have alowed to Thomas Agas for his fee for fyve yeres £1 5 0 upon his byll not charged in his acompte

[f. 27r]   **[1586-87]**

The acompte of John Symondes junior collector for the rentes & fermes of & for all the landes and tenementes belongyng to the townshepe of Wymondham acomptyng from the Feast of Saynt Mychaell Tharchangell in the yere of our Lorde God 1586 untyll the sayd feaste in the yere of our Lord God 1587 for one hoole yere then ended

Firste he doth acompte for tharerage of his laste acompte	1	15	10
Item of Edwar[d] Crane for the yere		3	0
Item of Agnes Wyseman for rent goyng out of her howse by yere		1	10

---

[7] Sir Edward Clere (1536–1606), of Blickling, a principal member of the Norfolk gentry, was a major landowner in Wymondham (see also n. 40).

[8] That is the guildhouse, sometimes referred to as the 'town hall', where the official business of the vestry was transacted.

	£	s	d
Item of Ales Frosten wedowe for rent goyng out of her howse		2	0
Item of Robert Mayhew for rent goyng out of his howse or yarde			4
Item of Peter Neve for rent goyng out of hys howse by yere			10
Item of Wylliam Grene for rent goyng out of his howse by yere			10
Item of Edmund Culliour for rent goyng out of a parcell of lande			1
Item of Wylliam Luce for ferme by yere	2	0	0
Item of John Castelton for the ferme of Teddes	6	0	0
Item of Richard Rawlyng for a cloase lyeyng at Bettes <Lane> *Dycke* and a parcell of medowe at Kyddes Wyllows & 2 acres of lande in the North Fylde & one acre in Byxlonde Fylde	2	3	4
Item of Robert Ryngwood for a medowe at Westwade & 4 acres of land in the Northe Fylde & one acre & a halffe in the Parke Fyllde by yere	1	19	0
Item of Thomas Grene for 2 porcels of medow at Salters Forde nere Westewade		16	8
Item of Henry Goche for a parcell of medow nere Hockhams Care		3	4

Summa   £15 7s 1d

	£	s	d
[*f. 27v*] Item of John Symondes junior for 8 acres <of> 1 rode of land in the Northe Fylde by yere	1	12	4
Item of Wylliam Sparham for a parcell of grownd somtyme a grove & one acre of lande by yere		6	0
Item of Thomas Agas for halffe one acre of lande by yere		2	0
Item of Wylliam Kett for 2*½* acres of lande in Byxelond Fylde by yere		8	4
Item of Robert Hobbes for 2 acres of lande in Byxelond Fylde & a parcell of medowe at Wade Brigge		7	0
Item of Abbacooke Lawrence for a closse at Ryvaldes & 3 rodes of land there	1	0	0
Item of John Vynyoure gent for one acre of lande in Claxwel Furlonge		4	0
Item of Peter Pitcher for a close cawled Howlyns by yere		14	0
Of Robert Wyseman for 2 acres 3 rodes of lande in the Northe Fylde by yere		11	0
Of Loye Agas for 7 acres of lande by yere	1	8	0
Of Robert Appleton for for [*sic*] 2 acres of lande at Hellanes Ende		6	8
Of John Sayer for 3 acres of lande in the Northe Fylde ner the wyndemylle		9	0
Of John Symondes for an orteyarde		1	0
Of Henry Norton for 2 acres 3 rodes of lande in the North Fylde		10	0
Of Thomas Woodcocke for 3 rodes in Suton		2	0

	£	s	d
Of John Kensey for one cloase next Dyggebeke Comon & 2 acres of lande nere Crownshaughe		16	0
Of Robert Thornton gent for a parcell of medowe nere Wade Brygge		4	0
Of John Busshe for 2 acres of lande nere Westewade by yere		6	0

Summa £9 7s 4d

	£	s	d
[f. 28r] Of Thomas Smyth for 2 acres of lande nere Tedds in Sylfylde		10	0
Of John Kett for 3 roodes of lande in the North Fylde ner Becks Dyck		3	0
Of Thomas Talbott gent for one acre of land lyeng in his cloase at the Game Place		4	0
Of Antony Caryngton vyker of Wymondham for a cloase next Norwoode Moore	1	0	0
Of Christopher Foxe for a cloase nere Hockhams	1	0	0
Of Wylliam Daynes for the guylde howses and the vessell by yere	3	0	0
Of Raignolde Kene for the howse he dwelyth in	1	10	0
Of Antony Engleshe for the howse at Blackenham		16	8
Of Randoll Downyng for the towne shoppe		12	0
Of Edmund Fedemonde his howse *nere the Fayer Lond* by yere		6	8
Of Robert Bettes for his howse theare by yere		6	8
Of Jone Symondes for her howse		6	8
Of Wylliam Cooke for his howse by yere		6	8
Of John Smyth for his howse by yere		6	8
Of the wedowe Meyes for her howse		6	8
Of the wedowe Ferme for her howse		6	8
Of Richard Cotton for his howse by yere		6	8
Item receyvyd of John Kensey gent for one oke		9	6
Item receyv[d] of Nycholas Dyckerson *8s* John Poll *8d* Thomas Woodcocke senior *4s 4d* & Nycholas Stocton [4d] chirche wardens this yere upon the determynacion of ther accompte		13	4
Item receyvyd of Edward Crane *8d* John Dorantt *1s 6d* Nycholas Baxeter *6s 9d* & Thomas Blys *6s 10d* chirche wardens upon the determynacion of ther acompte		15	9
Item receyvyd moare *of* Nycholas Baxter upon the determynacion of his acompte for the pore		1	8

Summa £13 9s 3d

The hole some rec. in this acompte is £38 3s 8d

Whereof he askythe to be alowed of fre rent on payd 9s 11d

And so the hoole some receyvyd is £37 13s 9d   Whereof payd

	£	s	d
[f. 28v] /**Paymentes**/			
Firste payde to the Quens Majestyes balye for one hole yeres rent with a henn	1	7	11
Item payd to the balye for the manner of Cromwells for one hoale yeres rent		4	1
Item payd to the balye for the manner of Hethersettes for one hoale yeres rent			6
Item payd to Master Leveryngton scolemaster for his hole yeres wages	15	0	0
/☞/ Item payd to Wylliam Edwardes proctor[9] without Saynt Benettes Gates for takyng in of Martha Meyes of our towne	1	7	4
/☞/ Item payd to Mr Cooke for his fee being of cowncell with the towne		10	0
Item to Robert Coleman for a bonde			4
Item payd to Thomas Sporle for kepyng of a towne chylde		1	8
Item payd to Mr Leveryngton for William Kett	4	0	0
/☞/ Item payd for the prechers charges		7	1
Item payd to Robert Marshall to make up his forty shelynges for kepyng the chylde		5	6
Item payd to the sheryff for takyng of knowledge of charter[10]		5	0
Item payd to Loye Agas of an oulde dett		7	6
Item payd to Robert Symondes for a planke for to make a dresser for the towne howse		7	0
Item payd to Thomas Stubbes for bringyng home of a <chalder of lyme> *fudder of leade*		2	4
Item payd to John Gedney for a quarte of wyne for the bysshope of Londons chaplen when he preched here			8
Item payd to Nycholas for the taske for the towne landes			8

Summa £24 7s 7d

	£	s	d
[f. 29r] /☞/ Item payd to Mr Godfrye beyng of cowncell with the towne		10	0
/☞/ Item payd to Robert Marshall for kepyng of Hornes chylde		13	4
Item payd to Henry Davy of Norwitche for one fudder & syxeten pownd of leade	10	1	6
Item payd to Robert Bettes for reparyng of the well wheare he dwellyth		3	4

[9] A proctor in this sense was an agent acting for a lazar house or hospital; one who collected alms on behalf of a former lazar house now turned charity hospital taking in poor people who were sick; the steward of a lazar house.

[10] See Introduction p. 23.

	£	s	d
Item payd Edmund Fedemonte for 2 dayes worke of a thacester &			
his man and for strawe		3	4
Item payd to John Symondes for his fee		13	4

Summa £12 4s 10d

And so the receytes excede the paymentes £1 1s 4d

Over & besydes eight shelynges receyvyd of the chirchewardens 8s

[f. 29v]   **[1587-88]**

The acompte of John Symondes junior collector for the rentes & fermes of & for all the landes and tenementes belongyng to the townshepe of Wymondham acomptyng from the Feaste of Saynt Michaell Tharchangell in the yere of our Lord God 1587 untyll the sayd feaste in the yere of our Lorde God 1588 for one hoale yere then ended

/Fre rentes/

Firste he doth accompte for tharerage of his laste accompte	1	1	4
Item of Edwarde Crane by yere		3	0
Of the wedow Wyseman for rent of her howse by yere		1	10
Of the wedowe Frostyn for rent by yere <4d>		2	0
Of Robert Mayhew for rent by yere			4
Of Peter Neve for rent by yere			10
Of Wylliam Grene for rent by yere			10
Of Edmund Culliour for rent by yere			1
Of Wylliam Luce for ferme by yere	2	0	0
Of <Ales> John Castelton for Teddes Cloase	6	0	0
Of Richard Rawlyng for a cloase at Beckes Lane & parcell of medowe at Kyddeswyllows and 2 acres of land in the North Fylde and one acre in Byxlonde Fylde	2	3	4
Of Robert Ryngwood for a medowe nere Westewade & 4 acres of lande in the North Fylde & one acre & a halffe in the Parkefylde	1	19	0
Of Thomas Grene for parcell of medowe nere Saltersforde & a medow nere Wyndams Cloase by yere		16	8
Of Henry Goche for a parcell of medowe nere Hockhams Carre		3	4
Of John Symondes junior for 8 acres <of lande> and one roode of land by yere	1	12	4

Summa £16 4s 11d

[f. 30r] Of Wylliam Sparham for a parcell of lande sometyme a grove & one acre of lande by yere		6	0
Item of Thomas Agas for halffe an acre of lande		2	0
Of Wylliam Kett for 2½ acres of lande in Holme Fylde by yere		8	4

	£	s	d
Of Robert Hobbes for 2 acres of lande in the same fylde & a parcell of medow nere Wade Brigge		7	0
Of AbbacookeLawrence for a cloase & 3 rodes of lande nere Ryvaldes	1	0	0
Of John Vynour gent for one acre of lande in Claxwell Furlong by yere		4	0
Of Peter Pitcher for a cloase caulde Howlyns		14	0
Of Robert Wyseman for 2 acres 3 rodes of lande in the North Fylde		11	0
Of Loye Agas for 7 acres of lande by yere	1	8	0
Of Richard Apleton for 2 acres of land at Hellans Ende		6	8
Of John Sayour for 3 acres of land in the Northe Fylde		9	0
Of John Symondes senior for an orteyarde		1	0
Of Henry Norton for 2 acres 3 roodes of lande		10	0
Of Thomas Woodcocke senior for 3 roodes of lande in Suton		2	0
Of John Kensey gent for a cloose nexte Dygbecke Comon & 2 acres of lande at Crowneshaughe		16	0
Of Robert Thornton gent for a parcell of medowe nere Wade Brigge		4	0
Of John Busshe for 2 acres of lande		6	0
Of Thomas Smythe for 2 acres of land nere Teddes		10	0
Of John Kett for 3 roodes of lande at Beckes Deike		3	0
Of Thomas Talbott gent for one acre of land in his cloose at the Game Place		4	0
Of Antony Caryngton for a cloase at Norwoode Mere nere the Claye Pittes	1	0	0

Summa £9 12s

[f. 30v] Of Cristopher Foxe for a cloase nere Hockhams	1	0	0
Of Wylliam Daynes for *all* the guylde howses and the pewter & other implementes	3	0	0
Of Raignolde Kene for his howse by yere	1	10	0
Of Antony Engleshe for the howse nere Blacke Inham		16	8
Of Randoll Downyng for the towne shoppe		12	0
Of Edmund Fedemond for the howse nere the Fayer Lande		6	8
Of Robert Bettes for the howse he dwellyth in		6	8
Of Jone Symondes for the howse she dwellyth in		6	8
Of Wylliam Cocke for the howse he dwellyth in		6	8
Of the wedow Meyse for the howse she dwellyth in		6	8
Of Mother Ferme the howse she dwellyth in		6	8
Of Richard Cotton for the howse he dwellyth in		6	8
Of John Smyth for the howse he dwellyth in		6	8
Item rec. for 2 hundered woode	1	0	0
Item rec. of the chirche wardens of the arerage of ther accompte		8	0

	£	s	d

Summa £11

The hoole some rec. this yere is   £36 16s 11d

Whereof he aske to be allowyd of rent on payd   9s 11d

And so the hoole some rec. <is> this yere is   £36 7s   Whereof paid

[*f. 31r*] /**Paymentes**/

	£	s	d
Firste payd to the Quenes balye for one hoole yeres rent with a rent henne	1	7	11
Item payd to the balye for the manner of Cromwells for one hoole yeres rent		4	1
Item payd to the balye for the manner of Hethersetes for one hoale yeres rent			6
Item payd to Mr Leveryngton scolemaster for his hoale yeres wages	15	0	0
/☞/ Item payd for Mr Townesendes charges for hym and his companye when he toke the muster on the Assencyon Daye	1	1	10
Item payd to Nycholas Baxter	1	4	0
/☞/ Item payd to Jone Lenard for kepyng one of John Frances chyldrn		6	8
Item payd to Richard Elder for stackyng of wood		1	0
Item payd to Mr Lovell for a muskett for the towne	1	13	4
Item to Nycholas Baxter for the taske of the towne landes in Downham			8
Item payd to Henry Appleyard gent for a corselett for the towne	2	0	0
Item payd to Mr Funston for dychargeyng of Wymondham men at Mychaelmes Sessyons		3	4
/☞/ Item payd to hym for recordyng the charter in the Excheker	4	0	0
/☞/ Item payd to Edwarde Crane for a well curbyll		3	0
Item payd to Symond Johnson for sawyng of the <well c> tymber for the well			10
Item payd to Bartyllmew Reade for makyng of the well howse at Wyll Daynes and for hewyng of a tree		4	8
Item payd for a planke for the keyes of the curbyll		1	0
Item payd to George Norton for halffe a hundered borde & 4 fotte		4	4
Item payd to Robert Symondes for ten foote of borde			7

Summa £27 17s 9d

	£	s	d
[*f. 31v*] Item payd to John Quayntrell for one hundered nayles			8
Item payd to Robert Carre for parte of his wages sence John Palmer was chirchewarden		14	10
/☞/ Item payd for the townsmens charges when they went to my Lord Bysshopps with the lybertye		3	10
Item to Peter Harvy for his fee		2	0

	£	s	d
Item payd to John Symondes for his fee		13	4

Summa £1 14s 8d

The hoale some of the paymentes is   £29 12s 5d

And so the receytes excede the paymentes   £5   15s

[*f. 32r*]   **[*1588-89*]**

The acompte of John Symondes junior collector for the rentes & fermes of & for all the landes and tenementes belongyng to the townshepe of Wymondham acomptyng from the Feaste of Saynt Mychaell Tharchangell in the yere of our Lord God 1588 ontyll the sayd feaste in the yere of our Lord God 1589 for one hoole yere then ended

/Fre rentes/

Fyrste he doth acompte for the arerage of his laste acompte	5	15	0
Item receyvyd of Edward Crane by yere		3	0
Item rec. of the wedowe Wyseman for rent goyng out of her howse by yere		1	10
Item of Ales Frostyn wedow for rent goyng owte of her howse by yere		2	0
Item receyvyd of Robert Mayhew for rent goyng out of his howse by yere			4
Item rec. of Peter Neve for rent goyng out of his howse by yere			10
Item of Wylliam Grene for rent goyng out of his howse by yere			10
Item of Edmund Culliour for rent of a parcell of his lande *by yere*			1
Item rec. of Wylliam Luce for ferme by yere	2	0	0
Of John Castylton for Teddes Close by yere	6	0	0
Of Richard Rawlyn for one closse at Beckes Lane one medowe at Kydeswelowes 2 acres of land in the North Fylde and one acre in Byxelond Fylde	2	3	4
Of Robert Ryngwood for a medowe nere West Wade 4 acres of land in the North Fylde and one acre & a halfe in the Parke Fylde	1	19	0
Of Thomas Grene for a parcell of medowe nere Salters Forde & another parcell there nere Wyndames Close by yere		16	8

Summa £19 2s 11d

[*f. 32v*] Of Henry Goche for a medowe nere Hockhams Care		3	4
Of John Symondes junior for 8 acres <of> and one rode of land by yere	1	12	4
Of Wylliam Sparham for a parcell of lande sometyme a grove & one acre of lande		6	0
Of Thomas Agas for halfe an acre of lande		2	0
Of Wylliam Kett for 2 acres & halfe of lande		8	4

	£	s	d
Of Robert Hobbes for 2 acres of lande and a parcell of medow at Wade Brigge		7	0
Of Abbacoke Lawrence for a closse and 3 rodes of lande nere Ryvaldes	1	10	0
Of John Venyour gent for one acre of lande		4	0
Of Peter Pitcher for a cloase in Hungate		14	0
Of Robert Wyseman for 2 acres 3 rodes of lande by yere		11	0
Of Loye Agas for 7 acres of lande	1	8	0
Of Richard Appleton for 2 acres of lande at Hellanes Ende		8	0
Of John Sayer for 3 acres of lande		9	0
Of John Symondes senior for an orteyarde nere the gylde howse		1	0
Of Henry Norton for 2 acres 3 rodes of lande		10	0
Of Thomas Woodcocke senior for 3 rodes of lande		2	0
Of John Kensey gent for a cloase nere Dykbecke Comon and 2 acres of lande nere Crowneshaughe *within his growndes*		16	0
Of Mr Thornton <of> for a parcell of medowe nere Wade Brygge by yere		4	0
Of John Busshe for 2 acres of lande		6	0
Of Thomas Smyth for 2 acres of lande		6	0
Of John Kett for 3 rodes of lande		3	0
Of Thomas Talbotte for one acre of land lyeng in his closse at the Game Place		4	0
Of Antony Caryngton for a closse at the Claye Pyttes nere Norwood Comon	1	0	0

Summa £11 9s

[f. 33r] Of Crystopher Foxe for a cloosse nere Hockhams	1	0	0

/Tenementes/

Of Wylliam Daynes for all the guylde howses and all the vessell & other implementes kepyng the sayd howses in good reparacions	3	0	0
Of Raignolde Kene for the howse over a gaynste the guylde howse kepyng it in reparacons	1	10	0
Of Antony Engleshe for the howse & grownd nere Blackinham		16	8
Of Randoll Downyng for the towne shoppe		12	0
Of Edmund Fedymond for the howse nere the Fayer Londe		6	8
Of Wylliam Bettes for another howse there		6	8
Of Jone Symondes wedowe for a howse		6	8
Of Wylliam Cocke for the howse he dwellyth in		6	8
Of John Smyth for the howse he dwellyth in		6	8
Of the wedowe Meyes for the howse she dwellyth in		6	8
Of Mother Ferme for the howse she dwellyth in		6	8

	£	s	d
Of Richard Cotton for the howse he dwellyth in		6	8

Summa £9 12s

The hoole some receyvyd this yere is   £40 3s 11d

Whereof he aske to be alowed of rentes onpayde   9s 11d

And so the hole some receyvyd this yere is   £39 14s

Whereof payd

[f. 33v] /**Paymentes**/

	£	s	d
Firste payd to the clarke of the market for dyschargeyng of the towne for a busshell and weyghtes		8	6
Item payd to the scolemaster for his hoale yeres wages	15	0	0
Item payd to the Quenes Majesties balye for one hole yeres rent with a rent hene	1	7	11
Item payd to the balye for the manner of Cromwells for one hole yeres rent		4	1
Item payd to the baly for the manner of Hethersettes for one hole yeres rent			6
Item payd to Robert Ryngwood for certen tymber for the howse in the chirche yarde	1	0	0
Item payd to hym moare for sparres for the same		2	4
Item payd for reste of the tymber for the same howse and for the caryage	3	0	0
Item payd Robert Reder for makynge of the chymney & pynnyng of the towne howse	1	0	0
Item payd to Andrewes & Engleshe for dawbyng & floryng of the same howse		14	0
Item payd for 3 pownde & halfe of hempe to splente the same howse			5
Item payd to Henry Gaye for 2 hundered splentes with the caryage		5	0
Item payd to Wylliam Clarke for settyng up of the same howse & fynysshyng of it	2	0	0
Item payd to Wylliam Daynes for meate and drynke for the carpendors & other company when the howse was raysed		6	0
Item payd for barly strawe for the claye and for the caryage		1	4
Item payd to John Queyntrell for nayles for the same howse			11
Item payd for 3 loades of straw with the cariage		13	6
Item payd for 6 loades of claye with the cariage		3	0
Item payd for 2 loades of sande with the cariage		2	0

Summa £26 9s 6d

	£	s	d
[f. 34r] Item payd to Elwyn for thackyng the same		12	0
Item payd for 4 fadome of rede for the same		2	0

	£	s	d
Item payd for 2 loade of sande with the cariage		2	0
Item payd for 2 chalder of lyme with the cariage		13	4
Item payd for broches & byndynges		1	6
Item payd to Mr Talbott for 2 thowsand brycke	1	0	0
Item payd for caryeng of the same breke		2	0
/☞/ Item payd for 2 gallons of wyne & one pownd of suger for my			
lorde juge		7	0
Item payd to John Queyntrell for 4 hundered & fortye leade nayles		5	10
Item payd moare to hym for halffe a hundred thre peny nayles			3
Item payd moare to hym for 4 pownd and a quarter of greate			
nayles		1	5
Item payd to hym for one hundered fower penye nayles & one			
hundered 3 pennye nayle		1	2
Item payd for 2 mandyltres for the howse		4	4
Item payd to Mr Talbotte for seven hundered brycke with the			
cariage		9	6
Item payd to Fraunces Queyntrell for halfe a hundered 3 penny			
nayle & thre peny worth of fower penye nayle			6
Item payd to Bartylmew Kett for castyng of claye		1	0
Item payd to John Queyntrell for 2 payer of hokes & hengyls for the			
dores		2	0
Item payd to hym sneckes ryngles and staples for the same dores			8
Item payd to Robert Foster for 2 payer of gemowes for the vyce			
dore of the same howse			8
Item payd to Waulter Queyntrell for one hundred & a halffe of			
4 penye nayle& one hundred <of> & alffe of 3 peny nayle &			
one [sic]		1	10

Summa £4 9s

	£	s	d
[f. 34v] Item payd for castyng of fower loades of claye			6
Item payd for caryeng of the same		2	0
Item payd for 2 harthe tres			6
Item payd to Andrewes for makyng of the 2 harthes & for stoppyng			
of 3 holes in the pynyng			10
Item payd Wylliam Clarke for nayles wiche he fetched for the			
chirche			9½
Item payd to him for 2 steppes			3
Item payd for shetyng the leade		3	4
Item payd to hym for 4 hundred borde for the chirche & the howse	1	10	0
Item payd for halffe a hundred & ten pales for Kenes yarde		4	0
Item payd for a quarter of pales and a rayle & the settyng		2	4

	£	s	d
Item payd to John Queyntrell for barres for the chirche wyndowes & mendyng of oulde barres & for nayles that Clere occupyed a bought the wyndowes		7	3
Item payd to Wylliam Pratt for thynges that he bought for the chirche that is to saye for byllett for woode for the plomer and a planke for the glaser & other thynges		14	2
Item <for> payd to Raphe Fytlyng for borde & other thynges for the plomer		3	9
Item payd to the chirche wardens for mony wiche theye layde out when the plomer was here	4	0	0
Item for a quarte of wyne & a quarter of suger when Mr Chanceler was here		1	0
Item payd John Symondes junior for his fee		13	4
Item payd to Peter Harvy for his fee		2	0

Summa   £8 6s ½d.

The hole some of the paymentes is   £39 3s 6½d

And so the receptes exced the paymentes   9s 5½d

[f. 35r]   **[1589-90]**

The accompte of John Symondes junior collector for the rentes & fermes of & for all the <towne> *landes* and tenementes belogyng [sic] to the towneshepe of Wymondham accomptyng from the Feaste of Saynt Mychaell Tharchangel in the yere of our Lorde God <1590> 1589 ontyll the yere of our Lord God 1590 for one hole yere then ended

/Fre rentes/

First he doth [acompte] for the arerage his laste acompte		9	5½
Item of Edwarde Crane by yere		3	0
Of Agnes Wyseman for the rent of her howse		1	10
Of Ales Frosten for fre rent of her howse		2	0
Of Robert Mayhew for fre rent goyng out of his howse by yere			4
Of Peter Neve for fre rent of his howse			10
Of Wylliam Grene fre rent of his howse			10
Of Edmund Culliour for fre rent by yere			1
Of Wylliam Luce for ferme by yere	2	0	0
Of John Castelten for Teddes Closse	6	13	4
Of Robert Rawlyn for a cloase at [?Beckes] Lane a parcell of medowe at Kyddes Wyllowes 2 acres of land in the North Fylde and one acre in Byxlond Fylde nere Beast Brygge	2	3	4
Of Robert Ryngwood for a medowe nere Westwade & 4 acres of land in the North Fylde & one acre & halffe in the Parke Fylde	1	19	0

	£	s	d
Of Thomas Grene for a parcell of medowe nere Saltersforde & another parcell nere Wyndames Closse by yere		16	8
Of Henry Goche for a parcell of medowe nere Hockhams Carre		3	4
Of John Symondes junior for 8 acres of lande & one rode by yere	1	12	4
Of Wylliam Sparham for a parcell of lande sometyme a grove & one acre of lande		6	0

Summa £16 12s 4d

	£	s	d
[*f. 35v*] Of Thomas Agas for halffe an acre of lande		2	0
Of Wylliam Kett for 2 acres & a halffe of lande		8	4
Of Robert Hobbes for 2 acres of lande and a parcell of medowe nere Wade Brygge		7	0
Of Thomas Busshe for a cloase & 3 rodes of lande nere Ryvaldes	1	3	4
Of John Vynor gent for one acre of lande		4	0
Of Peter Pitcher for a cloase in Hungate		14	0
Of Robert Wyseman for 2 acres <of ?> & 3 rodes of lande in the North Fylde		11	0
Of Loye Agas for 7 acres of [land] there	1	8	0
Of Richard Apleton for 2 acres of lande		8	0
Of John Sayour for 3 acres of lande		9	0
Of John Symondes senior for an ortyarde		1	0
Of Henry Norton for 2 acres 3 rodes of lande		10	0
Of Thomas Woodcocke senior for 3 rodes of lande		4	0
Of John Kensey gent for a closse at Dygbeke More & 2 acres of land nere Crownshaughe amonge his landes there		16	0
Of Mr Thornton for a parcell of medowe nere Wade Brygge		4	0
Of John Busshe for 2 acres of lande		6	0
Of Thomas Smyth for 2 acres of lande at Teddes		10	0
Of John Kett for 3 rodes of lande		3	0
Of Thomas Talbott gent for one acre of lande lyeng in his closse at the Game Place		4	0
Of Thomas Poker for a closse at the Clayepyttes	1	6	8
Of Thomas Funston gent for a closse nere Hochams at Bekes Lane	1	6	8

/**Tenementes**/

	£	s	d
Of Wylliam Daynes for all the guylde howses and all the vessell & other implementes kepyng the howses in good reparacons	3	0	0
Of Raygnolde Kene for the howse that he dwelyth in kepyng the howses in good reparacons	1	10	0

Summa £15 16s

	£	s	d
[*f. 36r*] Of Antony Engleshe for the howse & grownd at Blackinham		16	8
Of Randoll Downyng for the towne shoppe		12	0

	£	s	d
Of Edmund Fedemonde for the howse he dwell in		6	8
Of Thomas Queyntrell for the howse he dwellyth in		6	8
Of John Clere[11] for the howse he dwellyth in		6	8
Of Wylliam Cocke for his howse		6	8
Of John Smyth for the howse that he dwellyth in		6	8
Of the wedowe Meyse for the howse she dwellyth in		6	8
Of Mother Ferme for her howse		6	8
Of Richard Cotton for his howse		6	8

Summa   £4 2s

The hole some rec. this yere is   £36 <?s 8½d> 10s 4½d
Where of he aske to be alowyd of fre rentes on payd   9s 11d
And so the hole some rec. this yere *is*   £36 [cancelled figures] 5½d

Where of payd

/ **Paymentes** /

	£	s	d
Firste payd to Clere for his fees for glasyng the chirche wyndowes		6	8
Payd to Thomas Queyntrell for makyng of the bell clapper & mendyng of it dyverse tymes & for other worke	1	0	4
Item payd to Thomas Corball[12] scolemaster for his hole yeres wages	15	0	0
Payd to Robert Foster for scoryng the towne armor		5	0
Payd to Wylliam Ovyngton for mony he layde out when he was chirchewarden		11	0
Payd to Wylliam Pratt for mony wich he layd out when he was chirchewarden		9	4
Payd to John Barnard beyng warden lykewyse		2	2
Payd to Thomas Rudland lykewyse for the same tyme		6	0

Summa   £18 0s 6d

	£	s	d
[f. 36v] Payd to Robert Symondes for the markett busshell the chenes & the locke		5	10
Payd to the Quenes Majestyes balye for one hole yeres rent with a rent hene	2	7	11
Payd to Mr Pagraves balye			6
/☞/ Payd to Robert Kett for the comyssyoners dynners	3	0	0
Payd to John Gedneye for Mr Otes charges when he preched here		2	0

---

[11] John Clare, glazier, was provided with a town house rent free in return for keeping the church windows in repair. He was regularly paid for work on the church which exceeded the value of his rent (6s 8d), for frequent attention to the windows of the schoolhouse and for occasional work on town houses.

[12] Mr Thomas Corball, schoolmaster from 1589 until his probable discharge (p. 51) 1590–91.

	£	s	d
/☞/ Payd for a pottell of wyne for Ser Artur Hevenyngham & his company		1	4
Payd to <the> Robert Ryngwood for mony he layd out to the clarke of the markett		5	0
Payd to Richard Rawlyn for an oke for to make mantre for the kechyn chymnye at the gyldhouse		13	4
Payd to Robert Foster for scoryng of the towne corslett		2	6
Payd Chykerynges wyffe for kepyng of Lawrence daughters childe		5	0
Payd to her moare for one monyth		4	0
Payd to her one other monyth		4	0
Payd more to her for one weke		1	0
Payd to Robert Marshall for the same chylde	2	0	0
Payd to Thomas Francys for caryeng of a letter to Ser Edward Cleres knyght		1	0

<Summa>

	£	s	d
Item lente to the vycker by the consent of the towne	1	13	4
/☞/ Item payd to Mr Funston for the towneshepe of Wymondham for 3 petecions to Master Setherton in the tyme of Ser John Payton shreve & for rulyng the same & for dyschargyng the issues to Mr Bedyngfylde[13] in the Exchecker		19	4
Item payd to hym for his fee		3	4
Item payd to hym for a petecyon in the tyme of Master Paston shreve & for dychargeyng the same <in that> to Master Beddyngfylde		15	4
Item payd to Mr Funstone for his fee		3	4

Summa   £12   12s   2d

	£	s	d
[f. 37r] /☞/ Item payd for a writte agaynste Thomas Tyrrell & Walter Queyntrell & for 2 warantes		5	9
Item payd for a declaration & the copye		1	8
Item payd Mr Funston for his fee		3	4
Item payd to the proctor of Saynt Stephens Gates when he came to se Chambelen		1	0
Item payd to John Gyllyngforde for & towardes the helyng of the sayd Chambelen	1	10	0
Item payd to Robert Marshall for Abbacooke Lawrence doughters chyldes kepyng		6	8
Item payd to Robert Kett for Master Knevetes charges & his men when he came to confer with the towne	1	2	0

[13] Mr Bedingfield was an official in the Exchequer. See A.Hassell Smith and G.M.Baker eds, *The Papers of Nathaniel Bacon of Stiffkey III, 1586–1595* (Norfolk Record Society, liii, 1987 and 1988), p. 332, n. 61.

	£	s	d
Item payd to John Symondes for his fee		13	4
Item payd to Peter Harvye for his fee		2	0

Summa £4 5s 9d

The hole some of the paymentes is £34 18s 5d

And so the receytes exced the paymentes £1 2s ½d

Over & besydes thre pownds lente to Thomas Terrell & ten shelynges
nyne pence spent in sute for recover the same £3 10s 9d

And also £1 13s 4d lent to the vycker £1 13s 4d

All wiche somes the towne wyll nott alowe

[*f. 37v*]   **[1590-91]**

The acompte of John Symondes junior collector for all the rentes & fermes of & for all the landes and tenementes belongyng to the townshepp of Wymondham accomptyng from the Feaste of Saynt Mychaell Tharchangell in the yere of our Lord God 1590 untyll the yere of our Lord God 1591 for one hole yere then ended

And firste he doth acompte for tharerage of his laste acompte	1	2	½

/Fre rentes/

	£	s	d
Item Edward Crane for fre rent by yere		3	0
Item of Agnes Wyseman for the rent of her howse		1	10
Item of Ales Frostyn for the rent of her howse		2	0
Item of Robert Mayhew for rent goyng out of his howse			4
Item of Peter Neave for fre rent goyng out of howse			10
Item of Wylliam Grene for fre rent goyng out of his howse			10
Item of Edmund Culliour for fre rent			1
Item of Ser Thomas Knevet knyght for the increase of £20 wiche was in the handes of Wylliam Luce	2	0	0
Item of John Castelten for Teddes Closse	6	13	4
Item of Richard Rawlyn for one closse at Bettes Lane a parcell of medow at Kyddeswyllowes and 2 acres of lande in the Northefylde	1	19	4
Item of Robert Crismas for one acre in Byxelond Fylde		4	0
Item of Robert Ryngwood for a medowe at Westwade & 4 acres of lande in the Northfyllde & one acre and a halfe in the Parke Fylde	1	19	0
Item of Thomas Grene for one acre and 3 rodes of medowe nere Salters Forde*and one pece of medowe nere Wyndoms Closse*		16	8
Item of Henry Goche for a parcell of medow at Hockhams Care		3	4
Of John Symondes junior for 8 acres and one rode of lande	1	12	4
Of Wylliam Sparham for one acre of land & a nother parcell of land some tyme a grove		6	0
Of Thomas Funston gent for a cloase	1	0	0

Summa £18 4s 11½d

	£	s	d
[f. 38r] Of Thomas Agas for halffe an acre of lande		2	0
Of Wylliam Kett for 2 acres & halfe of lande		8	4
Of Robert Hobbes for 2 acres of land & a percell of medow nere Wade Brigge		7	0
Of Thomas Busshe for one cloase & thre rodes of lande nere Ryvaldes	1	3	4
Of Fraunces Cusyng gent for one acre of lande		4	0
Of Peter Pytcher for a cloase in Hungate		14	0
Of Robert Wyseman for 2 acres 3 rodes of lande in the Northe Fylde		11	0
Of Loye Agas for 7 acres of lande there	1	8	0
Of Richard Appylton for for [sic] 2 acres of lande		8	0
Of John Sayer for 3 acres of lande		9	0
Of John Symondes senior for an orteyarde		1	0
Of Henry Norton for 2 acres 3 rodes of lande		10	0
Of Thomas Woodcocke senior for 3 rodes of lande		4	0
Of John Kensey gent for one cloase in Dygbecke and 2 acres of lande nere Crownshaughe		16	0
Of Robert Thornton gent for a percell of medowe nere Wade Brigge		4	0
Of John Busshe for 2 acres of lande & pasture		6	0
Of Thomas Smythe for 2 acres of lande		10	0
Of John Kett for 3 rodes of lande		3	0
Of Thomas Talbott doctor of the lawe for one acre of lande lyeng in his close at the Game Place		4	0
Of Thomas Poker for a cloase at the Claye Pyttes	1	6	8
Of Wylliam Daynes for all the guylde howses all the vessell & other implementes	3	0	0
Of Raignolde Kene for the howse he dwellyth <in with> kepyng the sayd howses in reparacons	1	10	0
Of Antonye Engleshe for the howse & growndes at Blacke Inham		16	8
Of Randoll Downyng for the towne shoppe		12	0
Of Thomas Fedymond for the howse he dwelyth in		6	8

Summa £16 4s 8d

	£	s	d
[f. 38v] Of Thomas Queyntrell for the [house] he dwellyth in		6	8
Of John Clere for the howse he dwelyth in		6	8
Of Wylliam Cocke for the howse he dwelyth in		6	8
Of Cristen Smyth for the howse she dwelyth in		6	8
Of John Smyth for the howse he dwelyth in		6	8
Of Mother Ferme for the howse she dwelyth in		6	8
Of Richard Cotton for the howse he dwelyth in		6	8

	£	s	d
Item recyvyd of dyverse men *&* of the streete of Wattylfylde for the fetchyng home of Mr Wells[14]		7	8
Recyvyd Mr Corball upon his acompte for certen skolers		1	6
Receyvyd of Loye Agas for forty fagotes of wood		3	4

Summa £2 19s 2d

The hole some rec. this yere is   £37 8s 9½d

Whereof he aske to be allowyd of fre rentes onpayd 9s 11d

And so the hole some rec. is   £36 18 10½d

Whereof payd

	£	s	d
[f. 39r] Paymentes. Firste payd to the Quenes Majestyes balye for one hole yeres rent	1	7	11
Item payd to the balye for the manner of Cromwels for one hole yeres rent		4	1
Item payd to Mr Pagraves balye			6
Item payd to the skolemaster for his hole yeres wages	15	0	0
Item payd to John Clere for his fee for kepyng the glase wyndowes of the chirche		6	8
Item payd serchyng the regester at Norwitche for the vycker		6	6
Item payd to the clarke of the market for the towneshepe of Wymondham	1	0	0
Item payd to Robert Marshall for the chylde	1	0	0
/☞/ Item payd to Thomas Bell for layeng 2 brigges at Westwade			4
/☞/ Item payd for the charges of Mr Stookes and Docter Talbott & others upon Witson Tewseday to sett downe order for dyverse persons <fo> beyng in sute for ther tythes		6	0
Item payd for charges of sute agaynste Thomas Terell to Mr Fonnstone	1	14	7
Item payd for a quarte of wyne for Mr Hunson when he preched here			8
Item payd to Benet Botye for fetchyeng home of Mr Wells his stuffe	1	6	8
Item payd for a galon of wyne geven to my Lord Chefe Justice		2	8
/☞/ Item payd to Raignolde Kene for kepyng of Mr Woodfalles childe[15]	2	5	0
Item payd to William Clarke for growndsyllyng of the towne shoppe for one new stothe and for settyng it ryght		3	8
Item payd to Fraunces Queyntrell for nayles			1

[14] Mr Simon Wells, schoolmaster c. 1590–1603. Williams claims 1595–1603, but the 'fetching home' of Wells and Knyvett's presence at the new schoolmaster's appointment in 1590–91 (p.51) argues for that year. Wells was vicar of Wymondham 1590–1607. A respected figure, he was left personal bequests as well as payments to preach funeral sermons and to see testators 'decently buried'.

[15] This may have been the child of Mr John Woodfall, vicar of Wymondham 1589–90.

	£	s	d
Item payd to John Queyntrell for 2 ankers & for braddes & one peny			
worth of nayles		2	2
Item payd to Jeffery Steward for a planke for the same shoppe			4
Item payd for splentes for the same shoppe			4
Item payd to Thomas Browne for bringyng of 2 growndsyls from			
the chyrche to the shoppe			1

Summa   £25 8s 3d

	£	s	d
[*f. 39v*] Item payd to the Quenes Majesties surveyor for entryng of			
the towne copyes		2	6
Item payd to Robert Garade for a pyeke for the towne		3	4
Item payd to Mr Heyward for entryng the towne copyes in			
Cromwells courte		2	6
Item payd Mr Duffylde for a serche in the Tower[16] for the vycker		10	0
Item payd to Mr Godfre for a cowncell fee for the towne		10	0
Item payd to Mr Duffylde for the answeryng of the letters wiche			
cam from my Lordes Grace of Canterbury	1	0	0
/☞/ Item payd to Robert Kett for Mr Knevettes charges & others			
for his dyete when he came to receyve solgeors & for placyng of			
the skolemaster[17] & other thynges	4	0	0
Item payd to Mr Funston for the dyschargeyng of the iseues loste by			
the townsmen at the Assyses & Sessyons	1	11	0
Item payd to hym for the wrytte of execusyon[18] agaynste Terell		1	0
/☞/ Item payd to Mr Cleres baly for a fyne	1	0	0
Item payd to Mr Smyth before Mr Chancelor for dychargeyng the			
skolemaster		2	6
Item payd to James Bettes for mendyng of the locke & makyng of a			
new keye for the skole dore			9
Item payd to Joseffe Bullocke for kepyng of Buckenhams chylde	3	0	0
Item payd to Loye Agas for a pyeke for the towne		3	4
Item payd to John Bushe for mony by hym layd out to John Nevell			
for 2 dayes traynyng in the towne armor		1	4
Item payd to hym for a sworde gyrdell			10
Item payd to hym fir stuffe & frynge for to arme the pykes			8
Item payd for oyle to skore the corselett			2

Summa   £12 9s 11d

[16] The Tower of London was used until the late 1850s to store a variety of national records.

[17] This is the only reference in this volume of the Town Book to the attendance by a member of the leading local gentry, Thomas Knyvett the younger of Ashwellthorpe, at the official appointment of a new schoolmaster.

[18] A writ of execution is the command of a court that a legally recognised debt be recovered by the seizure and sale of the debtor's goods. Sheriffs issued bailiffs with these writs.

£   s   d

[Pages have been torn out of the document at this point. It resumes at folio 43.]

[f. 43r]   **[1594-95]**

The acompte of Nycholas Dyckerson collector for all the rentes & fermes of
<all> *&* for all the landes & tenementes belongyng to the townshepe of
Wymondham acomptyng from the Feaste of Saynt Mychaell Tharchangell in
the yere of our Lord God <1595> *1594* ontyll Feaste of Saynt Mychaell
Tharchangell <1596> *1595* for one hoale yere then ended as folowyth

/Fre rentes/

	£	s	d
Firste of Edward Crane for fre rent by yere		3	0
Of Agnes Wyseman for the rent of her howse by yere		1	10
Of Ales Frostyn for free rent goyng out of her howse		2	0
Of Robert Mayehew for fre rent			4
Of Peter Neve for fre rent			10
Of Wylliam Grene for free rent			10
Of Edmund Culliour for fre rent			1
Of Margaret Ryngwood	2	0	0
Of Thomas Smyth for Teddes	7	10	0
Of hym for 2 <ack> acres of land there nere		10	0
Of Richard Rawlyng for 3 roodes of medowe at Kydes Wyllowes & 2 acres of land in the North Fylde		12	8
Of Thomas Haste gent for a medowe at West Wade nere Salters Forde	1	0	0
Of John Flowerdew for a <th> cloase at the Popyles	1	6	8
Of hym for 3 acres of medow at Salters Forde nere Weste Wade		16	8

Summa £14 4s 11d

	£	s	d
[f. 43v] Of John Symondes the sonne of John Symondes the yonger for a cloase at Beckes Lane	1	0	0
Of Wylliam Ovyngton for 3 acres and a halfe of lande in the Northe Fylde		18	6
Of Margaret Ryngwood for one acre *dimidia* in the Parke Fylde & one acre in the North Fylde		10	0
Of Robert Cristmas for one acre in [*sic*] of lande in Byxelonde Fylde		4	0
Of John Burde for a pyghtell of medow at Hockhams Carre		3	4
Of John Symondes the yonger for 6 acres one rode of lande in the Northfylde	1	4	4
Of Wylliam Sparham for one acre of lande and a parcell of grownde sometyme a grove		6	0
Of Thomas Carre & Wylliam Payne for 2 acres & halffe in Holme Fylde		10	0

	£	s	d
Of them for 2 acres in the same fyllde late in the ferme of Robert Hobbes		8	0
Of Robert Hobbes for a parcell of medowe at Wade Brigge lyeing within his medow there		1	0
Of Thomas Busshe for a cloase & thre roodes of lande at Ryvaldes	1	6	8
Of Thomas Seaberne for one acre of lande lyeing at Clackewell Furlong		5	0
Of Jeffery Sturmyn for a cloase lyeng in Hongate		14	0
Of hym for one acre of land in the North Fylde		4	0
Of Symonde Booth for halfe an acre of lande		2	4

Summa £7 16s 2d

	£	s	d
[f. 44r] Of Robert Wyseman for 2 acres 3 roodes of land in the North Fylde		11	0
Of Loye Agas for 7 acres of lande in the North Fylde	1	8	0
Of Richard Appleton for 2 acres of lande at the Hell Lanes ende		10	0
Of Henry Kett for 3 acres of lande in the North Fylde		12	0
Of John Symondes sennior for an orteyarde nexte the guylde howse		1	0
Of Thomas Woodcoke for 3 roodes of land		4	0
Of Henry Norton for 2 acres 3 roodes of lande in the North Fylde		11	0
Of Henry Spenlove gent for one cloosse in Diggebeke & 2 acres of lande nere Crowneshawe		16	0
Of Robert Thornton gent for a parcell of medowe nere Wade Brigge		4	0
Of John Busshe for 2 acres of lande in the Northe Fylde		6	0
Of John Kett for 3 roodes of lande at Beckes Dyke		4	0
Of Thomas Talbott doctor of the lawe for one acre of land lyeng [in] his cloase at the Game Place		4	0
Of Thomas Poker for a cloasse at the Claye Pyttes	1	6	8
Of Artur Wylliams gent for a parcell of medow or pasture late in the ferme of John Busshe		[blank]	

Summa £6 16s 8d

	£	s	d
[f. 44v] Of Wylliam Daynes for all guyldehowses and all the pewter & all other implymentes kepyng the howses in reparacyons	3	0	0
Of Raignolde Kene for the howse dwellyth in kepyng it in good reparacyon [sic]	1	10	0
Of Randoll Downyng for the towne shoppe		12	0
Of Edmund Fedymonde for the howse he dwellyth in		6	8
Of Thomas Queyntrell for a howse there		13	4
Of John Clare for the howse he dwellyth in to kepe the chirche wyndowes in reparacyon		6	8
Of Wylliam Cocke for his howse		6	8

	£	s	d
John Smythe for his howse		6	8
Of the wedow Smeth for her howse		6	8
Of Mother Ferme for her howse		6	8
Of Elizabeth Leche & Jane Cotton for ther howse		6	8
Of Robert Lynckon for the howse at Blacke Inham	1	4	0

Summa £9 6s 0d

The hoole some receyvyd this yere   £38 3s 9d

/*Arrerages*/

Whereof he aske to be alowyd of free *rentes* onpayd   <9s> *8s* 11d

Where of

<and so the hoole some recyvyd is   £37 14s 10d>

Item of 4s <in> of Thomas Talbott doctor of the lawe for the ferme of one acre of lande

<whereof payd>

/*Memorandum the arrerage of Margarett Ringwood ys dischardged by generall consent*/

In the handes of Robert Hobbes 12d in the handes of Margaret Ryngwood 4s in the handes of John Symondes 20s in the handes of Thomas Haste 20s in the handes of the wedow Carre 4s in the handes of John Kett 3s in the handes of Thomas Queyntrell 13s 4d

Summa of this is   £3 18s 3d

And so the hoole some receyvyd this yere is   £34 5s 6d

Whereof payd

[*f. 45r*] /*Payementes*/

	£	s	d
Firste payd to the Quenes Majestyes balye for one hoale yeres rent	1	7	11
Item payd to the balye of the manner of Cromewells for one yeres rent		4	1
Item payd to the skole master for thre quarters wages ended at the Feaste of Saynt Mychaell	11	5	0
Item payd Wylliam Stocton for layeng in of the mandelltre in kytchyn chymney at the towne hall		5	0
Item payd towardes the bryngyng up of Barkers chylde		13	0
Item payd to Robert Bale for lyme & cariage		8	2
Item payd to Walter Kyng workyng up of the kytchyn chymney at the towne hall		15	0
Item payd for makyng clene the towne hall			6
Item payd moare to Robert Borell for Barkers chylde	2	0	0
Item payd Master Funston for serchyng of rolles & for wrightyng		13	0
Item payd to John Danny for wryghtyng out of the tenement boke dyverse parcells of lande to be sett downe in the coppye		2	6

	£	s	d
Item payd to John Kett for the taske of the guylde howses			8
Item payd to the Quenes balye for the fynne of dyverse landes newly taken up	5	6	8
Item payd to Bettes for skoryng the towne armor		4	0
Item payd to Foster Nevell & Sadde and a nother for 2 dayes traynyng in the towne armor		8	0

Summa £23 13s 6d

[f. 45v] Item payd to John Sadde to have the towne armor agayne wiche he hadde kepte ever sence he was constabyll		7	4
Item payd for thre pownd of poder for the muskettes		4	0
Item payd to Master Debney for a copye		4	6
Item payd to Henry Blake for a copye of his warant wiche he hadde for grantyng of the towne landes		1	8
Item payd to the balye of the manner of Cromewells for a fynne	1	0	0
Item payd Master Heyward wryghtyng and other thynges		5	0
Item payd for issues of our landes holden of the manner of Cromewells		5	0
Item alowyd to John Clere for kepyng of the chirche wyndowes		6	8

Summa £2 14s 2d

The hoole some of the paymentes is £26 7s 8d

And so the receytes excede the paymentes £7 17s 10d

Unde allocatur eidem compoto pro filio Henrici Barker 7s
Et sic debet in toto £7 10s 10d

[f. 46r]   **[1595-96]**

The accompte of Nycholas Dickerson collector for all of the rentes & fermes of & for all the landes and tenementes belongyng to the towneshepp of Wymondham acomptyng from the Feast of Saynt Mychaell the Archangell in the yere of our Lorde God 1595 ontyll the sayd feaste in the yere of our Lord God 1596 for one hoale yere then ended as folowyth

*First he doth acompt the arerages of his laste acompte	7	10	
10*			
Firste of Edward Crane for free rent for one yere then ended		3	0
Item of Agnes Wyseman for the rent of her howse that yere		1	10
Item of Ales Frostyn for fre rent goyng owte of her howse by yere		2	0
Item of Robert Mayhew for fre rent by yere			4
Item of Peter Neve for free rent by yere			10
Item of Thomas Nyckeson for free rent goyng out of his howse by yere			10
Item Edmund Culliour for fre rent by yere			1

	£	s	d
Item of Magaret Ryngwood for the ewse of twentye pownde	2	0	0
Item of Thomas Smyth for Teddes Closse and 2 acres of lande there nere	8<10>		0
Item of Richard Rawlyng for 3 roodes of medow at Kyddes Wellowes & 2 acres of land in the North Fyllde		12	8
Of hym a medowe Westewade Chapell[19]	1	0	0
Of John Flowerdew for a cloase at the [word cancelled] Popylles	1	6	8
Of hym for 3 acres of medow at Salters Forde		16	8
Of hym for thre acres *one roode* of land in the Northe Fylde		13	0
Of Richard Engleshe for a cloase at Beckes Lane	1	0	0
Of Wylliam Ovyngton for 3 acres & a halffe of land in the Northe Fylde		17	6
Of hym for a cloosse at the Claye Pyttes	1	6	8

<Summa   £18 2s 2d>

Summa   £25 12s 11d

	£	s	d
[f. 46v] Of Margaret Ryngwood for halffe an aker of lande in the Parke Fylde		2	6
Of Robert Cristmas for one acre of land in Byxelond Fylde		4	0
Of John Burde for parcell of medow at Hockhames Carre		3	4
Of John Symondes the yonger for one aker & a halffe lyeng in his crofte		6	0
Of Thomas Coale for one acre of land in the Northe Fylde nere the Baroughes		5	0
Of hym for one acre in Holme Fylde late in the ocupyeing of Thomas Carre		4	0
Of Thomas Crane for one acre & halffe nere Stevens Medowes		7	6
Of Wylliam Sparham for one acre of lande and a parcell of lande some tyme a grove		6	0
Of Wylliam Payne for 2 acres of land in Holme Fylde		8	0
Item of Thomas Hobbes for 2 acres in the same fyllde		8	0
Of Robert Hobbes for a parcell of medow at Wade Brigge		1	0
Of Thomas Busshe & Thomas Kyng for a closse & 3 [sic] of lande nere Ryvalde	1	6	8
Of John Venyour gent for one acre of of [sic] lande lyeng nere Claxewell		5	0
Of Jeffery Sturmyn for one cloose in Hungate & one acre of lande lyeng nere Tolyes Crosse		19	0
Of Robert Wyseman for 2 acres <of land> and 3 roodes of land in			

---

[19] The remains of a chapel, built by Wymondham Priory on a bridge over the Westwade stream.

	£	s	d
the North Fylde		11	0
Of Loye Agas for seven acres of lande in the North Fylde	1	8	0

Summa £7 5s

	£	s	d
[f. 47r] Of Richard Appylton for 2 acres of lande at Hellanes end		10	0
Of Henry Kett for 3 acres of lande in the Northe Fyllde		12	0
Of John Symondes sennior for one orteyard		1	0
Of Henry Norton for 2 acres 3 roodes of lande in the Northe Fyllde		11	0
Of Thomas Woodcocke for 3 roode of lande		4	0
Of Henry Spenlove gent for one cloase in Dygbecke & 2 acres of lande at Croughaughe		16	0
Of Robert Thorneton gent for a parcell of medowe nere Wade Brygge		4	0
Of John Busshe for 2 acres of lande		6	0
Of John Kett for 3 roodes of lande		3	0
Of Thomas Talbott doctor of lawe for one acre of lande in his close at the Game Place		4	0
<Of Wylliam Daynes>			
Of Artur Wylliam gent for a parcell of medow or pasture at Myle Poole late in the ferme John Busshe		[blank]	
Of Wylliam Daynes for the towne howse and the lettyng of the pewter	3	0	0
Of Raignolde Kene for his howse	1	10	0
Of Randoll Downyng for the towne shoppe		12	0
Of hym for one acre & a halffe of lande in the Parke Fylde		7	6
Of Edmund Fedemonde for his howse		6	8
Of Elizabeth Tolye for the howse she dwellyth in		13	4
Of John Clare for the howse he dwelyth in he in [sic] kepe the chirche wyndowes in reparacions		6	8

[sum cancelled]
Summa £10 7s 2d

	£	s	d
[f. 47v] Of Wylliam Cocke for the <the> *howse he* dwellyth in		6	8
Of John Smythe for the howse he dwellyth in		6	8
Of Cristen Smyth for the howse she dwellyth in		6	8
Of Mother Ferme for the howse she dwellyth in		6	8
Of Elizabeth Leche & Jane Cotton for ther howse		6	8
Of Robert Lyncon for the howse at Blackeinham	1	4	0

Summa £2 17s 4d

	£	s	d
The hoole some of the receytes with the arerages of the laste acompte is	46	2	5

	£	s	d
Whereof he asketh to be alowyd of certen rentes & fermes on payd as followyth			
Firste in the handes of Agnes Wyseman		1	10
In the handes of Ales Frostyn *vidua*		2	0
In the handes of Robert Mayehew			4
In the handes of Peter Neve			10
In the handes of Wylliam Grene			10
In the handes of Edmund Culliour			1
In the handes of Doctor Talbott gent		4	0
In the handes of Robert Hobbes		1	0
In the handes of Robert Lynkon	1	6	0
wiche is forgeven			

Summa of this is   £1 16s 11d

and so in this acomptantes handes   £44 5s 6d

whereof payd

[*f. 48r*] /**Payementes**/

Firste payd to the Quenes Majesties baly for one hoale yeres rent	1	7	6
Item payd to the balye for the manner of Cromewells for one hoale yeres rent		4	1
Item payd to Master Welles skolemaster	15	0	0
Item payd to Shefyld & Mannyng for fagotte bondes		5	4
Item payd to Shefylde & Leche for nyne hundered 23 fagottes of woode		19	6
Item payd to Robert Tolye & others for caryeng of eight hundred woode	1	2	0
Item payd to 2 men traynyng in the towne armor the syxte of Maye		2	0
Item payd to Robert Foster for traynyng		1	0
Item payd to Robert Culliour for a corselett	1	4	0
Item payd to Robert Foster for skoryng and mendyng the towne armur		8	0
Item payd to hym for kepyng the[?m] clene and in good reparacions & servysabyll		1	0
Item payd to Stephen Nevell for 2 dayes traynyng in the towne armur		2	0
/☞/ Item payd to hym that toke Barkers chylde to kepe the forte of Julye	1	15	6
Item payd to John Gedney for wyne for my Lorde Bysshoppe[20]		8	0
Item payd to Richard Rawlyng makyng the brigges at Weste Wade Chappell		5	0
Item payd payd [*sic*] to Thomas Flemyng for the taske of the towne howse			8
Item payd to Richard Rawlyng for that he was indytted for the			

---

[20] William Redman, Bishop of Norwich 1595–1602.

	£	s	d
brigges afforesayd		4	4
Item payd to Wylliam Norton for gonne powder and matche		3	10

Summa £23 15s 2d

	£	s	d
[f. 48v] Item payd to Thomas Crane for powder and mache			[blank]
/☞/ Item payd to Thomas *Crane* for mony by hym layde out			
when the towne was in sute with my Lorde Bysshoppe	5	0	0
Item payd to Neves doughter for kepyng of her syster			6
Item payd to Andrewes for pitchyeng of 2 loades of strawe			4
/☞/ Item payd Artur Wylliams *gent* for his charges when he			
folowyde the sute aforsayd	2	4	1
/☞/ Item payd to Thomas Armes for kepyng and dyschargeyng the			
towne of Neves chylde	1	0	0
Item payd for 3 loades of strawe for the towne howses in Townegrene		12	0
Item payd to Robert Culliour for caryeng the same		2	0
Item payd to Benton for seven dayes & halfe thakkyng with his borde		7	6
Item payd to John Kytemey & Andrewes for servyng hym the same			
tyme		5	3
Item payd for broches & byndeyng		1	0
Item payd to Fraunces Queyntrell for a locke for the vaulte dore at			
the towne howse			4
Item payd to Nelyng for Fedemondes chylde		3	4
/☞/ Item payd Artur Wylliams *gent* for Dowes daughter	2	0	0
Item payd to hym for caryeng of her to Norwitche		1	8
Item payd to Turner of Dysse for the change of pewter	1	5	0
Item payd to Robert Foster for a stampe to marke the pewter with all			8
Item payd to Artur Wylliams gent for a markett busshell		3	4

Summa £13 7s 1d

	£	s	d
[f. 49r] Item payd to Rotherames wyffe for the conveayeng her			
chylde out of the towne		1	6
Item payd to Esaye Freman for 3 loades of strawe		15	0
Item payd to Claryngton for 7 dayes thackyng the same with his			
borde		7	0
Item payd to John Kytmey servyng hym the same tyme with his borde		5	3
Item payd for broches & byndynges		1	2
Item payd to Clare for glasyng the chirche wyndowes		6	8

Summa £1 16s 7d

The hoole some of the paymentes is £38 18s 10d
And so the receytes exced the paymentes is [sic] £5 6s 8d

[f. 49v blank]

	£	s	d

[f. 50r]   [1596-97]

The accompte of Nycholas Dickersone collector for all the rentes & fearmes of & for all the landes & tenementes belonginge to the towneshippe of Wymondham accomptinge from the Feaste of Sanct Mychaell the Arckeanngell in the yere of our Lorde God 1596 untill the seyde feaste in the yere of our Lord God 1597 for one whole yere then ended as followethe

	£	s	d
Firste he dothe accompte the arerages of his laste acompte	5	6	8
Item for free rente of Edwerde Crane by the yere		3	0
Item of Agnes Wyseman for the rente of her howse that yere		1	10
Item of Ales Frosten for the rente of her howse by yere		2	0
Item of Robert Mayhew for his rente by yere			4
Item of Peter Neave for free rente by yere			10
Item of William Greene for free rente by yere			10
Item of Edmunde Cullior for free rente by yere			1
Item of Margrete Ryngwoode for the use of £20 by yere	2	0	0
Item of Thomas Smythe for Teades Cloose by yere	7	10	0
Of him for twooe acres of lande by yere		10	0
Item of Richard Rawlinge for three roodes of medow at Kyddes Willowes & 2 acres of lande in the Northe Feylde by yere		12	8
Item of John Flowerdewe for the cloose at the Popples	1	6	8
Of him for a medowe of 3 acres at Sallters Forde		16	8
Item of <John Symondes> *Richard Englishe* for a cloose by yere	1	0	0
Item of <Thomas Haste gent> *Richard Rawlinge* for one medowe neere Westewerde Chappell by yere	1	0	0
Item of William Ovington for 3 acres & a halfe of lande in the Northe Feilde by yere		17	6
Of him for a cloose at the Claye Pittes	1	6	8
Item of John Flowerdewe for 3 acres of lande in the Northe Feilde		14	10
Item of Thomas Jafferye for one acre of lande in Byxlande Feilde		4	0
Item of John Burdye for a parcell of medowe		3	4
Item of John Symondes for one acre & a halfe of lande lyinge in his crofte		7	6
Item of William Sparham for one acre of lande & a parcell of grownde somtyme a groove		6	0

£24 11s 5d

	£	s	d
[f. 50v] Item of William Payne for 2 acres of lande in Holme Feilde		8	0
Item of Thomas Hobbes for 2 acres of lande in the same feilde		8	0
Item of Robert Hobbes for a parcell of medowe near Wade Brigge		1	0
Item of Thomas Kinge for a cloose at Ryballes and 3 roodes of			

	£	s	d
lande by yere	1	6	8
Item of Mr Vyniord for one acre of lande		5	0
Item of Jafferie Stirmine for a cloose by yere		14	0
Item of Robert Wyseman for 2 acres & 3 roodes of lande in the Northe Feilde		11	0
Item of Loye Agas for seven acres of lande in the Northe Feilde	1	15	0
Item of Richard Appleton for 2 acres of lande at Hell Lanes ende		10	0
Of Henry Kette for 3 acres of lande in the Northe Feilde		12	0
Item of John Symondes for an archeyerde		1	0
Item of George Norton for 2 acres & 3 roodes of lande		11<4>0	
Item of Henry Spenlowe gent for one cloose & 2 acres of lande		16	0
*Item of Thomas Woodcoke for 3 rodes		4	0*
<Item of [blank] Coole for one acre of lande		4	0>
Item of John Bushe for 2 acres of lande		6	0
Item of John Kette for 3 roodes of lande		3	0
Item of Mr Doctor Talbotte for one acre of lande in his cloose at the Game Place		4	0
Item of Mr Williams for a parcell of medowe			6
Item of William Daynes for the towne howses	3	0	0
Item of Reynolds Kene for the towne howse	1	10	0
Item of Randolfe Downinge for the towne shoppe		12	0
Of him for one acre & a halfe of lande		7	6
Item of Edmunde Fidemonde for his howse		6	8
Item of the wedowe Toolye for hir howse		13	4
Item of John Clere for his howse		6	8
Item of William Cocke for his howse		6	8
Item of John Smythe for his howse		6	8
[f. 51r] Item of the wedowe Smythe for hir howse		6	8
Item of Mother Fearme for hir howse		6	8
Item of the widdowe Leeche for hir howse		6	8
Item of Lincone for his howse at the comon	1	4	0
Item of Thomas Crane for one acre & a halfe with the grove		8	6
Item of Thomas Coole for one acre of lande		5	0
Of him for one other acre of lande		4	0
Item receyved of Phillipe Culliors accounte <£2 12s 8d>			
[total on right in arabic numerals]	2	19	8

For arrerages *videlicet* of John Flowerdewe *26.8.* & Loy Agas 28s & of B. Norton 5s

Summa £22 10s 10d

Summa totalis <£47 2s 3d>

over is £47 2s 3d

Allowances to be made out of the some aboveseyd

	£	s	d
Of Edward Crane for free rent		3	0
Annys Wyseman		1	10
Alyes Frosten		2	0
Robert Mayehewe			4
Peter Neve			10
Wylliam Grene			10
Edmund Culyer			1

<Some   8s 11d>

Mr Doctor Talbotte		4	0
Robert Hobbes		1	0

<Ultra in folio sequente>

Some   13s 11d

Ultra in sequente

[f. 51v] /**Paymentes**/

	£	s	d
Firste payde unto Thomas Kette for the Quenes rente	1	7	5
Item payde unto Russells for Cromwells rente		4	1
and for a helper			6
Item payd to Robert Bettes for Fidemondes chylde		4	0
Item payde to Mr Williams for his charges for the chylde	1	1	10
Item payd to Thomas Crane for his charges		2	0
Item for my owne charges		2	0
Item payd to Father Allaine towerdes his howse rente		3	4
Item payde to Mr Williams for Dowes daughter	5	0	0
Item to Stephen Nevell for halfe a pownde of gunpowder			8
Item payd to Ashemer			6
Item payd to the currior for Cobbes chylde		10	0
Item payd to Broune for grownesellinge the crosse	2	16	0
Item payd to Mr Welles scoolemaster	15	0	0
Item payd to the fower churchewardens	4	13	0
Item paid to Clere for glasing		6	8
Item for his fee		13	4

Somma totalis for allowances & paymentes   £32 19s 3d

Et sic debet

Somma debita   £14 3s

[f. 52r]   **[1597-98]**

The acompte of Nicholas Dickersone collector for all the rentes & fermes of &
for all the landes and tenementes belonginge to the towneshipp of Wymondham
acomptinge from the Feaste of Sanct Mychaell the Arckeanngell in the yere of
our Lord God 1597 untill the seyde feaste in the yere of our Lord God 1598 for
one whole yere then ended as followethe

	£	s	d
Firste he doth acompte for the arerages of his laste acompte	14	3	0
Item for free rente of Edwerd Crane by yere		3	0
Item of Agnes Wyseman for free rente by yere		1	10
Item of Ales Frosten for free rente by yere		2	0
Item of Robert Mayhew for rente by yere			4
Item of Peter Neave for free rente by yere			10
Item of Thomas Nyckson for free rente by yere			10
Item of Edmunde Cullior for free rente by yere			1
Item of Margret Ryngwood for the use of £20 by yere	2	0	0
Item of Thomas Smythe for Teades by yere	7	10	0
Of him for 2 acres of lande		10	0
Item of Richard Rawlinge for 3 roodes of medowe and 2 acres of lande		12	8
Of him for a medow neare Westwarde Chappell	1	0	0
Item of John Flowerdewe for the cloose at the Pooples	1	6	8
Of him for three acres of medowe at Westewarde Chappell		16	8
Of him for 3 acres of lande in the Northe Feilde		14	10
Item of Richard Englishe for a cloose at the Pooples	1	0	0
Item of William Ovington for 3 acres & a halfe of lande in the Northe Feilde		17	6
Of him for the cloose at the Claye Pittes	1	6	8
Item of Robert Crismas for one acre of lande		4	0
Item of John Burdye for a parcell of medowe at Hockames Carre		3	4
Item of John Symondes for one acre & a halfe of lande lyinge in his crofte		7	7
Item of William Sparham for one acre of lande & a parcell of grounde somtyme a grove		6	0
Item of William Payne for 2 acres of lande in Holmefeilde		8	0
[f. 52v] Item of Thomas Hobbes for 2 acres of lande in the same feilde		8	0
Item of Robert Hobbes for a parcell of medowe neare Wade Brigge		1	0
Item of Thomas Kinge for one cloose & 3 roodes of lande near Rybaldes	1	6	8
Item of Mr Vynior for one acre of lande		5	0
Item of Jeffrye Stirmyn for one cloose		14	0
Of him for one acre of lande		5	0
Item of Robert Wyseman for 2 acres & 3 roodes of lande in the Northe Feilde		11	0
Item of Loye Agas for 7 acres of lande ther	1	15	0
Item of Richard Appleton for 2 acres of lande at Hell Lanes ende		10	0
Item of Henry Kette for 3 acres of lande in the Northe Feilde		12	0

	£	s	d
Item of John Symondes for an archeyerd		1	0
Item of George Norton for 2 acres & 3 roodes of lande		11	0
Item of Thomas Woodcocke for 3 roodes of land		4	0
Item of Henrye Spendlowe gent for a close in Dickbecke & 2 acres of lande		16	0
Item of Robert Thornton gent for a parcell of medowe neare Wadebrigge		4	0
Item of John Bushe for 2 acres of lande		6	0
Item of John Kette for 3 roodes of lande		3	0
Item of Thomas Tallbotte doctor of the lawe for one acre of lande in his cloose at the Gamplace		4	0
Item of Arthur Williams gent for a parcell of medowe		[blank]	
Item of William Daynes for the towne howse	3	0	0
Item of Reynolde Kene for the towne howse	1	10	0
Item of Randolphe Downinge for his shoppe		12	0
Of him for one acre & a halfe of lande in the Parcke Feilde		7	6
Item of Edmonde Fidemonde for his howse		6	8
Item of Mother Toolye for hir howse		6	8
Item of John Clere for his howse		6	8
Item of William Cocke for his howse		6	8
Item of Peper & the widdowe Smythe		6	8
Item of the widdowe Smythe for hir howse		6	8
[f. 52r, bis] Item of Dowsinge & Marchall for a howse		6	8
Item of the widdowe Leeche for hir howse		6	8
Item of Edmonde Frosdicke for the howse at the Comon	1	4	0
Item of Thomas Crane for one acre & a halfe of lande with the grove		7	6
Item of Thomas Coole for 2 acres of lande		9	0
Item for Dowes howse	2	13	4

Summa oneris pro arreragiis et redditibus   £55 15s 9d

Woode solde owt of Teades this yere

	£	s	d
Firste to Robert Symondes 18 for	1	0	0
Item to John Whitle 23 for	1	10	0
Item to Thomas Smythe a parcell of woode	1	13	4
Item to Thomas Spinke a grove for	1	3	4
Item to Mr Williams all the hether grove	2	13	4
Item more to him as muche as come to		10	0
Item to George Acton as muche as comethe to	1	3	4
Item solde to William Sparham a bargayne of woode growinge aboute his pytell for		18	0

Some   £10 11s 4d   *Ultra*

Receptum de Thome Hast pro arreragiis pro firma prati apud Westewade Chappell que debuit

	£	s	d

in anno 1595 £1
<*Et sic*> *Somma* *debit in toto* £67 7s 1d

Allocaciones eciam pro redditu non soluto ut antea in compoto precedento		8	11
Et pro una acre terre Mistress Talbott		4	0
Et similiter pro Hobbes		1	0
Et pro domo Johannis Clere allocatum in glasing		6	8

Summa <17s> £1 0s 7d

[*f. 52v, bis*] **/Paymentes/**

Firste payde to Mr Wells scoolemaster for this yeares wages	15	0	0
Item to William Queyntrell for the iron worcke of the towne busshell		6	4
Item to the oulde woman for Fosters chylde		4	0
Item to Mother Allen for Hipersones chylde			6
/☞/ Item to Elizabeth Kitmer when she lay sicke			8
Item to Mr Welde attorney[21] for Mr Herne to followe Mr Palgraves[22] sute	1	0	0
Item to Gybbes when he went to Loye Kett		10	6
Item payd to Thomas Kett for the Quenes rente	1	7	5
& ther was owinge him for 2 hennes		1	0
Item to Mr Bucke for healinge of Crampes feete		10	0
Item payd to Boothe for the chylde the 30 of Aprill		13	8
Item payd to Clearke for mendinge of Frosdickes howse		1	8
Item payd to Robert Colman for a duble taske for the towne howse		1	4
Payde to him more for taske			8
Item payd for the prechers charges		9	8
Item payd to Walter Kinge for pinninge the crosse	1	6	0
Item payd to Rogers the mason for mendinge the towne welles[23]		10	0
Item payd to Agnes Gedney for wyne since the laste yere		4	0
Item payd to John Bunne for Cromwells rente		4	1
Item payd to Russells for Dowes rente			4
<Item sente to Mr [*word illegible*]	5	0	0>
/☞/ Item for Durrantes charges for Mr Palgraves sute	4	0	0
Item to Auger for servinge a subpena of Mr Palgrave		1	0
Item payd to Rycherd Rawling for fower planckes & for making a			

---

[21] Thomas Weld gent. of Wymondham, (bn. *c.* 1563), father of the Parliamentarian Thomas Weld (*c.* 1598–*c.* 1662) of Cavick House, Wymondham, also an attorney and good servant of the town.

[22] John Pagrave (*c.* 1531–1611) of North Barningham, J.P. 1579, commissioner for subsidies and lord of Hethersett's manor in Wymondham. See A.Hassell Smith, *County and Court: Government and Politics in Norfolk, 1558–1603* (Oxford, 1974), p. 388.

[23] There were two town wells, one in the Market Place and the other in Town Green.

	£	s	d
bond for the securytie of Howchinges children		3	4
Item for the *accomptantes* fee		13	4
Item to Mr Castleton for charges in thexchequr		12	8
Item paid to Thomas Godfrey for Widowe Swayns houserent		13	4

Summa £33 15s 6½d <recept>

<*Summa redditi allocati* £1 0s 7d>

Summa totalis allocacionum £34 16s 1½d

Et sic idem accomptor debet super compotum suum pro annis preteritis £37 11s

[*f. 53r*]   **[1598-99]**

The acompte of Nycholas Dyckerson collector for all the rentes & fermes of & for all the landes & tenementes belongyng to the towneshyppe of Wymondham acomptyng from the Feaste of Saynt Mychaell the Archangell in the yere of our Lorde God 1598 untyll the yere of our Lord God 1599 for one hoole yere then ended as folowyth

	£	s	d
Firste he dothe acompte for the arerage of his laste accompte	37	11	0
Of Edward Crane <fre> for free rent by yere		3	0
Of Agnes Wyseman for free rent by yere		1	10
Of Ales Frostyn for free rent by yere		2	0
Of Robert Mayhew for free rent by yere			4
Of Peter Neve for free rent by yere			10
Of Wylliam Grene for fre rent by yere			10
Of Edmund Culliour for free rent by yere			1
Of Margaret Ryngwood for the interest of twentye pownd in her handes	2	0	0
Item of Thomas Smythe for the ferme of Teddes Cloase & 2 acres of lande there nere	9	0	0
Item of Richard Rawlinge for thre rodes of medow at Kyddes Wyllowes & 2 acres of lande in the Northe Fylde		12	8
Of hym for a medow at Westewade Chapell	1	0	0
Item of John Flowerdewe for a cloase at the Poples	1	6	8
Of him for 3 acres of medowe at Salters Forde		16	8
Of hym for 2 acres of land in the North Fylde		10	0
Of hym for one acre in 2 peces in the same fylde		4	10
Item of Richard Engleshe for a cloase at the Popylles	1	0	0
Item of William Ovyngton for 3 acres of lande in the <Nothe> Northe Fylde		17	6

Summa £55 8s 3d

	£	s	d
[*f. 53v*] Item of hym for the cloase at the Claye Pyttes	1	6	8

	£	s	d
Item of Robert Cristmas for <acre> acre of lande in Byxelonde Fylde		4	0
Item of John Burde for a medowe at Hochams Care		3	4
Item of John Symondes for one acre and a halfe at Stephens Crofte		7	6
Item of Wylliam Sparham for one acre of lande & an other pece			
sometyme a grove		6	0
Item of Wylliam Payne for 2 acres of land in Holme Fylde nere			
New Mylles		8	0
Item of Thomas Hobbes for 2 acres theare		8	0
Item of Robert Hobbes for a parcell of medow near Wade Brigge in			
his medow		1	0
Item of Thomas Coale for a cloose <at R> & thre rodes of lande			
nere Ryvaldes	1	6	8
Item of John Vynyor for 1 acre of lande lyeng in Claxewelle Furlonge		5	0
Item of Jefferye Sturmyn for a cloose in Hunegate		14	0
Of hym for one a & halffe with a grove in the este ende in Claxewell			
Furlong		7	6
Of hym for one acre nere Tolyes Crosse		5	0
Item of Robert Wyseman for 2 acres thre roodes of lande in the			
Northe Fylde		11	0
Item of Loye Agas for 7 acres of lande in the Northe Fyllde	1	15	0
Item of Richard Appylton for 2 acres of lande at Hell Lanes ende		10	0
Item of Henry Kette for 3 acres of land in the Northe Fylde		12	0
Item of John Symondes for an o[r]teyard nere guylde hall		1	0

Summa £9 11s 8d

[*f. 54r*] Item of George Norton for 2 acres 3 roodes of land in the			
Northe Fylde		11	0
Item of Thomas Woodcoke senior for 3 roodes of land		4	0
Item of Henry Spenloue gent for a cloose in Digebeck & 2 acres of			
land nere Crownsawghe		16	0
Item of Robert Thornton gent for a parcell of medow nere Wade			
Brigge by yere		4	0
Item of John Busshe for 2 acres of lande		6	0
Item of John Kette for 3 roodes of lande		3	0
Item of Thomas Talbott doctor of the lawe for one acre of lande			
lyeng in his close nere the Game Place		4	0
Item of Artur Wylliams gent for a parcell of med & pasture late in			
the ferme of John Busshe		[*blank*]	
Item of William Daynes for the towne howses called the guylde			
howse & the pewter & brasse & other thynges	3	0	0
Item of Raignolde Kene for the towne howse	1	10	0
Item of Randole Downyng for the towne shoppe		12	0

	£	s	d
Of hym for one acre of lande in the Parke Fylde		5	0
Item of Edmund Fedemond for a towne howse		6	8
Item of Robert Toly for for [*sic*] a towne howse		13	4
Item of John Clare for a towne howse he kepe the chirche wyndowes with glaseyng		6	8
Item of Wylliam Cocke & Robert Garrade for ther howse		6	8
Item of Margaret Hunteley & Cristen More for a towne howse		6	8
Item of Cristen Smythe for a towne howse		6	8
Item of Ales Smyth & others for a towne howse		6	8
Item of the wedowe Leche & Jone Cotton for a howse		6	8
Item of John Gaye for the howse at Blackenham	1	4	0
Item of Thomas Coole for one acre at Barowes Hedd		5	0
Of him for one acre in Holme Felde		4	0
Item of Henry Turner for Dowes howse	2	13	4

Summa £15 1s 4d

The hoole some of the receytes this yere is   <£80 12s 11d> £80 1s 3d

Where of

[*f. 54v*] he aske to be alowyd of the free rentes and other rentes on payd by dyverse persons as folowyth

/Fre rentes/

	£	s	d
Firste in the handes of Robert Crane		<3	0>
In the handes of Artur Wylliams for that that was Agnes Wysemans		1	10
In the handes of Ales Frostyn wedow		2	0
In the handes of George Mayehew			4
In the handes Peter Neave			10
In the handes of Thomas Nykeson			10
In the handes of Edmund Culliour			1

Summa of this is   5s 11d

	£	s	d
In the handes of Thomas Talbott doctor of the lawe		4	0
In the handes of Robert Hobbes		1	0
Item he aske to be alowyd of Thomas Hastes ferme by the consent of the townesmen		10	0
Item he doth aske to be alowyd of the ferme of Randole Downyng not payd by thre yeres		7	6
Item aske to be alowyd oulde Frosedickes howse for the laste yere	1	4	0
Item he aske to be alowyd for the ferme of Wylliam Daynes for the guylde howses	3	0	0

The some of this is   £5 7s 6d

	£	s	d
And so the trew some receyvyd thys yere <is> with the areragis is	74	8	10

[*The above sum contains two cancellations and two figures for pounds which together add up to £74*]

whereof

[*f. 55r*] /**Payementes**/

	£	s	d
Firste payd to the Quenes Majestyes baly for rent	1	7	5
Item payd to hym for one rent henne			6
Item payd to the balye for the manner of Cromwells for rent		4	1
Item payd to Mr Welles the skolemaster for his yeres wages	15	0	0
/☞/ Item payd to Mr Welles the mynnestere by the consent of dyvers of the townesmen	6	0	0
/☞/ Item payd to Master Jubbes one of the chirchewardens toward the mendyng of the stepyll	6	0	0
/☞/ Item payd to Thomas Smyth one of the chirchewardens for to mend the stepyll	5	0	0
Item payd for makyng of tressells & formes and bordes & other reparasyons in thackyng dawbyng grownsyllyng pamentyng & mendyng of the sparres at the guyldehowse	3	2	10
Item payd for the charges of the sowlgers for traynyng coates cundyt mony powder shott a sworde & a hede pece	4	11	9
/☞/ Item payd to Bartylmew Bothe the 18 of January 1599 for kepyng the chylde	1	3	4
/☞/ Item payd to the wedow Buckenham for the chylde for 20 wekes at 16 pence a weke	1	6	8
/☞/ Item payd moare to her toward the bringyng up of the chylde tyll is abyll to shyfte for it selffe then she must have £4 wherof she hadd	1	0	0
Item payd to Master *Heyward* for a coppe of certen landes holden of the manner Cromweles		2	6
/☞/ Item payd to John Kensey & Thomas Agas to cary to Mr Herne for the sute for the towneland	2	0	0
Item payd to John Castelten for to have a mocyon for the towne lande		15	0
Item payd Robert Wyseman for the towne well		11	4
Item payd for mendyng of the harth where Elizabethe Leche dwellythe		2	4

Summa £48 8s 2d

	£	s	d
[*f. 55v*] Item payd for a coppye of Master Pagravys warant to Buttfylde			6
/☞/ Item payd for the townes mens charges when they went to Norwitche to be examyned at Mr Palgravis first comyssion for the taske	1	8	8

	£	s	d
Item payd for Master Baxters charges beyng of cownsell with the towne at the laste comyssion		2	8
Item payd for Henry Turners harth & the well		5	4
Item payd to Brownes wyffe for helyng the chylderens heades beyng skalde		5	0
Item payd to Stephen Wyseman for the preachers charges in Rogacion Weke		18	8
Item payd for makyng the chymney for Father Cocke & Robert Garrade		3	6
Item payd for healyng of Brownes daughters head		15	0
/☞/ Item payd for Crampes apparell & a payer of shoes		6	8
Item payd moare for Browns daughters head healyng		15	0
Item payd for a revesheppe to the manner of Cromwells for the Tenement Skorells		1	0
Item payd to the wedow Buckenham for the chylde for Cristemes quarter		10	0
/☞/ Item delyverd to Stephen Wyseman <and when> *and* Thomas Agas when they went to London to defend the sute agaynst Ser Henry Woodhowse for the towne lande the 16 of Januarye 1599	14	14	4
Item payd to Loye Agas for the taske of the guylde howses		1	4
Item payd to Master Leveryngton for a coppye of the landes holden of the Quene		1	0
Item payd to John Rudland for mony he was out of when he was chirchewarden	1	6	2

Summa   £21 14s 10d

	£	s	d
[f. 56r] Item payd to Edmund Barnard for lyke cause the same yere	1	6	8
Item payd moare to John *More* for lyke cause the same yere	2	4	6
Item delyvered to Robert Coleman by consent upon bonde	5	0	0
<Item I aske to be alowed for 20s I payd for Thomas Haste the ded grant I shulde have it back agayne [sic]	1	0	0>
/☞/ Item payd to Robert Crane for *a* horse for Thomas Agas to rydde to London on		10	0
/☞/ Item payd to Wylliam Culliour for bakyng of breade for the pore folke		15	4
Item payd to John Clare for glasyng the chirche		6	8

<*Summa*   £10 3s 2d>

	£	s	d
Item for my fee		13	4

Summa   £10 16s 6d

The hoole some of the payementes is   £80 19s 6d

And so the payementes exced the receytes   £6 10s 8d

	£	s	d

[1599-1600]

The acompte of Nycholas Dyckerson collector of & for all the rentes & fermes of all the landes and tenementes belongyng to the towneshepp of Wymondham acomptyng from the Feaste of Saynt Mychaell Tharchangell in the yere of our Lorde God 1599 ontyll the Feaste of Saynt Mychaell in the yere of our Lord God 1600 for one hoole yere then ended as folowyth

	£	s	d
First of Wylliam Crane for fre rent		3	0
Of Artur Wylliams for fre rent of the house late Agnes Wysemans		1	10
Of Ales Frostyn for fre rent		2	0
Of George Mayhew for fre rent			4
Of Peter Neave for fre rent			10
Of Thomas Nykson for fre rent of the howse late Wylliam Grenes			10
Of Edmund Culliour for fre rent			1
Of Margaret Ryngwood for the ewse of £20 by yere	2	0	0
Of Thomas Smyth for Teddes & 2 acres of land	9	0	0
Of Richard Rawlyn for 3 roodes of medowe at Kyddes Wyllowes & 2 acres of land		12	8
Of hym for a medow at Westewade	1	0	0
Of Agnes Flowerdew for a close at the Popylls	1	6	8
Of her for 3 acres of medow at Salters Forde		16	8
Of her for 2 acres of lande in the Deale		10	0
Of her for 2 halffe acres in the Northe Fylde		4	10
Of Richard Engleshe for a close at the Popyles	1	0	0
Of Wylliam Ovyngton for 3 acres & halffe of lande in the Northe Fylde		17	6

Summa £17 17s 3d

	£	s	d
[f. 57r] Of hym for a close at the Claye Pyttes	1	6	8
Of Robert Crisemes for an acre of land in Byxelond Fylde		5	0
Of John Birde for a medowe at Hochams Care		3	4
of John Symondes junior for one acre & halfe of land lyeng nexte his crofte		7	6
Of Wylliam Sparham for one acre of land and a parcell of grownde sometyme a grove		6	0
Of Wylliam Payne for 2 acres of land in Holme Fylde		8	0
Of Thomas Hobbes for 2 acres of land there		8	0
Of hym for parcell medow nere Wade Brigge		1	0
Of Thomas Coole for a close & 3 rodes of lande nere Ryvaldes	1	6	8
Of hym for one acre of lande in the North Fylde at Barowes Hedde		5	0
Of hym for one acre in Holme Fylde		4	0
Of John Venyor gent for one acre of lande nere Claxewell		5	0

	£	s	d
Of Jefferye Sturmyn for a close in Hungate		14	0
Of hym for one acre & a halffe of lande with a grove in the este ende		7	6
Of hym for one acre nere Tolys Crosse		5	0
Of Robert Wyseman for 2 acres 3 rodes of lande there nere		11	0
Of Loye Agas for 7 acres of lande in the Northe Fylde	1	15	0
Of John Apylton for 2 acres of lande at Hellanes ende		10	0
Of Henry Kett for 3 acres of lande in the Northe Fylde		12	0

Summa £10 0s 8d

	£	s	d
[*f. 57v*] Of John Symondes sennior for an orteyarde		1	0
Of George Norton for 2 acres 3 roodes of land		11	0
Of Thomas Woodecock for 3 roodes of lande		4	0
Of Henry Spenlove gent for one cloase in Dyggebecke & 2 acres nere Crownshaughe		16	0
Of Robert Thorneton gent for a parcell of medow nere Wade Brygge		4	0
Of John Busshe for 2 acres of lande		6	0
Of John Kett for 3 roodes of lande		3	0
Of Thomas Talbott doctor of the lawe for one acre of lande lyeng in his close at the Game Place		4	0
Of Artur Wylliams gent for a parcell of medowe		[*blank*]	
Of Alexesander Folsham for the towne howse & the pewter	5	0	0
Of Raignolde Kene for a towne howse	1	10	0
Of Randoll Downenyng for a shoppe		12	0
Of hym for one acre of land in the Parke Fylde		5	0
Of Edmund Fedemonde for a towne howse		6	8
Of Robert Tolye for a towne howse		13	4
Of John Clare for a howse he muste glase the chirche wyndowes		6	8
Of Wylliam Cocke & Robert Garrade for a howse		6	8
Of Robert Huntelye & Crysten More for a howse		6	8
Of Cristen Smythe wedow for a howse		6	8
Of Kateryn Bearte & Ales Smyth for a howse		6	8
Of Elyzabeth Leche & Jone Cotton for a howse		6	8
Of John Gaye for a howse nere Blacke Inham	1	4	0

Summa £14

	£	s	d
[*f. 58r*] Of Henry Turner for Dowes howse	2	13	4

Summa £2 13s 4d

The hole some receyvyd this yere is £44 11s 3d

Whereof he aske to be allowed of rentes on payd by dyverse persons as folowythe

	£	s	d

/Fre rentes/

Firste of Artur Wylliams gent for the howse late Agnes Wysemans
for fre rent | | 1 | 10
Of Ales Frostyn wedowe for her howse | | 2 | 0
Of George Mayhew | | | 4
Of Peter Neave for his howse | | | 10
Of Thomas Nyckeson for his howse | | | 10
Of Edmund Culliour for a pece of lande | | | 1
Of Thomas Talbotte doctor of the lawe for one acre of lande in his
cloose | | 4 | 0
Of Robert Hobbes for a parcell of medowe | | 1 | 0
and for the twenty pownde in the handes of Margaret Ryngwood | 2 | 0 | 0

The some of these parceles is   £2 10s 11d

And so the trew some receyvyd this yere is   £42 0s 4d

Where of payd

[f. 58v] */Payementes/*

Firste payde to Thomas Kett for the Quenes rente | 1 | 7 | 5
Item payd to hym one rente hene | | | 6
Item payd to Russelles for Cromewells rente | | 4 | 1
Item payd to John Clare for glasyng the chirche wyndowes | | 6 | 8
Item payd skole master for his wages | 15 | 0 | 0
Item payd to Raphe Fytylyn for a dubble taske for the guylde howses | | 1 | 4
Item payd to the wedowe Gedney for the prechars charges in
Rogacion Weke | | 9 | 0
Item payd to Raphe Fitlyng for Fosters and Goldynges trayenyng in
the towne armur the 25 of Aprill *anno* 1600 | | 1 | 8
Item payd to Cristopher Browne mendyng of John Gayes howse | | 7 | 0
Item payd to the wedowe Buckenham for 3 quarters *ended at
Cristemas* kepyng the chylde | 1 | 10 | 0
Item payde to Henry Turner for glasyng | | 3 | 4
Item payd to Raphe Jubbes toward the stepyll | 6 | 0 | 0
Item moare to hym for to paye Goodwyn | | 17 | 6
Item payd to Sturmyns wyffe for charges at the Asyzes | | 7 | 0
Item for my fee | | 13 | 4
Allowed <which> *[?]to* Nycholas Dykerson which he layd owte in
the yere before | 6 | 10 | 8

The hoole some of the paymentes is   <£27 8s 10d> £33 19s 8d

And so the receytes exced the paymentes all thynges
alowyde is<£14 11s 6d> £8 0s 10d

£   s   d

The acompte of Nycholas Dyckerson collector of and for all the rentes & fermes of all the towne landes and tenementes belongyng to the townsheppe of Wymondham acomptyng from the Feaste of Saynte Mychaell Tharchangell in the yere of our Lorde God 1600 ontyll the Feaste of Saynt Mychaell in the yere of our Lorde God 1601 for one hoale yere the[n] ended as folowyth

	£	s	d
Firste for the arerages of his last acompte <14 11 6>	*8	0	10*

/Free rentes/

	£	s	d
Firste of Wylliam Crane for free rent		3	0
Of Frances Neave <[two words illegible]> late Agnes Wysemans for free rent		1	10
Of Ales Frostyn wedow for free rent		2	0
Of Peter Neave for free rent			10
Of Thomas Nyckeson for free rent			10
Of <Rob> George Mayhew for free rent			4
Of Edmund Culliouor for free rent			1
Of Thomas Smythe for Teddes	9	0	0
Of Richard Rawlyn for 3 roodes of medow at Kydes Wyllowes & 2 acres of land		12	8
Of hym for a medowe at Weste Wade nere Sallters Forde	1	0	0
Of Agnes Flowerdew wedowe for a close at the Popylls	1	6	8
Of her for thre akers of medowe at Salters Forde nere Westewade		16	8
Of her for 2 akers of lande in the Dele		10	0
Of her for one acre of lande in 2 peces		4	10
Of Richard Engleshe for a close at the Popyls	1	0	0
Of Wylliam Ovyngton thre acres of land & a halffe		17	6
Of hym for a close at the Claye Pyttes	1	6	8
Of Robert Cristmas for one aker of lande in Byxeland Fyllde		5	0

Summa   <£32 0s 5d>   £25 9s 9d

	£	s	d
[f. 59v] Of John Burde for a medow at Hochmes Care		3	4
Of John Symondes the yonger for one aker and a halffe in <he> his crofte		7	6
Of John Gaye for one acre of lande and a parcell of grownde sometyme a grovet		6	0
Of Wylliam Payne for 2 acres of land in Holme Fylde nere New Mylles		8	0
Of Thomas Hobbes for 2 acres theare		8	0
Of hym for a parcell of medow at Wade Brigge		1	0
Of Thomas Coole for a close & 3 roodes of land nere Ryvaldes	1	6	8
Of hym for one acre of lande at Barowes Hede		5	0
Of [sic] for one acre in Holme Fylde		4	0

	£	s	d
Of John Venyor gent for one acre nere Claxwell		5	0
Of Jefferye Sturmyn for a close in Howngate called Howlyns Close		14	0
Of hym for one acre & a halfe of lande with grovet in the este ende in Claxwell Furlong		7	6
Of hym for one acre nere Tolyes Crosse		5	0
Of Robert Wyseman for 2 acres *3 rodes* of lande lyeng there nere		11	0
Of Loye Agas for 7 acres of land in the Northe Fylde	1	15	0
Of John Raygnolde for 2 acres at Hell Lanes end		10	0
Of Henry Kett for 3 acres in the Northe Fylde		12	0
Of John Symondes *senior* for an orteyarde at the guylde howse		1	0
Of George Norton for 2 acres 3 rodes of lande		11	0
Of Thomas Woodcock for 3 roodes of pasture		4	0
Of Henry Spenloue gent for a close & 2 acres of lande nere Crownsshaughe		16	0
Of Robert Thorneton gent for a parcell of medow at Wade Brygge		4	0

Summa   £10   5s

	£	s	d
[f. 60r] Of John Busshe for 2 acres of lande		6	0
Of Thomas Talbott doctor of the cevyll lawe for one acre of lande		4	0
Of John Kett for 3 roodes of lande nere Beckes Lane		3	0
Of Artur Wylliams for a parcell of medow at Myll Poole		[blank]	
Of Alexesander Foulesham for the towne howses	5	0	0
Of Raignolde Kene for the howse agaynst the guylde howse	1	10	0
Of Randoll Downyng for the towne shoppe		12	0
Of hym for one acre of lande		5	0
Of Edmund Fedemond for a towne howse		6	8
Of Robert Tolye for a towne howse		13	4
Of John Clare for a towne howse		6	8
Of John Swayne & Wylliam Cocke for a towne howse		6	8
Of Cristen More Margaret Hunteley & the wedowe Crosse for a towne howse		6	8
Of the wedowe Smyth & Thomas Alen		6	8
Of Agnes Brese Mother Berte Margery Goselyng & Ales Brewer for a howse		6	8
Of Elizabeth Leche & Jone Cotton		6	8
Of John Gaye for a towne howse	1	4	0
Of Henry Turner for Dowese howse	2	13	4

<div align="center"><<em>Summa</em>   £14   17s   4d></div>

	£	s	d
Item receyvyd for woode solde Master Spendloue	1	0	0
Of Robert Wyseman for woode & tymber	1	6	8
Of Thomas Cornewell for woode at Woodcockes close		6	0

	£	s	d
Receyvyd Esaye Freman for the arerages of his acompte beyng chirche warden		1	15	0

Receyvyd Esaye Freman for the arerages of his acompte beyng
   chirche warden   1 15 0

Receyvyd of John Queyntrell for 2 graves made in the chirche for
   Mystres Talbott & for Mr Talbottes mother   13 4

Summa £19 18s 4d

The hoole some receyvyd this yere is   <60 £62 4s 9d> *£55 13s 1d*

Whereof

[*f. 60v*] he askyth to be alowed of free rentes on payde as folowyth

/Respyted/

Firste of Fraunces Neave for the rent the howse late Agnes Wysemans
   now the sayd Fraunces   1 10

Of Ales Frosten wedow for her howse   2 0

Of George Mayhewe for grownd within his yard   4

Of Peter Neave for his howse   10

Of Thomas Nyckeson for his howse   10

Of Edmund Culliour for a pece of lande   1

Of Doctor Talbott doctor of the cevyll lawe for one acre of land or
   pasture   4 0

Of Robert Hobbes for a parcell of medowe   1 0

Item for Clares howse   6 8

Summa of this is   <10s 11d> 17s 7d

And so the trewe some receyvyd this yere is   £61 12s 10d

Whereof payd

/Payementes/

Firste payd to the Quenes Maiestyes bale for rent   1 7 5

Item to hym for a rent hene   6

Item payd to Thomas Howse heyward for the manner of Cromwells   4 1

Item payd to the scolemaster for his wages   15 0 0

/☞/ Item payd to Buckenhams wyffe and Master Well[s] for her
   for 2 quarters which is the payment for kepyng the chylde   1 0 0

Item payd to Master Welde for to geve Master Sheryffe to alowe
   our charter   10 0

Item lente to Robert Coleman upon his bonde   4 0 0

Item payd to John Queyntrell the 8 of Maye 1601 for the stepyll   3 0 0

Item payd to the wedowe Gedney for the prechers charges in
   Rogacion Weke   16 0

Item payd to Mr Cromewell for prechyng here   5 0

Item payd by Robert Wyseman to John Clare for glasyng the chirche
   wendowes   1 0 0

	£	s	d
[*f. 61r*] /☞/ Item payd to John Queyntrell by the wedow Flowerdewe for the stepyll	1	10	0
Item payd moare to John Queyntrell for the stepyll	1	4	0
Item lent moare to Robert Coleman	1	10	0
Item payd to Raphe Jubbes upon the determynacion of his acompte sence he was chirchewarden	1	10	0
Item payd for sewyng Henry Turner in the markett courte		3	0
Item payd moare to John Queyntrell upon the determynacion of his acompte sence he was chirchewarden	1	8	7
Item payd to Brownes doughter for her goyng to London		5	0
Item alowyd to Alexander Folsham for makyng 2 planchers in one stabyll and for other reparacions done at the towne howse as aperyth by a byll of parcells	4	0	0
Item payd Mr Welles for glasyng the skolehowse wyndowes as by his acompte delyvered to the Seventen		7	4
Item payd the good wyfe Crane by the appoyntment of John Clare for glasyng the skolehowse wyndowes sence Mr Welles was scolemaster		12	0
Item he aske to be alowyd of forty schelynges and sixe of Jefferye Sturmyns rent wiche is respyted	2	0	6
And for thre yeres rent of the tenement wherein John Swayne dewellyth also respyted	1	0	0
Item for my fee		13	4

The hoole some of the paymentes is   <£51 8s 7d>£44 4s 4d

And so the receytes execed the paymentes   <£10 15s 2d>£11 8s 9d

[*Below these totals at bottom right of page in Arabic numerals*]   44 : 4 : 5

Debet 11 : 8 : 8

[*f. 61v*]   **[1601-1602]**

The acompte of Nycholas Dickerson collector of and for all the towne landes & tenementes & for all the rentes & fermes belongyng to the towneshepe of Wymondham acomptyng from the Feaste of Saynt Mychaell in the yere of our Lorde God 1601 ontyll the yere of our Lorde God 1602 for one hoole yere then ended as folowyth

Firste he dothe acompte for the arerages of his laste acompte wiche is	11	8	9
Item of Wylliam Crane for fre rent by yere		3	0
Item of Fraunces Neve for fre rent of the howse lat Wysemans		1	10
Item of Ales Frostyn for fre rent		2	0
Item of George Mayhew for fre rent			4
Item of Peter Neve for fre rent			10
Item of Thomas Nyckeson for fre rent			10
Item of Edmund Culliour for fre rent			1

	£	s	d
Item of John Botye for the loone of seven pownde		14	0
Item Thomas Smythe for the ferme of Teddes and 2 acres of land there nere	9	0	0
Item of Richard Rawlyn for <land> 3 acr[es] of land & medowe		12	8
Item of Thomas Funston gent for a medowe at Weste Wade	1	0	0
Item of Agnes Flowerdewe wedow for a cloose at the Popyles	1	6	8
Item of her for thre akers of <lande> *medow* at Salters Forde		16	8
Item of her for 2 akers of land in the Dele in the Northe Fylde		10	0
Item of her for one aker in 2 peces in the same fylde		4	10
Item of Richard Engleshe for a close at the Popyles	1	0	0
Item of Wylliam Ovyngton for thre akers *dimidia* of lande in the Northe Fylde		17	6
Item of hym for a cloase at the Claye Pyttes	1	6	8
Item of Edward Lawes for one aker of lande in Byxelande Fylde		5	0

Summa is £29 11s 8d

	£	s	d
[*f. 62r*] Item of John Burde for a medow at Hochams Carre		3	4
Item of John Symondes for one aker & halffe lyeng in his crofte		7	6
Item of John Gaye for one aker of lande and another percell sometyme a grove		6	0
Item of Wylliam Payne for 2 akers in Holme Fylde		8	0
Item of Edmund Bucke for 2 akers there		8	0
Of Thomas Hobbes for a parcell of medowe nere Wade Brigge		1	0
Of Thomas Coole for a medow at Ryvalldes and thre rodes of lande there	1	6	8
Of hym for one aker of lande at Barowes Hed		5	0
Of hym for one aker in Holme Fylde		4	0
Of John Venyor for one aker of lande lyeng in Claxewell Furlong		5	0
Of [*blank*] Ysbelles for the cloase called Howlyns	1	0	0
Of hym for one aker & a halffe with a grove		7	6
Of hym for one aker at Tolyes Crosse		5	0
Of Robert Wyseman for 2 akers & 3 rodes of land in the Northe Fylde		11	0
Of Loye Agas for 7 akers of land in the Northe Fylde	1	15	0
Of John Raynolde for 2 akers inclosed at Hellanes end		10	0
Of Henry Kett for 3 akers of land in the Northe Fylde		12	0
Of John Symondes for an orteyarde at the towne howse		1	0
Of George Norton for 2 akers 3 rodes of lande in the Northe Fylde		11	0
Of Thomas Woodcock for 3 rodes of pasture lyeng in his close		6	0
Of Henry Spenlove for 2 akers of land nere Crongshaughe and one close in Dyggebecke nere his howse		16	0

Summa is £10 9s

	£	s	d
[*f. 62v*] Of Robert Thornton gent for a percell of medowe ner Wade Brigge		4	0
Of John Busshe for 2 akers of lande		6	0
Of Thomas Talbott doctor of the lawe for one aker of lande lyeng in his closse nere the Game Place		4	0
Of John Kett for 3 rodes of lande at Beckes Dyke		3	0
Of Artur Wyllmes gent for a parcell of medowe or pasture late in the ferme of John Busshe		[*blank*]	
Of Alexsander Foulsham for the towne howses	5	0	0
Of Raynolde Kene for the howse he dwellyth in	1	10	0
[*On the same line beyond the sum*] & reparacions			
Of Randoll Downyng for the towne shoppe		12	0
Of hym for one aker of lande in the Parke Fylde		5	0
Of Edmund Fedemond for a towne howse		6	8
Of Robert Toly for a towne howse		13	4
Of John Clare for a towne howse		6	8
Of John Swayen & Wylliam Cocke for a towne howse		6	8
Of Robert Hunteley & others for a towne howse		6	8
Of Cristen Smyth & Thomas Alen for a towne howse		6	8
Of Mother Berte Ales Smyth & others		6	8
Of Elizabeth Leche & Jone Cotton		6	8
Of John Gaye for the howse at Blacke Enham	1	4	0
Item receyvyd of Richard Engleshe for <thre> *4* skore & ten fagottes of woode		5	0

Summa is £12 13s 0d

The hoole some of this yeres rent with the arerages of the last yeres
acompte is £52 13s 8d

Whereof respeted of fre rentes & others on payd in dyverse mens handes as
folowyth

/Fre rentes/

First of *in* Fraunces Neves *handes*	1	10	
Of Ales Frostyn wedow	2	0	
Of George Mayhew		4	
Of Peter Neve		10	
In the handes of Thomas Nyckson		10	The some of all
In the handes of Edmund Culliour		1	respeites is 11s 11d
In the handes Doctor Talbotte	4	0	
In the handes of Robert Hobbes	1	0	
In the handes of John Symondes	1	0	

And so the trew some besydes the respeites is £52 1s 9d

	£	s	d

Whereof he aske to be allowyd as folowyth

[f. 63r] /**Paymentes**/

	£	s	d
Firste payd to the Quenes baly for rent	1	7	5
Item payd to hym moare for a rent henne			6
Item payd to the baly of manner of Cromweles		4	1
Item payd Clare for glasyng the chirche wyndowes		6	8
Item payd to the skolemaster for his yeres wages	15	0	0
/☞/ Item payd for 2 loades of strawe for the towne howses	1	5	0
Item payd to Byxe for syxe dayes thackyng for his boye & hym selffe		12	0
Item for broches and byndynges		1	4
Item payd to the shereve for alowyng the charter		10	0
Item payd to Richard Dyllan for mony that was owyng hym sence he was chirche warden		12	3
Item payd for the prechers charges on Gange Mondaye	1	0	0
Item payd to Clare for glasyng the scole howse wyndowes	1	18	5
/☞/ Item payd to Mr Welde for to renewe the towne charter	1	0	0
Item payd to Thorne Howse & Bucke for servyng and traynyng in the towne armor 2 dayes a pece in June 1602		5	0
Item payd for a sworde 2 dagers one gyrdell and a hanger for for [sic] the towne armor		6	0
/☞/ Item payd to Nycholas Kecheham to take one of Howelles boyes to be his prentyce for seven yeres	1	10	0
Item payd to John Raynolde for mony dewe to hym sence he was chirche warden		8	0
/☞/ Item payd to Robert More for aparell for Crosse		8	0
Item payd moare *for* clothynge of Bartylmew Blodde by the apoyntment of Mr Spenloue & others		11	8
Item payd to Robert Coleman for monye layde out by hym when he was chirche warden		3	6
/☞/ Item we muste allowe to Spynke for mony layd out by hym when he was destrayned for Tyfford Brygge & his cowe solde by the balye	1	0	0
Item yow must alowe me for mony layd owt by Alexsander Folssam for bryke & tyle	1	19	1
Item payd to Turpyn for a solgers coate		6	8

Summa is £30 15s 7d

	£	s	d
[f. 63v] Item payd to John for mony layd by hym when he was chirche warden		17	0
Item payd to Robert Toly for kepyng of Howeles chylderen	1	0	0
Item for my fee		13	4

£ s d

Summa is £2 10s 4d

The hoole some of the paymentes is £33 5s 11d

And so the receytes exced the paymentes £18 15s 10d

[*f. 64r*]   **[1602-1603]**

The acompte of Nycholas Dickerson collector of & for all the rentes & fermes of all the towne landes and tenementes belongyng to the townshepe of Wymondham acomptyng from the Feaste of Saynt Mychaell the Archangell in the yere of our Lorde God 1602 ontyll the Feaste of Saynt Mychaell in the yere of our Lorde God 1603 for one hole yere then ended as folowyth

Firste he doth acompte for the arerages of his last acompte wiche is 18 15 10

/Free rentes/

Item of Wylliam Crane for free rent	3	0
Of Fraunces Neave for free rent	1	10
Of Ales Frostyn wedow for free rent	2	0
Of George Mayhew for free rent		4
Of Peter Neave for free rent		10
Of Thomas Nyckson for free rent		10
Of Edmund Culliour for free rent		1
Of John Botye for the *euse* of 7 pownde	14	0

Of [*blank*] Spynke for Teddes & 2 acres of land 9 0 0

Of Richard Rawlyn for 3 rodes of medowe at Kyddes Wyllowes
  & 2 acres of land in the Northe Fylde 12 8

Of Thomas Funston gent for a medow at Weste Wade 1 0 0

Of Agnes Flowerdew *vidua* for a closse at the Popyles 1 6 8

Of her for 3 akers of medow at Westwade Chapell 16 8

Of her for 2 akers of lande in the Northe Fylde 10 0

Of her for halfe an aker in the same fylde 3 6

Of her for halfe an aker at the Pyttes 3 4

Of Robert Engleshe for a cloase at the Popyles 1 0 0

Of Wylliam Ovyngton for 3 akers & a halfe of lande in the
  Northe Fylde 17 6

Of hym for a cloase at the Claye Pyttes 1 6 8

Of Edward Lawes for one aker of lande in Byxeland Felde 5 0

Summa £36 18s 9d

[*f. 64v*] Of John Burde for a parcell of medow at Hockhams Carre 3 4

Of John Symondes for one aker & a halfe of lande in his crofte 7 6

Of <John> *Thomas Gaye* for one aker of land and a parcell of
  land some tyme a grove 6 0

Of Wylliam Payne for 2 akers of land in Holme Fylde 8 0

	£	s	d
Of Edmund Bucke for 2 akers there		8	0
Of Thomas Hobbes for a parcell of medow lyeng nere Wade Brygge		1	0
Of Thomas Coole for a medow & 3 rodes of lande nere Ryvaldes	1	6	8
Item of hym for one aker of land <in Holm Fylde> lyeng at Baroughes Heade		5	0
Of hym for one aker in Holme Fylde		4	0
Of Master Venyour for one aker nere Claxewell		5	0
Of [blank] Esbeles <word cancelled> for a pyghtell called Howlyns lyeng in Hungate	1	0	0
Of hym for one aker & a halfe of lande with a grove		7	6
Of hym for one aker of land nere Tolys Crosse		5	0
Of Robert Wyseman for 2 akers & thre roodes of land in the North Fylde		11	0
Of Loye Agas for 7 akers of lande in the Northe Fylde	1	15	0
Of John Raignolde for 2 akers of lande at Hellanes ende		10	0
Of Henry Kett for 3 akers of lande in the Northe Fylde		12	0
Of John Symondes for an orte yarde		1	0
Of George Norton for 2 akers 3 roodes of lande in the North Fylde		11	0
Of Thomas Wodecocke for 3 roodes of pasture		6	0

Summa   £9 13s

	£	s	d
[*f. 65r*] Of Henry Spenloue gent for 2 akers of land nere Crownsaughe & close nere his howse		16	0
Of Robert Thornton gent for a parcell of medowe nere Wade Brigge		4	0
Of John Busshe for 2 akers of land in the Northe Fylde		6	0
Of Thomas Talbott gent doctor of the lawe for one aker of land lyeng in his cloose nere the Game Place		4	0
Of John Kett for 3 rodes of lande nere the Popyles		3	0
Of Artur Wylliams for a parcell of medowe and pasture nere Myle Poole		[*blank*]	
Of Alexsander Folesame for the towne howses	5	0	0
Of Raynolde Kene for a towne howse	1	10	0
[*Following the sum for the above item*] & the reparasyons			
Of Randole Downyng for the towne shoppe		12	0
Of hym for one aker of lande in the Parke Fylde		5	0
Of Edmund Fedemond for a towne howse		6	8
Of Robert Tolye for a towne howse		13	4
Of John Clare for a towne howse		6	8
Of John Swayne & Wylliam Cocke for a towne howse		6	8
Of Robert Hunteley Cristen More and Eme Crosse for a towne howse		6	8
Of Thomas Alen & Cristen Smyth for a towne howse		6	8

	£	s	d
Of Margery Goselyng & others for a towne howse		6	8
Of Elizabethe Leche & Jone Cotton for a towne howse		6	8
Of John Gaye for a towne howse	1	4	0

Summa £13 4s 0d

The hoole some of all is £59 <12s 11d> *15s 9d*

Where of respyted of rentes & fermes onpayd as folowyth

/Fre rentes/

First in the handes Fraunces Neave	1	10
In the handes of Ales Frostyn	2	0
In the handes of George Mayhew		4
In the handes of Peter Neave		10
In the handes of Thomas Nyckson		10
In the handes of Edmund Culliour		1
In the handes of Doctor Talbott	4	0
In the handes of Robert Hobbes	1	0
In the handes of John Symondes	1	0

The some of all these are 11s 11d

And so the trewe some received thys yere besydes the respeites is £59 3s 10d

Where of payd

[f. 65v] **/Paymentes/**

Firste payd to the Kynges baly for rent	1	7	5
Item payd to hym for a rent henne			6
Item payd to the balye for the manner of Cromwelles for rent		4	1
Item payd to the scole master for his yeres wages	15	0	0
Item payd to Thomas Funston beyng sherife for to alow the towne charter		10	0
Item payd for the prechars charges in Rogasyon Weke		11	0
Item payd to Robert Crane John More and Robert More for gone powder agaynst the Crownacyon Daye & another daye of triumfe	1	0	0
/☞/ Item payd to Esaye Freman for 3 lodes of strawe	1	0	0
Item payd to Richard Byxe the tenth of Auguste for layeng of 2 loades of of [sic] strawe on the towne tenantres		12	0
Item payd to hym for layeng of thre loades on the towne howse the gylde howse		18	0
Item payd to Wylliam Payne for one loade of strawe		5	0
Item payd to Wylliam Grene *the 8 of October 1603* for buyldyng the bothe for the Justysys to sytt in at the Sesyons[24]	1	0	0

[24] These were petty sessions to deal with minor misdemeanours and the licensing of alehouses, a relatively new development in Norfolk (see Smith, *County and Court*, pp. 103–106).

	£	s	d
/*Sicknes* ☞/ Item payd Henry Kett to kepe in those where the syckeneswas the 15 of October *1603*	1	10	0
Item payd moare to hym the 22 of October for the same <pupose> purpose	1	0	0
Item payd moare to hym the syxte of November	1	10	0
Item payd to Stephen Burrell for halfe a barell of bere[25] agaynst the tryumfe daye		4	0
Item payd to Wetherley for Garrades howse rent		5	0
Item payd for ten water tankardes for the towne at 2s 6d a pece	1	5	0
Item payd to Peter Stafford for that he was dystraned for the towne well		8	8
Item payd to soweger			6
Item payd John Clare for glasyng the chirche wyndowes		6	8
/*Sicknes* ☞/ Item payd moare to Henry Kett the 5 of January	2	0	0

Summa is   £30 17s 10d

[*f. 66r*] <Item payd *gyven* Master Welles [*three words cancelled*]		10	0
Payd to the skolemaster for Cristmes quarter	3	15	0
Item for my fee		13	4

Summa is   £4 18s 4d

The hole some of paymentes are   £35 16s 2d

and so the receptes exced the paymentes   £23 6s 10d>

The accounte of Nicholas Dickersonn taken the 5th of Januarye 1603 for £29 1s 8d which was left in arrerage in his accompte made at Mihelmas in the yere aforesaide.

Whereof paid as followeth

/*Sicknes* ☞/ Inprimis to Henry Kett	2	0	0
Geven to Mr Wells in consideracion of buryinge the people in tyme of the visitacion		10	0
Paide to Mr Leverington[26] for his quarter ended at Chrismas	3	15	0
Geven to Roberte Toolye towardes the bringinge upp of Howells children	1	6	8
Paide to John Moore for gunpowder spent in tryumphinge for the Kinges Majestie		14	0
Geven to Mr Wells towardes his chardges in seekinge of some rightes supposed to be appertinente to his vicaridge	3	6	8

[25] A barrel of beer was 36 gallons until 1688. A half barrel was therefore 18 gallons. See D. Yaxley, *A Researcher's Glossary of words found in historical documents of East Anglia* (Larks Press, 2003), p. 8.

[26] Mr Thomas Leverington junior, schoolmaster 1603–06, was a graduate of Trinity College, Cambridge and a priest (see Williams, *The History of Wymondham Grammar School*).

	£	s	d

***/Sicknes* ☞/** Geven to diverse pore people in the tyme that ther
  howses were visited with the infection   3   6 <7> *6*

Delivered more by him to Henry Kett towardes the releevinge of
  the sicke people   1   0   6

> Some paid out of the abovesaide some of £29 1s 8d amounteth
> to   £15 19s 4d

The rest not collected by the saide accomptante butt referred to be collected by
John Raynoldes upon diverse men as hereafter followeth

[f. 66v]   *videlicet*

	£	s	d
Richard Rawlinge		12	8
Thomas Funstone *generosus*	1	13	0
Agnes Flowerdewe *vidua*	2	18	2
Katheringe Burley *vidua*		1	4
William Payne		8	0
John Vynyour *generosus*		5	0
Thomas Hobbs		8	0
Roberte Wyseman		11	0
Henry Kett	1	4	0
Thomas Woodcock		2	0
John Bushe		12	0
Alexander Fowlesham	3	10	0
John Swayne		6	8
Margarett Huntley *vidua*		5	6
Kristian Moore		5	0

> Some of tharrerages chardged upon John Raynoldes   £13 2s 4d
> *ut supra* wherof received

	£	s	d
Of Richard Rawlinge		12	8
Of Robert Wyseman		11	0
Of Henry Kett	1	4	0
Of Agnes Flowerdewe	2	18	2
Of Katheringe Burley in parte			4
Of John Vynyour		5	0
Of William Payne		8	0
Of John Swayne in parte		4	0
Of Margarett Huntley & Kristian Moore		3	4

> Some of tharrerages received of the said some of £13 2s 4d
> amountethe to   £6 6s 6d

Wherof laide out for the repayringe of the towne well belonginge
  to the towne houses in Townegreene   11   0

So restethe in thandes of John Raynoldes of tharrerages by him
  collected   5   15   6

	£	s	d

[f. 67r] And of tharrerages uncollected by the saide John Raynoldes
   rest   £6 15s 10d

Wherof alowed to Alexander Fowlsham for repracions of the howses
in his occupacion   3 10 0

So restethe uncollected as followeth

	£	s	d
Of Thomas Funstone *generosus*	1	13	0
Of Katheringe Burley *vidua*		1	0
Of Thomas Hobbs		8	0
Of Thomas Woodcock		2	0
Of John Bushe		12	0
Of John Swayne		2	8
Of Margarett Huntley *vidua*		3	10
Of Kristian Moore		3	4

Some uncollected   £3 5s 10d

Memorandum that Esaye Freman ded delyver into the handes of the townsmen the second daye of Januarye 1605 one obligacion wherin Robert Bale standeth bound to Richard Rawlinge Esaye Freman & Thomas Hobbes for the dischardgeinge the towne of Thomas Bale his brother for any chardge.

Memorandum that Thomas Leverington gent delivered the daye & yere aforesaid three severall obligacions, one for the payement of £5 by Andrew Hawes, the other two for the dischardinge the towne of children.

[f. 67v] These be the names of the seaventenn headborowghes agreed upon at the meetinge of the townsemen the 3 of Januarye 1604

Markettsteade:	<Arthure Williams *generosus*>*Phillip Cullyer* *mortuus*
	Nicholas Dickersonn
	John Moore
Damgatte:	<William Rowse> removed
	Richard Dillan
	<Thomas Agas>*Steven Agas* *mortuus*
Townegrene:	Richard Rawlinge *mortuus*
Chaplegate:	Thomas Leverington *generosus mortuus*
Downegham:	<Roberte Cullyer> *1606: removed into
	Brathewaighte*
	John Symondes
	Edmunde Barnard
Brawicke and	
Stanfilde:	Henry Gay
Suton:	Thomas Weld *generosus*
	Henry Blackborne *generosus mortuus*

	£	s	d

Sylfilde: Steven Wyseman *generosus*
<Frauncis Daynne *generosus*> *removed* *John Raven*
Spoonearowe and
Wattlefilde: Robert Dey
Edward Colman senior
<John Rudlande remove>
John Sheppard

[*f. 68r*]   **[1603-1604]**

The accompte of John Raynoldes collector for all the rentes & fearmes of all the landes & tennementes belonginge to the towneshippe of Wymondham accompt-tynge from the Feaste of Sanct Mychaell Tharchangell in *anno* 1603 untill the said feaste in *anno* 1604 for one hole yeere then ended as followeth

	£	s	d
Inprimis for tharrerage left uncollected in the accompte of Nicholas Dickersonn & referred to be collected by this accomptante which is received	5	15	6
Received of Phillippe Cullyer collector for the rentes & fearmes of the towne landes & tennementes in the yeres 1592 & 1593 which remained upon his accounte made for the foresaide yeres the some of		12	2

[*The pages which contained these accounts are torn out.*]

/Free rentes/	£	s	d
Received of William Crane for free rent		3	0
/<**These sixe not paide**>/			
Item of Frauncis Neave		1	10
Item of Ales Frosten *vidua*		2	0
Of Geordge Mayhewe			4
Of Peter Neave			10
Of Thomas Nicksonn			10
The landholders late Edmunde Culliers			1
John Bootye for the use of seaven poundes payable by bond		14	0
/Farme rentes/			
Of Thomas Spynck for the farme of Teddes Close & 3 acres of land nere adjoyninge	9	0	0
Of Richard Rawlinge for 3 roodes of medowe at Kyddes Willowes & 2 acres of land in the Northefelde		12	8
Of Thomas Funstone *generosus* for a medowe at Westewade	1	0	0
Of Agnes Flowerdewe *vidua* for a close at the Poples for 3 acres of medowe at Westwade Chappel & 3 acres of land in the Northefelde	2	18	2
Of William Ovyngton for a close at the Clay Pyttes & 3 acres *dimidia* of land in the Northe Felde	2	4	2

	£	s	d
Of Edward Lawse <of> for one acre of land in Bixtland Feld		5	0
Of Larrence Fletcher for a parcell of medowe at Hockhams Carre		3	4
Of Richard Inglish for a pightell neer Hockhams	1	0	0

Some   £24   13s   11d

<div align="center"><Besides these [<i>word illegible</i>] not paide></div>

	£	s	d
[<i>f. 68v</i>] Of John Symondes junior for an acre & a halfe of land in his crofte		7	6
Of Arthure Earle for on acre of land & a parcell of land some tyme a grove		6	0
Of William Payne for 2 acres of land in Holmefelde		8	0
Of Edmunde Buck for 2 acres ther		8	0
/<Not paide>/			
Of Thomas Hobbs for a parcell of medowe nere Wattbrigge		1	0
Of Thomas Cole senior for a medoue & 3 roodes of land neere Ryvaldes one acre at Barroughes Heade & one acre in Holmefelde	1	15	8
Of Raphe Foxe for one acre of land in Claxewell Furlonge		5	0
Of Thomas Isbells for a pightell called Howlyns in Hungate & 1 acre <i>dimidia</i> of land with a grove	1	7	6
Of Robert Wyseman for 2 acres & 3 roodes of land in the Northefelde		11	0
Of Loy Agas for 7 acres of land in the Northe Felde	1	15	0
Of John Raynoldes junior for a pightell at Hell Lanes end		10	0
Of Henry Kett for 3 acres of land in the Northefelde		12	0
/<Never paide>/			
John Symondes for an artcheyard		1	0
Of Geordge Norton for 3 acres <& 3 roodes> of land in the Northe Felde		11	0
Of Thomas Woodcock for 3 roodes of pasture		5	0
Of Henry Spendlowe gent for a pightell nere his howse & 2 acres of land<nere> which <Crowne> head upon the landes of Henry Meane		16	0
Of Robert Thorneton <i>generosus</i> for a parcell of medoue nere Wadebrigge		4	0
Of Robert Agas for 2 acres of land in Northefeld		6	0
/<Not paide>/			
Of Thomas Talbott generosus for one acre of land in his close neere the Game Place		4	0
Of John Kett for 3 roodes of land neere the Poples		3	0
Of Arthure Williams for a parcell of medowe & pasture neere Myll Poole		[<i>blank</i>]	

	£	s	d
Of Alexander Foulsham for the towne howses	5	0	0
Of Raynold Kene for a towne howse	1	10	0
Of Randoll Downynge for a towne shoppe & an acre of land in the Parkefelde		17	0
Of Edmund Fedymonte for a towne howse		6	8
Of Stephen Agas for an acre of land at Toolyes Crosse		5	0

Some £18 15s 4d

<div align="center"><Besides these the somes [<em>word illegible</em>] not paide></div>

		£	s	d
[f. 69r] Of Robert Tooly for a townehowse			13	4
Of John Cleere for a townehowse			6	8
Of John Swayne & William Cock for a townehowse			6	8
Of Robert Huntley Christian Moore & Em Crosse for a towne howse			6	8
Of Thomas Allyne & Christian Smythe for a towne house			6	8
Of Margery Goslinge & Ales Smythe alias Bruer for a towne house			6	8
Of El[i]sabethe Lietche & Jone Cotten for a towne howse			6	8
Of John Gay for a towne howse		1	4	0

Some £3 <12> 17s 4d

<Some totall of all these receytes

over & besides the free rentes & other somes menconed upon ther> [blank]

Some of tharrerages & rentes amountethe to the some of £47 6s 7d

More rec. by him of Lemman for parte of the <her> farme of the medoue at Westwade sett upon Mr Funstone	8	0
Rec. by him more for maples sold to Edmund Hamonde	8	0
Rec. by him of Thomas Cole for an okes topp & 3 old trees	3	0
Rec. by him of William Ovyngton for wood	4	6

Some totall of all the chardge £48 10s 1d

Wherof prayethe to be alowed as followeth

[f. 69v] **/Rentes not paide/**

Inprimis of rentes not received videlicet

	£	s
Of Frauncis Neave	1	10
Of Ales Frosten vidua	2	0
Of Geordge Mayhewe		4
Of Peter Neave		10
Of Thomas Nicksonn		10
Of the landholders late Edmund Culliors		1
Of Thomas Hobbs	1	0
Of John Symondes senior	1	0
Of Thomas Talbotte gent	4	0

[All rents not paid are bracketed and totalled on right margin at 11s 11d]

	£	s	d
/Paymentes/			
Payd for the reparacions of the howse wher Fowlsham dwellethe			
bestowed by the said Fowlsham	3	10	0
Geven to Fowlsham by the consente of the Seaventenn		12	0
Item alowed to Robert Tooly in consideracion of Howells children			
the rent of the howse wher he dwelleth *videlicet*		13	4
Item alowed to John Cleere in consideracion of glasinge the churtche			
wyndowes the rent of the howse wher he dwellethe *videlicet*		6	8
Paide to Mr Leveringtonn the schoolemaster for his whole yeres			
wages	15	0	0
/☞/ Paid to Mr Weld to be advysed upon the charter	1	3	8
Paid to Russells for Cromwells rent for one whole yeere		4	1
Paid for the preachers chardges upon Rogation Mundaye		9	2
Paide to Wade for bryck & tyle for the schoolehowse		13	6
Paid to Robert Colman for 2 loades of sand		1	8
Paide for carriadge of the same to Symond Howse			4
Paide for heare		1	4
Paide for carringe of lyme to the schoolehowse			4
Paide for makinge the wall at the schoolehowse & mendinge the walls			
within the schoole		12	0
Paide more for tyle pynne & nayles & beere			8
Paide more for whytinge the schoolehowse & shredes		7	0
Paide for 2 chalder of lyme		9	4

Some   £24 17s 0d

	£	s	d
[*f. 70r*] Paide for 2 loades of clay castinge & carringe		1	4
Paide to Esau Freman for strawe			4
Paide for carringe of sand & comminge twyse to the bryck kill		1	0
Paide for carringe of 2 chalder of lyme		5	4
Paide more for 2 bushels of lyme to whyte the schoole			6
Paide to Wytherley for amercemente for the towne for the bridges			
at Westwade			6
Paide for fellinge, shredinge, crowninge & ladinge a tree to make the			
bridges			6
Paide for cariadge of the same tree		1	0
Paide for sawinge the planck & hewinge & layinge the bridges		2	0
/☞/ Pade for lynnen & wollen clothe for Ashemans boy		18	10
Paide more for him for lynsey wollsey		2	6
Paide to Thriste for makinge his clothes & 2 shirtes		5	4
Paid for hose & shoes for him		2	8
Paide for a dublett for him		2	0
Paide to Mullarel for 3 loades carringe *videlicet*: one of lyme & planck,			
& one of brycke & one of sand		1	6

	£	s	d
Paide to Robert Colman for a loade of sand			10
Paide to Wade for 500 bryck for the churtche portche		5	10
Paide more to Wade for 200 tyle for the schoolehowse		2	5
Paide for 2 bushels of lyme for the churtche portche		1	6
Paide to Wade for 14 bryckes more			2
Paide to Mr Wells for an ashe		1	0
Paide for nayles & spyles & for one day *dimidia* of worke of Farrowe & his man		3	2
Paide for 15 yardes of lynnen clothe to apparell Bartholmewe Ubanck		7	6
/☞/ Paide for the Lord Byshopps[27] chardges at his visitation	8	0	0
/☞/ Paide to Thomas Browne for his howse in the tyme of the infection	1	0	0
Paide to Mr Shene the Kynges baylie for the rentes of the landes holden of his Majestie	1	7	5
/☞/ Paide for a petticote & a wastcote for Margarett Dunn		9	0

Some   £14 4s 8d

	£	s	d
[*f. 70v*] /☞/ Paide for 7 yardes of lynnen clothe for the saide Margarett		3	8
Paide more for a sheete for the saide Margarett		2	6
Paide to John Kett for 200 strawe		4	0
Paide to Richard Russells for issues for the towne landes		1	0
/☞/ Paide to Henry Kett to releeve the sycke howses in tyme of the visitation	6	1	9
Paide to Richard Farrowe for hewinge 2 bord <howse> stockes for the guilde howse		1	6
Paide for sawing 200 *dimidia* of bord		4	6
Paide for hewinge of a grounsell			6
Paide to John Raynoldes for carringe of 3 quarters of wood from the pightell & groundes in the occupacion of Mr Sckipp <&> *or* his farmors		2	6
Paide to him for carringe the bord & grounsells			6
Paide to John Appleton for dykinge & hedginge 15 rods at 5d a rod about Teddes Close		6	0
Paide to Godfrye & his man for 3 dayes worke at Teddes		6	3
Paide for hookes & hingles			10
Paide more for diking & hedginge 22 rodd at Teddes		9	1
Paide to Thomas Wells & his man for 6 dayes workes in thackinge the howses in Towngreene		10	0
Paide to John Appleton for makinge 400 wood		8	0
Paide more to him for making 200 3 quarters & 15 faggottes		5	9

[27] Bishop John Jegon 1603–18.

	£	s	d
Paide more to him for makinge 150 faggottes of brushe woode in			
Teddes & 10 faggottes in the Northefelde		2	3
Paide for fellinge of maples			2
Paide to John Raynoldes junior for carringe 200 & a quarter of wood			
from Teddes		9	0
Paide more to him for carring a loade of tymber & 40 faggottes			
of brushe		2	0
Paide to John Appleton for makinge of a quarter of brushe wood in			

the Northefelde, for a quarter & a halfe at Westwade &
15 faggottes of greate wood ther, for 3 score & 5 faggottes of
brushe at the groundes occupyed by Mr Skypp or his farmors &
25 faggottes of greate wood ther   2   5

Some   £10 4s 2d

[f. 71r] Paide to John Wyllies for carringe up the towne chyste into
the portch[28]   4
Paide for a bushel of charcole   8
Paide for 2 loade of strawe   8   0
Paide for carringe of 3 loades of strawe   2   0

Some   11s

Some totall of the alowances & paymentes   £49 16s 10d

So the alowances & paymentes exceede the
receyptes which is disbursed by John Raynoldes   £1 6s 9d

[f. 71v]   **[1604-1605]**

The accompte of John Raynolds collector for all the rentes and fearmes of all the landes and tennementes belonginge to the towneshippe of Wymondham accomptinge from the Feaste of Sanct Michaell Tharchangell in *anno* 1604 untill the sayde feaste in *anno* 1605 for one whole yere then ended as followeth

/Arreragium nihil/

/Free rents/

Received of William Crane for fre rent	3	0
Of Frauncis Neave	1	10
Of Ales Frosten *vidua*	2	0
Of Geordge Mayhewe		4
Of Peter Neave		10

[28] This seems to refer to keeping parish documents in a locked chest in the parvise above the porch of the parish church. A chest with three locks was required under Elizabethan legislation. For detailed instructions of how to open the locks of the seventeenth-century parish chest see the second volume of the Wymondham Town Book, 1627–62, NRO, ACC 2002/156.

	£	s	d
Of Thomas Nicksonn			10
The landholders late Edmunde Culliors			1
Of John Bootie for the use of seaven poundes		14	0
Of Henry Kett for Teddes close & 2 acres of land therto adjoyninge & for 3 acres of land in the Northefelde	9	12	0
Of Richard Rawlinge for 3 roodes of medowe at Kyddes Willowes & 2 acres of land in the Northefelde		12	8
Of [blank] Lemmon for a medowe at Westwade	1	6	0
Of Agnes Flowerdewe vidua for a close at the Poples, 3 acres of medowe *& pasture* at Westwade & 3 acres of land in the Northefelde	2	18	2
Of William Ovyngton for a close at the Clay Pyttes & 3 acres dimidia of land in the Northefelde	2	4	2
Of Stephen Agas for 2 acres of land one in Bixtland Feld & one at Toolies Crosse		10	0
Of Larrence Fletcher for a parcell of medowe at Hockhams Carr		3	4
Of Richard Inglishe for a pightell neere Hockhams	1	0	0
Of John Symondes junior for an acre & a halfe of land in his crafte		7	6
Of Arthure Earle for an acre of land & a parcell of land sometymes a grove		6	0
Of William Payne for 2 acres of land in Holmefelde		8	0
Of Edmunde Buck for 2 acres ther		8	0

Some   £20 18s 9d

	£	s	d
[f. 72r] Of Thomas Hobbs for a parcell of medowe neere Wattbrigge		1	0
Of Thomas Cole senior for a medowe & 3 roodes of land neere Ryvaldes, one acre at Barroughs Heade & 1 acre in Holmefelde	1	15	8
Of Raphe Foxxe for one acre of land in Claxewell Furlonge		5	0
Of Thomas Isbells for a pightell called Howlyns in Hungate & 1 acre dimidia of land with a grove	1	7	6
Of Robert Wyseman for 2 acres & 3 roodes of land in the Northefelde		11	0
Of Loy Agas for <7 acres> 7 acres of land in the Northefeld	1	15	0
Of John Raynoldes junior for a pightell at Hell Lanes end		10	0
<Of Henry Kett for 3 acres of land in the Northefelde		12	0>
Of John Symondes *senior* for an artchyard		1	0
Of Geordge Norton for 3 acres of land in the Northefelde		11	0
Of Thomas Woodcock for 3 roodes of pasture		5	0
Of <Henry Spendloue gent> *Mr Sckipp* for a pightell neere his howse & 2 acres of land which heade upon the landes of Henry Meane <16s>	1	5	0
Of Roberte Thorneton generosus for a parcell of medowe at Wattbrigg		4	0

	£	s	d
Of Robert Agas for 2 acres of land in Northefeld		6	0
Of Thomas Talbotte *generosus* for one acre of land in his close neere the Game Place		4	0
Of John Kett for 3 roodes of land neere the Poples		3	0
Of Arthure Williams for a parcell of medowe & pasture neere Myll Poole		[*blank*]	
Of Alexander Foulsham for the towne houses	4	1	0
Of Raynolde Kene for a towne howse	1	10	0
Of Randoll Downynge for a towne shoppe & an acre of land in the Parke Felde		17	0
Of Stephen Jackson for a townehowse		6	8
Of Robert Toolye for a townehouse		13	4

Some   £16 13s 2d

	£	s	d
[*f. 72v*] Of John Cleere for a townehowse		6	8
Of John Swayne & William Cock for a townehouse		6	8
Of Robert Huntley Christian Moore & Em Crosse for a townehowse		6	8
Of Thomas Allyne & Christian Smythe for a townehowse		6	8
Of Margery Goslynge & Ales Smythe *alias* Brewer for a towne howse		6	8
Of Elisabethe Lietche & Jone Cotton for a house		6	8
Of John Gay for a howse agaynst the Common	1	4	0
Of the landholders late Thomas Leverington for a parcell of the scholehowse *steple* to make a seller		1	0

Some   £3 5s 0d

	£	s	d
Rec. more of John Bushe for rent before due		6	0

Some totall of the chardge   £41 1s 11d

Wherof prayeth to be alowed as followeth:

/Rentes not paide:/

Inprimis of rentes not received *videlicet*

	£	s	d
Of Frauncis Neave		1	10
Of Ales Frosten *vidua*		2	0
Of Geordge Mayhewe			4
Of Peter Neave			10
Of Thomas Nicksonn			10
The landholders late Edmund Culliours			1
Of Thomas Hobbs		1	0
Of John Symondes senior		1	0
Of Thomas Talbotte *generosus*		4	0
Item alowed to Robert Tooly in consideracion of Howells children the rent of the howse wher he dwell *videlicet*		13	4

	£	s	d
Item alowed to John Cleere in consideracion of glasing the churtche			
wyndowes the rent of the howse wher he dwelleth *videlicet*		6	8

Some   £1 11s 11d

[*f. 73r*] /**Paymentes**/

	£	s	d
Inprimis paid for breade & beere at the meetinge of the Seaventenn		1	0
Paid to Alexander Fowlsham for carringe of 400 *dimidia* &			
15 faggottes of wood from Teddes		18	6
Paid to him for carringe of 150 faggottes of brushe woode		4	6
Paide to him for 160 faggots bondes		5	4
Paide for 6 bunches of broatchons & byndinges		2	0
Paide for stackinge of wood layd in for the pore		8	7
Paide to Richard Wytherley for amercement imposed upon the			
towne for the buttes		2	6
/☞/ <Paid> Lent by the consente of the townsemen to Andrewe			
Hawes	5	0	0
for which bond was taken by Thomas Leverington *generosus* senior			
Paide to Mr Wells for a rayle for pale		1	4
<Paide> Geven to Mr Shrieffe in the alowance of the charter		10	0
Paid to Mr Weld which he layd out aboute the charter also		10	0
Paid to Mr Thomas Leverington junior for his whole yeres wages			
being scholemaster	15	0	0
Paide to Sewall heyward for Cromwells for the whole rent		4	1
Paide to Henry Kett for the farme of the barne to lay in wood for			
the pore	1	0	0
Paide for the preachers charges upon Rogation Mundaye, dynner,			
supper, & breakfaste, with his horsemeate, with the company that			
dyned with him	1	2	8
Paide to Goodman Rawlinge for an oke to make a ladder for the			
towne		5	6
Paide to Henry Wade for a hundred bryck for the guilde howse &			
for worke		2	6
Paide to Christofer Browne for layinge of the plancher in the buttry			
at the guildhowse & for nayles		6	6
Paide to Stephen Agas cunstable for mendinge the towne armor[29]		4	0

Some   £26 8s 11d

	£	s	d
[*f. 73v*] Paide for 3 swordes for the towne		9	0
Paide for 3 souldiors cotes		15	6

[29] Stephen Agas was one of the parish or petty constables and was responsible for looking after the parish armour. This was worn by the two men who were taken to the annual muster of the Forehoe Hundred's militia.

	£	s	d
Paide for cotten to gard them		1	6
Payde for reade clothe to arme the pykes			4
Paide for makinge the cotes		3	0
Paid for 12 yardes of inckle for them			6
Paide for fryndge & for arminge the pikes			10
Paide for lether for the corslettes		2	0
Paide for skoringe the corselettes & triminge of them		4	4
Paide for 3 daggars		4	6
Paide for halfe a pounde of gunpowder			7
Paide for soldiors wages at the trayninge		6	0
Paide to Mr Shene the Kynges baylie for the whole yeres rent for			
the landes holden of the Kynges manner with a rent henn	1	7	11
Paide to the stuard at the Kynges court for entry of a surrender			
made to diverse feoffees		6	0
/☞/ Delivered to Mr Weld to renewe the charter	4	0	0
Paide for brackettes & nayles to hang the towne armor			6
Paide for hanginge a dore over the churtche dore for 2 hyngles & a			
plate of iron		1	0
Paide to the Lady Knyvett[30] *for 100* wood to make the wood at			
sutche proportion that the pore might have yt at 2d a faggotte	1	0	0
Paide to Henry Wade for layinge of a threshold over the portche			
of fre stone			6
Paide to John Farme for fellinge of a tree for the pillerye			4
Paide to old Hammonte for makinge the wood of the same tree			4
Paide to Goodman Howse *alias* Symonde Howse for carringe of the			
same wood			8
Paide for the tryminge of the pentise over the towneshoppe		3	4
Payd for paper at the meetinge			1

Some   £9 8s 9d

[f. 74r] Alowed him which he this accomptante in his last accounte
   disbursed more than he receyved as aperethe upon the *foote of
   the* saide accompte   1   6   9

Some totall of the alowances & paymentes   £38 16s 4d

So ther remaynethe in this accomptantes handes,
all thinges alowed, upon this accompte   £2 5s 7d

[30] Murial, wife of Sir Thomas Knyvett (*c.* 1539–1617) of Ashwellthorpe, J.P. 1578, deputy
lieutenant 1585 (see A. H. Smith, *County and Court*, p. 386).

£ s d

[*1605-1606*]

The accompte of John Raynolds collector for all the rents and farmes of all the landes and tennements belonginge to the towneshipe of Wymondham accomptinge from the Feaste of Sanct Michaell Tharchangell in *anno* 1605 untill the saide feaste in *anno* 1606 for one whole yere then ended as followeth

/*Arrerags*/

Inprimis the arrerage remayning in the handes of this accomptante
    ut supra   2 5 7
Rec. by him of Thomas Hobbs upon an old arrerage (by which all
    arrerages in the former accountes specified upon the heades of
    the said Thomas Hobbs & Robert Hobbs his father ar acquyted)
    the some of   3 8

/*Free rents*/

Rec. of William Crane for fre rent   3 0
Of Frauncis Neave   1 10
Of Ales Frosten *vidua*   2 0
Of Geordge Mayhewe   4
Of Peter Neave   10
Of Thomas Nicksonn   10
Of the landholders late Edmund Cullyours   1

        Some   £2 18s 2d

[*f. 74v*] /*Farme rents*/

Of Frauncis Plummer for Teddes Close & 2 acres of land therto
    adjoininge   9 0 0
Of Richard Rawlinge for 3 roodes of medowe at Kydds Willowes &
    2 acres of land in the Northe Felde   12 8
Of Steven Wyseman *generosus* for a medowe at Westwade   1 6 0
Of Agnes Flowerdewe *vidua* for a close at the Poples, 3 acres of
    medowe & pasture at Salters Ford (before tymes wrytten at
    Westwade) & 3 acres of land in the Northe Felde   2 18 2
Of William Ovyngton for a close at the Clay Pyttes & 3 acres
    dimidia of land in the Northe Felde   2 4 2
Of Stephen Agas for 2 acres of land one in <the Nort> Brixelond
    Feld & one at Toolyes Crosse   10 0
Of Larrence Fletcher for a parcell of medowe at Hockhams Carr   3 4
Of Richard Inglishe for a pightell nere Hockams   1 0 0
Of John Symondes junior for an acre & a halfe of land in his crafte   7 6
Of Arthure Earle for an acre of land & a parcell of land sometymes
    a grove   6 0
Of William Payne for 2 acres of land in Holme Felde   8 0

	£	s	d
Of Edmunde Buck for 2 acres ther		8	0
Of Thomas Hobbs for a parcell of medowe neere Watt Brigge		1	0
Of Thomas Cole senior for a medowe & 3 roodes of land at Ryvaldes, one acre at Barrowghes Head & one acre in Holme Felde	1	15	8
Of Raphe Foxx for an acre of land in Claxewell Furlonge		5	0
Of Abraham Hedgeman for a pightell called Howlyns in Hungate	1	0	0
Of Thomas Isbells for an acre *dimidia* of land with a grove in Claxewell Furlonge		7	6
Of Robert Wyseman for 2 acres & 3 roodes of land in the Northe Felde		6	0

Some   £23 4s 0d

	£	s	d
[*f. 75r*] Of Loy Agas for 7 acres of land in the Northe Felde	1	15	0
Of John Raynoldes junior for a pightell at Hell Lanes end		10	0
Of Henry Kett for 3 acres of land in the Northe Felde		12	0
Of [*two words cancelled*] Geordge Norton for 3 acres of land in the Northe Felde		6	0
Memorandum: the artcheyard heretofor sett upon the heade of John Symondes senior is <not so> *nowe* conteyned in the rent of Alexander Foulsham & he useth the same		[*blank*]	
Of Thomas Woodcock for 3 roodes of pasture		5	0
Of Mr Sckipp for a pightell neere his howse which he purchased of Mr Spendlowe & 2 acres of land which head upon the landes of Henry Meane	1	5	0
Of Robert Thorneton *generosus* for a parcell of medowe at Wattbrigg		4	0
Of Robert Agas for 2 acres of land in the Northe Felde		6	0
Of Thomas Talbotte *generosus* for an acre of land in his close nere the Game Place		4	0
Of [*two words cancelled*] William Edwardes for 3 roodes of land neere the Poples		3	0
Of Arthure Williams for a parcell of medowe & pasture nere Myll Poole		[*blank*]	
Of Alexander Foulsham for the towne houses wherin he nowe dwelle the & the artchyard heretofor sett upon the heade of John Symondes senior	4	1	0
Of Raynolde Kene for a towne howse	1	10	0
Of Randoll Downynge for a towne shoppe		12	0
Of William Burrell for an acre of land in the Parke Felde		5	0
Of Stephen Jackson for a towne howse		6	8
Of Robert Tooly for a towne howse		13	4
Of John Cleere for a towne howse		6	8

Some   £13 9s 8d

	£	s	d
[*f. 75v*] Of John Swayne & the *vidua* Cock for a towne howse		6	8
Of \<Robert\> the *vidua* Huntlye Christian Moore & Em Crosse for a townehowse		6	8
Of Thomas Allyne & Christian Smythe for a townehowse		6	8
Of Margery Goslinge & Ales Smythe *alias* Bruer for a towne howse		6	8
Of Elisabethe Lietche & Jone Cotten for a towne howse		6	8
Of John Gay & Robert Cullyor for the *vydua* Tooly for the howse agaynst the Common	1	4	0
Of the landholders late Thomas Leverington for a parcell of the scholehowse steeple to make a seller		1	0

Some   £2 18s 4d

Received by him for a quarters use of £7 of John Bootye		3	6

Some totall of the chardge   £42 13s 9d

Whereof prayethe to be alowed as followeth

/Rents not paide/

	£	s	d
Inprimis of rentes not rec. *videlicet* of Frauncis Neave		1	10
Of Ales Frosten *vidua*		2	0
Of Geordge Mayhewe			4
Of Peter Neave			10
Of Thomas Nicksonn			10
Of the landholders late Edmund Cullyors			1
Of Thomas Talbotte *generosus*		4	0
Item alowed to Robert Tooly in consideracion of Howells children the rent of the howse wher he dwellethe *videlicet*		13	4
Item alowed to John Cleere in consideracion of glasinge the churtche wyndowes the rent of the howse wher he dwellethe *videlicet*		6	8

Some   £1 9s 11d

[*f. 76r*] **/Paymentes/**

	£	s	d
Paide to Kynge & his man for pyninge & castinge & mendinge the wyndowes at the guildhowse		2	0
Paide for 2 bunches of lathe		2	4
Paide for to the Kynges baylie for the yeres rent of the landes holden of his Majestie with a henn	1	7	11
Paide to old Clarck for worke at the howse wher Tooly dwellethe & layinge of a well curble		5	4
Paide to Mr Leverington scholemaster for his wages for one whole yeere with 30s to Mr Gary[31] for parte of the last quarter	15	0	0

[31] Mr Gary, schoolmaster 1606–08, acted as usher to Mr Leverington for part of the last quarter of 1605–06.

	£	s	d
/☞/ Geven to the Lord Byshopps secretary for the alowance of the pryvlledge		10	0
/☞/ Paide to Mr Weld for chardges layd out about the charter		13	4
Paide for <carien> 8 hundred strawe		16	0
Paide to John Raynoldes for carringe of the same		4	0
Paide to him more for 2 hundred strawe		4	0
Paide to him for carringe of ytt		1	0
Paide to Thomas Wells for 8 dayes workes in thackinge		10	4
Paide to John Kytmur for 8 dayes servinge		5	4
Paide to Alexander Fulsham for 5 burdens of broatchons & byndinges		1	8
Paide to him for strawe, & thackinge, broatchewons & bindinges	1	6	2
Paide to John Vyncente for the towne for chardges in standinge agaynst the paymente of bridges		8	0
<Paide> Geven to Mr Shriefe in the alowance of the charter		6	8
Paide for carringe a well curble & other peces to Toolyes howse			6
Paide for fower foote of tymber for a grounsell ther		1	8
Paide for the preatchers chardges upon Rogatyon Munday		14	0
Paide to John Wells upon an assumpcion for the dischardge of a childe from the towne			2
/☞/ Paide for wyne, beere, & cakes to intertayne the Lord Byshoppe comming through the towne		10	0

Some   £23 10s 5d

	£	s	d
[f. 76v] /☞/ Paide more to Mr Weld at the bringinge downe of the charter, renewed	1	0	4
Paide to Nycholas Whelpsdale for makinge cleane the leades <of> over the churtche			2
Paide to John Raynoldes junior for carring a loade of sand unto Toolyes		1	0
Paide to Goldsenye for helpinge to loade blockes at the woode		2	0
Payde to John Raynoldes for carringe 200 bryck to Toolyes, & 500 tyle to Foulshams		1	0
Paide for the towne for 100 wood to make the wood at sutche a proportion that the pore might have it at 2d a faggotte	1	0	0
Paide to Henry Kett for a barne for the wood	1	0	0
Paide to John Raynoldes for carringe a loade of stone from churtche to Toolyes			8
Paide to olde Clarck for a threshoulde			6
Paide for 2 chalder of lyme		10	0
Payde for 13 dayes workes of Wade & his man		13	0
Paide for caringe of 2 chalder of lyme		5	0
Paide for 200 well brycke		3	0

	£	s	d
Paide to Wade for 500 & a quarter of tyle		6	3
Payde for a loade of sand to Fowlsham & 200 bryckes endes		1	8
Paide for a 1000 lathe nayles		1	8
Payd for a 1000 tyle pynne			6
Paide for planck for eves bordes		1	4
Payde for nayles for them			1
Payde for breade & beere at the meetinge of the Seaventenn		1	6
Payde to Christofer Browne for hewinge & sawinge thinges for the pillery		4	0
Payd to Goldsenye for caring of itt into his yarde			2
Payd to Mr Leverington for a boxx to putt the bondes in			6
Payde to Alexander Foulsham for caring of the tree		2	0

Some £5 17s

[*Due to faulty page numbering, there is no folio 77.*]

	£	s	d
[*f. 78r*] /☞/ Payd to the Lady Knevett for 500 wood, for the bennefytt of the poore as aforesaide		10	0
Payd for boringe the ladder pece & for the sawinge		1	4
Payd for fower foote of tymber for ladder stafes		1	8
Paide to old Hammonde for makinge of 200 brushe woode at Earles		2	8
Paide to him for makinge of forty faggottes of two bond woode ther also			8
Payd to Symonde Howse for carringe of the wood		4	8
Payd to olde Hammonte for makinge of 300 brush woode in the medowe at Ryvaldes		4	0
Payd to him for makinge of 40 faggottes of 2 bond ther also			8
Payd for throwinge downe of the dyke & dyking of it agayne, for a gap to cary out the wood			4
Payd to Symonde Howse for caring of ytt		6	0
Payd to old Hammonte for making halfe a hundred brushe wood in the medowe in the occupacion of Mr Thorneton			10
Payd for 5 foote of tymber for keyes for the towne well		1	8
/☞/ Delyvered & geven to a pore prentise, the sonne of Christian Smythe, & servante to <Christ> Christopher Browne, being lame & diseased, towardes his going to the bathe	1	0	0
/☞/ Payd for a kirbell for the towne well		4	0
/☞/ Payd to Symonde Howse for caringe of halfe a hundred brushe woode		1	0
/☞/ Payd to Robert Cullyer for halfe a yeres rent for Cromwells		2	0
Payd to Mr Pyttes for a byll for the receypte of the Kynges rent			2
/☞/ Payd to him for a fyne for the towne landes holden of the Kynges Majesties mannor	4	0	0

	£	s	d
/☞/ Payd to Godfry for ryvinge & rayling of a tree		4	0

Some   £7 <1s 8d> 5s 8d

[f. 78v]   Some totall of the alowances & paymentes £38 3s 0d

So ther remayneth in the accomptantes handes
all thinges alowed upon this accompte   £4 10s 9d

Memorandum that this aforesaide arreradge of £4 10s 9d, chardged upon this accomptante at the yeldinge up of his accompte *videlicet* the 5 of Januarye in *anno* 1606 was at the requeste of the Seaventenn made by this accomptante the some of fyve poundes, which said some was lent unto one Larrence Fletcher by bond for one whole yere with John Symondes junior being his suertye & upon the occasion of the greate chardge of shootinge the bells & other chardges about the churtche, the said fyve poundes presently recalled out of the handes of the said Larrence Fletcher, & paid unto the churtche wardens then beinge, *videlicet*: Richard Rawlinge, John Hawes, Edward Colman junior & Fraunces Moore, wherupon the bond was immediately cancelled & the said accomptante to be dischardged of the said arreradge & the towne indebted to this saide accomptante nyne shillinges & three pence.

[f. 79r] Memorandum that the seaven poundes which was late in the handes of John Bootye is nowe remayninge as followeth: *videlicet* in the handes of Alexander Foulsham the some of fyve poundes for which Henry Kett standeth bound with the said Alexander for the repayment of the said fyve poundes with the use after 18d in the pound: & forty shillinges to William Gold, for which Edward Colman junior standeth bound for the said William, which bondes remayne in the chiste, with the use in like sort after 18d in the pound.

These three last former accountes <was> were entred & taken by us, at the assignemente of the Seaventenn or the moste parte of them, in testimonye wherof we have concluded the same & subscribed our names the eighte day of June in *anno* 1607.

Memorandum besides all these last recyted accountes, ther remaynethe in the accomptantes handes, which is not mencioned in any of the said accomptes, as a stock remayninge only for the buyinge of wood for the pore to the some of £12 7s 11d

[*Signed*]   *per me Stephanum Wiseman*
                          per me Johannem Symondes juniorem

[f. 79v]   **[1606-1607]**

The accompte of John Raynoldes collector for all the rentes and farmes of all the landes and tennements belonginge to the towneshippe of Wymondham accomptinge from the Feaste of Saint Michaell Tharchanngell in *anno* 1606 untill the saide feaste in *anno* 1607 for one whole yeere then ended as followeth

	£	s	d
Arrerages			
Inprimis of arrerages			nil
Free rentes			
Received of William Crane for free rent		3	0
Of Frauncis Neave		1	10
Of Ales Frosten *vidua*		2	0
Of Geordge Mayhewe			4
Of Peter Neave			10
Of Thomas Nicksonn			10
Of the landholders late Edmunde Cullyers			1
Farme rentes			
Of Frauncis Plomer for Teddes Close & 2 acres of land therto adjoyninge	9	0	0
Of Richard Rawlinge for 3 roodes of medowe at Kydds Willowes & 2 acres of land in the Northefelde		13	4
Of Steven Wyseman for a medowe at Westwade	1	6	0
Of Agnes Flowerdewe *vidua* for a close at the Poples, 3 acres of medowe at Salters Ford & 3 acres of land in the Northefelde	3	0	0
Of William Ovington for a close at the Clay Pittes & 3 acres [*two words cancelled*] of land in the Northefelde	2	16	8

Some   £17 4s <11d> 3d

	£	s	d
[*f. 80r*] Of Stephen Agas for 2 acres of land one in Bixtlond Feld & one at Toolyes Crosse		11	8
Of Larrence Fletcher for a parcell of medowe at Hockhams Carr		3	4
Of Richard Inglishe for a pightell nere Hockhams	1	4	0
Of John Symondes junior for an acre & a halfe of land in his crafte		10	0
Of Arthure Earle for an acre of land & a parcell of land sometymes a grove		12	0
Of William Payne for 2 acres of land in Holmefeld		12	0
Of Edmunde Buck for 2 acres ther		12	0
Of Thomas Hobbs for a parcell of medowe nere Wadebridge		1	0
Of Thomas Cole senior for a medowe & 3 roodes of land at Ryvaldes, one acre at Barrowhes Heade & one acre in Holmefelde	2	0	0
Of Raphe Foxx for an acre of land in Claxewell Furlonge		6	0
Of Thomas Seabborne for a pightell called Howlyns in Hungate	1	4	0
Of Abraham Hedgeman for an acre *dimidia* of land with a grove in Claxewell Furlonge		10	0
Of Robert Wyseman for 2 acres & 3 roodes of land in the Northefelde		14	0
Of Loy Agas for 7 acres of land in the Northefelde	2	9	0

	£	s	d
Of John Raynoldes junior for a pightell at Hellanes end		14	0
Of Henry Kett for 3 acres of land in the Northefelde		15	0
Of Geordge Norton for 3 acres of land in Northefelde		16	6

Some £13 14s 6d

	£	s	d
[f. 80v] Of Thomas Woodcock for 3 acres of pasture		7	6
Of Mr Skipp for a pightell neere his howse which he purchased of Mr Spendlowe & 2 acres of land which heade upon the landes of Henry Meane	1	16	8
Of Robert Thorneton *generosus* for a parcell of medowe at Wadebridge		5	0
Of Robert Agas for 2 acres of land in the Northefelde		12	0
Of Thomas Talbott *generosus* for an acre of land in his close neere the Game Place		6	8
Of William Edwardes for 3 roodes of land neere the Poples		5	0
Of Arthure Williams for a parcell of medowe & pasture neere Myll Poole	[blank]		
Of Alexander Fowlsham for the towne howses wher he nowe dwellethe & the artcheyard heretofore sett upon the heade of John Symondes senior	4	1	0
Of Raynold Kene for a towne howse	3	0	0
Of Randoll Downynge for a towne shopp		12	0
Of William Burrell for an acre of land in the Parkefelde		6	0
Of <Stephen Jackson> Thomas Plummer for a towne howse	1	0	0
Of Robert Tooly for a towne howse		13	4
Of John Cleere for a towne howse		13	4
Of John Swayne & the *vidua* Cock for a towne howse		6	8
Of *vidua* Huntly, Christian Moore & Em Crosse for a towne howse		6	8
Of Thomas Allyne & Christian Smythe for a towne howse		6	8
Of Margery Goslynge & Ales Smythe *alias* Bruer for a towne howse		6	8

Some   £15 18s <10d> 6d

	£	s	d
[f. 81r] Of Elsabethe Lietche & Jone Cotten for a towne howse		6	8
Of Robert Cullyer for the wydowe Tooly for the howse agaynst the Common	1	13	4
Of the landholders late Thomas Leverington *generosus* for a parcell of the schoolehowse steeple to make a seller	1	0	
Received of Thomas Cole for an old tree			6

Some   £2 1s 6d

Some totall of the chardge   £48 <16s [?]9d> *18s 9d*

Wherof prayeth to be alowed as followeth

	£	s	d
/Rents not paide/			
Inprimis of rentes not rec. *videlicet* of Frauncis Neave		1	10
Of Ales Frosten *vidua*		2	0
Of Geordge Mayhewe			4
Of Peter Neave			10
Of Thomas Nickson			10
Of the landholders late Edmund Cullyers			1
Of Thomas Talbotte *generosus*		6	8
Item alowed to John Cleere in consideracion of glasinge the churtche wyndowes the rent of the howse wher he dwelleth *videlicet* for the yere past	1	6	8

Some *[first sum cancelled]* £1 19s 3d

[f. 81v] /Paymentes/

	£	s	d
Inprimis paid for bread & beere when the Seaventenn did mete		2	0
Paid to Mr Leverington that was owinge him when he gave his accompte		1	4
Paid to the shriefe for chardges		7	0
Paid for John Raynoldes his chardges		1	0
Paid to Arthure Williams for a debt synce he was churchewarden		2<11>9	
Paid to Foulsham at the second meetynge		2	4
/☞/ Paid to Henry Kett for money laid out at the Sessions		11	0
Paid when the 17 did meete to abuttell the towne land		3	6
Payd to Master Gary	3	15	0
Payd to Samuell Cullyer for rent for the last yeere		2	1
Paid for the last yeere for stackinge of wood		8	0
Paid to Richard Russells for Cromwells rent		2	0
Paid for caringe of fyve hundred strawe by Garrad & Nevell to the towne howses		2	0
Paid for sixe burthens of broatchons & byndinges		2	0
Paid to Esau Freman for a ladder		5	0
Paid to Garrad & Nevell for caring more of fyve hundred strawe		2	0
Payd for the preatchers chardges & the townsemen that did accompany him		17	4
/☞/ Paid to Master Freeman for a thowsand of rye strawe	1	5	0
Payd more for 200 strawe		5	0
Paid for four burthen of broatchons & bindinges		1	4
Paid for 12 dayes of the thackster & his man	1	2	0
Geven them to drynck			4

Some £10

	£	s	d
[f. 82r] Paid to Garrad for caring 200 strawe			10

	£	s	d
Paid at the meetinge of the Seaventenn at the guildhowse[32] upon the towne busynes		2	2
Paid for the Kynges rent		13	8
/☞/ Paid to Mr Weld for a sute for the towne land	2	0	0
Paid for fetching of a plank			4
Payd for breakefast dynner & supper for Steven Wyseman & John Symondes & other of the townsemen being imployed in fynishinge the accountes for the towne		5	9
Paid to Mr Gary	3	15	0
Paid to Robert Crane draper for a chalder of lyme		5	0
Payd to Garrades boy for making cleane of the leades			2
Paid for broomes to sweepe the guildhowse			1
Payd to Goulsnye for polls & cuttings to make fyre		1	5
Payd for heare to the glover & tanner		2	0
Payd for nayles			6
Paid for sawinge of planck & stooles & stooles feete for the guildhowse		7	4
Paid to the Rusbrookes masons		2	0
Paid to Kytnner for 5 dayes workes		4	2
Paid to Henry Wade for 200 brycke		2	4
Paid to him for 20 pammontes		2	0
Paid to him for 6 ruff tyles			9
Paid for 4 foote of okynge tymber		1	8
Paid for 3 peces of ashe for stooles feete		1	0
Paid for a bunche of lathe		1	2
Paid for nayles			2
Paid for beerestooles, a dresser, & a pece to make pillars		4	0
Paid for 4 payr of trussells		2	0
Paid for mending of 2 caudrons		2	0
Paid for tackes & hingles			6

Some   £8 18s

	s	d
[f. 82v] Paid for sawinge of trussells feete		6
Paid for shredes		4
Paid for mendinge the back of the kytchine chymney		6
Paid for nayles		2
Payd for 2 peces of ashe		8
Paid for a lock & a key for the iron chyste	1	0
Paid for 2 trussells	1	0
Paid for crampittes for the tables		4

[32] This entry makes it quite clear that the vestry is calling itself 'The Seventeen' and that the guildhouse is its regular meeting place, indeed it is sometimes referred to as the 'town hall'.

	£	s	d
Paid for makyng of tables trussells & formes & 5 dayes worke		5	0
Paid for paper for a booke to inventory the goodes at the guildhowse			1
Paid to the sparrowe katcher		3	4
Paid to Thorne for 2 dayes work		2	0
Paid to Browne for 2 dayes work & a halfe of his 2 boyes & halfe a day of him selfe at the guild howse		4	4
Paid to 3 souldiors when they did showe		3	0
Paid for skoring of the muskettes & daggardes			8
Paid to Henry Wade for whytinge & tryminge of the guildhowse		5	0
/☞/ Layd out for Margarett Dunne	2	0	0
Paid to Mr Blackborne for 4 yeres rent for the towne land holden of him			4
Paid to Mr Gary	3	15	0
Paid to the Kynges baylie for the halfe yere rent		13	9
Paid for a henne			6
Paid to the sparrowe catcher		3	4
Paid for carring of a chalder of lyme		2	4
/☞/ Paid for the arest of Frauncis Plomer		2	0
Paid to Henry Wade for bryck for a harthe at the *vidua* Toolies & for the makinge		1	6

Some   £8 6s 8d

[*f. 83r*] Paid to the sparrowe catcher		3	4
Paid for a tree to make a table at the guildhowse of 37 foote		18	6
Payd for hewinge of the same		1	0
Paid to Johnson for breakinge of yt		3	8
Paid to Russells for rent		2	1
Paid for a helper in an office chardged upon the towne landes			8
Paid for a loade of strawe & cariadge to the howse wher the wydowe Toolye dwelleth		6	0
Paid to the thackster & his man for layinge of ytt		3	8
Paid for broatcheones & byndinges			10
Paid to Mr Gary	3	15	0
Paid for the fee of the baylie for gathering the towne rent		13	4

Some   £6 8s 1d

<Some totall of the alowences & paymentes   £35 12s>

Alowed to him upon an old acounte disbursed by him for the use of the towne		9	3
More to be alowed to the said accomptant in losse of wood sold to the pore	4	15	9

Some totall of the alowances & paymentes   £40 17s

£   s   d

So ther remaynethe in the accomptantes
handes all thinges alowed upon this accompte   £8 1s 9d

<Besides the stock of wood some of £12 7s 11d remayninge in his handes for a
stock of wood for the releefe of the pore.>

[*f. 83v*] Also remayninge in the handes of the said accomptante more
which he receyved of Alexander Fowlsham for the use of fyve
poundes 7s 6d & of William Gold for the use of forty shillinges
3s *in toto*   10   6

Et sic debet in toto   £8 12s 3d

Besides the some of £12 7s 11d which is for a stock to be contynued for the
releefe of the pore & for provision of wood.

[*f. 84r*]   **[*1607-1608*]**

The accompt of John Reynoldes collector for all the rentes and farmes of all the
landes and tenementes belonginge to the townshipp of Wymondham
accomptinge from the Feast of Saint Michaell Tharkangell in *anno* 1607 untill
the saide feaste in *anno* 1608 for one wholl yere then ended as followeth

/Arrerages/
Inprimis in arrerages   <3s 1d> *nullum*

/Free rentes/
Received of William Crane for free rent   3   0
Of Frauncis Neave   1   10
Of Alys Frosten *vidua*   2   0
Of George Mayhewe   4
Of Peter Neave   10
Of Thomas Nixon   10
Of the land holders late Edmonde Cullyers   1

/Farme rentes/
Off Frauncis Plomer for Teddes Close otherwise called Tenement
   Brixy in Silfilde and twoe acres of land thereto adjoyninge   9   0   0
Off Richard Rawlinge for 3 roodes of meadowe att Kyddes
   Willowes and twoe acres of lande in the North Feilde   12   8
Off Steven Wiseman for a meadowe att Westwade   1   6   0
Off Agnes Flowerdewe *vidua* for a close att the Poples, three acres
   of meadowe at Salters Forde and thre acres of land in the
   North Feilde   3   0   0
Off William Ovington for a close att the Claye Pyttes and thre
   acres *dimidia* of lande in the North Feilde   2   16   8
Off Stephen Agas for twoe acres of lande one in Bixland Feild &
   one at Toolyes Crosse   11   8

Summa   £17 <19s> 15s 11d

	£	s	d
[*f. 84v*] Off Lawrence Fletcher for a parcell of meadowe at Hockhams Carre		3	4
Off Robert Rawlinge for a pictell nere Hockhams	1	4	0
Off John Symondes senior for one acre and a halfe of land in his crafte		10	0
Off Arthure Earle for one acre of land and a parcell of lande sometymes a grove		12	0
Off William Payne for twoe acres of lande in Holme Feilde		12	0
Off Edmond Bucke for twoe acres <there> of lande there		12	0
Off Thomas Hobbes for a parcell of meadowe nere Wadebridge		1	0
Off Thomas Cole senior for a meadowe and three roodes of lande<s> att Ryvaldes, one acre at Barrowes Heade & one acre in Holme Feilde	2	0	0
Off Raphe Fox for one acre of lande in Claxewell Furlonge		6	0
Off Thomas Sebborne for a pightell called Howlyns in Hungate	1	4	0
Off Abraham Hedgman for one acre & *dimidia* of land with a grove att thend thereof lyeinge in Claxwell Furlonge		14	0
Off Robert Wyseman senior for twoe acres and three roodes of lande in the North Feilde		15	0
Off Loy Agas for seaven acres of land in the North Feilde	2	9	0
Off John Reynoldes senior for a pictell att Hellanes end		14	0
Off Henry Kett for thre acres of land in the North Feilde		15	0
Off George Norton for thre acres of land in North Feilde		16	6
Off Thomas Woodcocke for thre <acres> *roodes* of pasture lyeing in Wattlefeild		7	6

Summa £13 14s 4d

[*f.85r*] Off Mr Skipp for a pightell nere his howse which he purchased of Mr Spendlowe and twoe acres of land which heade upon the landes of Henry Meane	1	16	8
Off Robert Thornton *generosus* for a parcell of meadowe at Wade Bridge		5	0
Off Robert Agas for twoe <yeres> acres of land in the North Feilde		12	0
Off Thomas Talbott *generosus* for one acre of land lyeinge in his close neere the Game Place		6	8
Off William Edwardes for thre rodes of land nere the Poples		5	0
Off Arthure Williams *generosus* for a parcell of meadowe & pasture neere Myll Poole		[*blank*]	
Off Alexander Foulsham for the towne howses where he nowe dwelleth & the ortcharde	4	1	0
Off Reynolde Keene for a towne howse	3	0	0
Off Randoll Downynge for a towne shopp		12	0

	£	s	d
Off William Burrell for one acre of land in the Park Feilde		6	0
Off Robert Bettes for a towne howse	1	0	0
Off Robert Tooley for a towne howse		13	4
Off John Clere for a towne howse	1	6	8
Off John Swayne & the wydowe Cocke for a towne howse		6	8
Off the wydowe Huntlye Christian Moore and Eme Crosse for a towne howse		6	8
Off Thomas Allyne & Christian Smythe *vidua* for a towne howse		6	8
Off Alys Bruer *alias* Smythe & the wydowe Beart for a towne howse		6	8

Summa   £15 11s

	£	s	d
[*f.85v*] Off Elizabeth Leache and Joane Cotton for a towne howse		6	8
Off Robert Cullyor for the wydowe Tooley for a howse against North Wood Common adjoyninge to Blackinham	1	13	4
Off the lande houlders late Thomas Leverington *generosus* for a parcell of the schoolehowse steeple to make a seller		1	0
Receyved more for money lent to diverse persons	1	2	6

Summa   £3 3s

Some totall of the charge   £50 4s 3d

Whereof prayeth to be allowed for rentes not payde and other disburssementes for the towne as followeth

/Rentes not paide/

	£	s	d
Imprimis of Frauncis Neave		1	10
Off Alys Frosten *vidua*		2	0
Off George Mayhewe			4
Off Peter Neave			10
Off Thomas Nickson			10
Off the landholders late Edmond Cullyers			1
Off Thomas Talbott *generosus*		6	8

/Super/

	£	s	d
Item allowed to John Clere	1	6	8
Off John Symondes for one whole yere		10	0

Summa for rentes not receyved   £2 9s 3d

[*f. 86r*] /Disbursmentes/

	s	d
Imprimis paid for beere cakes and fier when the hedborrowes did take the accompt in the yere 1608	4	0
Payd att the second meetinge of the headborrowes upon the towne busines	1	6
Payd for strawe and for the caryeinge of the same to the wydowe Toolyes howse	4	0

	£	s	d
Payde to William Crane for a pese of eshe to undersett a billder		1	4
Payd to Christopher Browne and his boye for twoe daies worke		4	0
Payd to the newe clarke when he was hyered		1	0
Payd for the third metinge of the headborrowes			8
Delivered to Mr Blackborne of the towne money	5	0	0
Payd for 400 fagott bondes		1	4
Payd to the sparrowe ketcher		3	4
Delivered to Henry Kett to gyve to the sheriff for alloweinge of the charter		5	0
/☞/ Payd to Mr Welde to retayne councell att the Assizes	1	0	0
Payd for making of 100 twoe bonde woode		2	0
Payde for makinge of 100 *dimidia* of brushe wood		2	0
Payd for makinge of 3 quarters of twoe bond wood		1	6
Payd for makinge of 3 quarters of brushe wood		1	1
Payd to Mayston for carieinge of 8 leadinges of wood		8	0
Payd for makinge of a quarter of twoe bonde wood			6
Payd for makinge of 28 brush fagottes			4
Payd for thre hundred of fagott bondes		1	0
/☞/ Delivered to Mr Welde more	3	0	0
Payd to Hamond and Mayde for makinge of 3 & *a* quarter of brushe wood in the pictelles late that the wydowe Flowerdewe & Inglishe had		4	11
Payd to Francis Quayntrell for the carieinge of 200 wood		3	4
Payd to Stephen Agas for the carieinge of one hundred & a quarter of wood		2	0

Summa £11 12s 11d

	£	s	d
[*f. 86v*] Payd for the carieinge and throwinge of the wood out of the pictelles		1	4
Payd for stackinge fyve hundred wood that came out of the towne grownd		1	8
Payd to Mr Garye for his wages	3	15	0
Payd to John Woodcocke the Kinges Majesties baylyff		13	8
Payd for twoe payer of hookes and hyngens att the wydowe Toolyes			8
Payd for twoe gate postes		2	0
Payd for the ledges harthtree & claptree & other peces		1	8
Payd to Mihell Rix for makinge the gate & hanginge of the same		1	9
Payd to Mayston for caryeinge of the gate and the gate postes and board to the guildhowse			6
Payd for nayles for the plancher att the clarkes howse			8
Payd for fower peeces of tymber to make pillers and stoyles for the wyndowes		2	2
Payd for 100 & fortie foote of board to make the plancher		12	0

	£	s	d
/☞/ Payd to Frauncis Plomer for his expences att the Assizes		3	0
Payd more to him for makinge of a peticion		1	0
Payd more to him which he layd out to the jury		1	0
Payd to Knyghtes and his boye for layeinge the playncher for the clarkes chamber and for lyntelles for the glasse & for footinge the beere stooles		5	0
Payd for heweinge and saweinge of the tymber for the tables and formes & for thre dayes and a halfe worke		5	10
Payd for a peece of square tymber & for nayles			5
Payd to John Clere for glazeinge the fower wyndowes att the guilhowse		13	4
Payd for the dynner and supper for the preachers		14	4

Summa £7 16s <9d> 14d [sic]

	£	s	d
[f. 87r] Payd to Farrer for twoe tables feete			8
Payd to Robert Knyghtes and his boy for fower daies worke		6	8
Payd more to his man for three dayes worke		3	4
Payd more to him selfe and his boye for twoe dayes worke		3	4
Payd more to him for glewe			6
Payd more to his man for twoe dayes worke		2	4
Payd for lathe nayles			2
Payd for great nayles			2
Payd to Cooper for fetchinge the newe clarke		8	0
Payd to the clerke for his wages		15	0
Payd to Mr Gary for his wages	3	15	0
Payd to Francis Quayntrell for nayles			4
Payd to Thomas Fuller for splent yarne			4
Payd to Robert Crane for a chaldern of lyme		5	4
Payd to him for the cariage thereof		2	8
Payd to him for loame		1	0
Payd to him for carieinge thereof		1	0
Payd to Robert Carr for loame		1	0
Payd to Francis Quayntrell for carieinge thereof			8
Payd to Cooper for halfe a dayes worke			8
Payd to Alexander *Foulsham* for the strawe			8
Payd to Lawrence Swayne for workinge the claye		1	0
Payd for thre quarters of splentes		2	6
Payd to Foulsham for carieinge of a loade of claye and a loade of sand		1	4
Payd for a load of claye castinge			2
Payd to Bunne for *4* daies worke		4	8
Payd to Martyn for 4 dayes worke		4	8
Payd to Swayne for one dayes worke		1	2

Summa £7 4s 6d

	£	s	d
[f. 87v] Payd for fower bushelles of heare for the guilhowse		1	8
Payd to Proctor for 2 calves skynnes to mend the organs		3	0
Payd for halfe a chaldron of lyme		2	8
Payd for caryeinge of the same		1	4
Payd to twoe of Wades men for twoe daies castinge the guilhowse		5	0
Payd to three of Wades servers for twoe daies worke		6	0
Payd to Catchpowle for a locke for the guilhowse		1	6
Payd to him more for a locke for the clarkes doore		1	2
Payd to Page for three bushelles of heare		1	3
Payd to Cowper and his wyfe for makinge cleane of the guilhowse		1	0
Payd to Agnes Hallywaye for washeinge of tables and stooles there			8
Payd to Knightes and Clayborne for mendinge the organs		5	0
Payd to Stacye for draweinge of the Kinges armes that are in the hall		5	0
Payd to him more for cloathe to drawe the same upon		1	3
Payd for ashe to make trusselles feete		2	0
Payd for thirtie dozen of trenchers		10	0
Payd to Christopher Browne and twoe of his boyes for makinge of			
trussles & footinge of stooles		3	4
Payd for six formes and six payer of trussles		5	0
Payd to Francis Quayntrell for <makinge> mendinge of a locke & to			
Anne Pells for makinge cleane of the guildhowse			8
Payd to Catchpoole for mendinge of the scorslettes		1	0

Summa £2 18s 6d

	£	s	d
[f. 88r] /☞/ Payd to Mr Weld when I reckoned with him for the			
suyte concernynge Teddes Close	1	1	8
Payd to the clarke for his wages		15	0
Payd to Mr Garye for his wages	3	15	0
Payd to the Kinges Majesties baylyff		13	9
Payd to him more for a rent henn			6
Payd to the sparrowe catcher		3	4
/☞/ Payd more then wee receyved for fyve hundred great wood for			
the poore	1	0	0
Payd more for stackinge of the same		2	6
/☞/ Payd more then wee receyved for 11 hundred brushe woode for			
the poore	1	2	0
Payd more for the stackinge the same		4	0
Payd for Cromwelles rent		2	0
Payd to Mr Garye for his wages	3	15	0
Payd to the clarke for the like		15	0
/☞/ Payd for a dorman for the churche		13	6
Payd for caryeinge the sand to the churche		1	0

	£	s	d
Payd to Wytherley and John Rawlyn beinge constables for the mendinge of the armor & powder and other thinges imployed about the trayninge and the souliours wages		13	4
Payd for papier			1
For my fee for gatheringe the towne rentes		13	4

Summa £15 11s

Besides he prayeth to be allowed which was delivered to
the churchewardens towardes the shotinge of the great bell   £2   4s

Summa totalis of his allowance is   £49 16s 11d

Soe rest in the accomptantes hand   7s 4d

	£	s	d
Besides there remayneth in the accomptantes handes with the some of £12 7s 11d in the former accompt mencioned with the addinge of a some of £3 12s 4d made of wood out of the towne landes this yere \<to be\> which in the total is £16 3d to be imployed for a stocke to buye wood for the poore	16	0	3

[*f. 88v*]   **[1608-1609]**

The accompt of John Reynoldes collector for all the rentes and farmes of all the landes and tenementes belonginge to the towneshipp of Wymondham accomptinge from the Feast of Saint Michaell Tharchangell in *Anno Domini* 1608 untill the said feast in *Anno Domini* 1609 for one wholl yere then ended as followeth

/Arrerages/

Inprimis in arrerages in anno presedenti		7	4

/Free rentes/

	£	s	d
Receyved of William Crane		3	0
Of Frauncis Neave		1	10
Of Alys Frosten *vidua*		2	0
Of George Mayhewe			4
Of Peter Neave			10
Of Thomas Nixon			10
Of the land holders later Edmond Cullyers			1

/Farme rentes/

	£	s	d
Receyved of Frauncis Plomer for Teddes Close otherwise called Tenement Brixy in Silfield and twoe acres of land therunto adjoyninge	9	0	0
Of Richard Rawlynge for thre roodes of meadowe att Kyddes Willowes and twoe acres of land in the Northfeild		12	8
Of Stephen Wiseman for a meadowe in Westwade	1	6	0
Of Agnes Flowerdewe *vidua* for a close at the Popples, thre acres			

	£	s	d
of meadowe at Salters Forde & thre acres of land in the Northfeilde	3	0	0
Of William Ovington for a close at the Clay Pyttes & thre acres of land in the Northfeilde	2	16	8
Of Stephen Agas for twoe acres of land one in Bixland Feild and one att Tolyes Crosse		11	8
Of Lawrence Fletcher for a parcell of meadowe at Hockhams Carre		3	4
Of Robert Rawlinge for a pictell nere Hockhams	1	4	0
Of John Symondes senior for one acre & a halfe of land in his crafte		10	0
Of Arthure Earle for one acre of land and a parcell of land sometymes a grove		12	0

Summa £20 12s 7d

	£	s	d
[f. 89r] Off William Payne for twoe acres of land in Holmefeild		12	0
Off Edmond Bucke for twoe acres of land there		12	0
Off Thomas Hobbes for a parcell of meadowe nere Wadebridge		1	0
Off Thomas Cole senior for a meadowe & three roodes of land at Ryvaldes, one acre att Barrowes Heade & one acre in Holme Feilde	2	0	0
Off Raphe Fox for one acre of land in Claxwell Furlonge		6	0
Off Thomas Sebborne for a pictell called Howlyns in Hungate	1	4	0
Off Abraham Hedgman for one acre & dimidia of land with a grove att thend thereof lyinge in Claxwell Furlonge		14	0
Off Robert Wiseman senior for twoe acres & three roodes of land in the North Feilde		14	0
Off Loy Agas for seaven acres of land in the North Feilde	2	9	0
Off John Reynoldes senior for a pictell att Hellanes end		14	0
Off Henry Kett for thre acres of land in the North Feild		15	0
Off George Norton for thre acres of land in the North Feild		16	6
Off Thomas Woodcocke for thre roodes of pasture lyeinge in Wattlefeilde		7	6
Off Mr Skypp for a pictell nere his howse which he purchased of Mr Spendlowe and twoe acres of land which heade upon the landes of Henry Meene	1	16	8
Off Robert Thorneton gent for a parcell of meadowe att Wadebridge		5	0
Off Robert Agas for twoe acres of lande in the North Feilde		12	0
Off Thomas Talbott generosus for one acre of land lyeinge in his close nere the Game Place		6	8

Summa £14 5s 4d

	£	s	d
[f. 89v] Of William Edwardes for three roodes of land neere the Popples		5	0

	£	s	d
Off Arthure Williams *generosus* for a parcell of meadowe & pasture nere Mill Poole		[*blank*]	
Off Alexander Foulsham for the towne howses where he nowe dwelleth & the ortchard	4	1	0
Off Reynold Keene for a towne howse	3	0	0
Off Randoll Downynge for a townshopp		12	0
Off William Burrell for one acre of land in the Park Feilde		6	0
Off Robert Bettes for a townehowse	1	0	0
Off Robert Toolye for a towne howse		13	4
Off John Clere for a towne howse	1	6	8
Off John Swayne and the wydowe Cocke for a towne howse		6	8
Off the wydowe Huntley Christian Moore and Eme Crosse for a towne howse		6	8
Off Alys Brewer *alias* Smythe & the wydowe Beart for a towne howse		6	8
Off Thomas Alleyn & Christian Smyth *vidua* for a towne howse		6	8
Off Elizabeth Leache & Joane Cotton for a towne howse		6	8
Off Robert Cullyer for the wydowe Tooley for a howse against North Wood Common adjoyninge to Black Inham	1	13	4
Off the lande houlders late Thomas Leverington *generosus* for a parcell of the schoole howse steeple to make a seller		1	0
Receyved more *of Alexander Foulsham* for the use of £5		7	6
Receyved more of William Gould for the use of 40s		3	0

Summa £15 2s 2d

Summa totalis of the charge £50 10s 1d

with the *super* charged upon J. Sym [*sic*] John Symondes which this accomptaunt hath receyved.

[*f. 90r*] Whereof this accomptaunt prayeth to be allowed for rentes not payd & other disburssementes for the towne as followeth:

/Rentes not paide/

Inprimis of Frauncis Neave	1	10
Of Alys Frosten *vidua*	2	0
Of George Mayhewe		4
Of Peter Neave		10
Of Thomas Nickson		10
Of the land holders late Edmond Cullyers		1
Of Thomas Talbot *generosus*	6	8
Of John Clere	1 6	8

[*In right hand margin against last entry above written in Arabic numerals*] 39s 3d

/Disbursementes/

Inprimis for breade and beere when the hedborrowes & the rest of the inhabitantes of the towne did meete to take this accompt	4	0

	£	s	d
/☞/ Payd for six yardes of cloath for Gouldnyes boye to put him			
to service		3	0
Payd for 140 foote of board to repayer the guilhowse		12	0
Payd for nayles to laye the same boarde			7
Payd to Robert Dixon for 200 faggots bondes			10
Payd to Christopher Browne for layeinge the foresaide board & to			
Foulsham for carieinge the same		1	4
Payd to John Rawlynge for 100 & *dimidia* of faggots bondes			9
Payd to John Appleton for makinge of 200 thre quarters &			
15 fagottes of wood		4	8
Payd more to him for makeinge of halfe a hundred wood		1	0
Payd to Mr Browne for careinge the same woode		8	0
Payd for stackinge the same woode		1	4
Payd to Robert Kett of Downeham for Cromwelles rent		4	1
Payd to the clarke		15	0
Payd to Mr Garye	3	15	0
Payd for rent to the Kinges Majesties baylye		13	8
Payd to the sparrowe ketcher		3	4
Payd more when the headborrowes did meete		1	2
/☞/Payd to William Cullyer beinge a churche warden towardes the			
belles	1	0	0

Summa £10 9s

[f. 90v] **/Disbursementes/**

	£	s	d
Payd upon Gann Munday for the preachers dynners		16	0
Payd for carieinge 300 & *dimidia* of wood from my howse to the barne		5	0
Payd for stackinge of the same		1	6
Payd for 500 of twoe bonde wood		[blank]	
Payd more then I receyved for the foresaid 500 of woode		11	0
Payd for the careinge thereof	1	2	0
Payd for stackeinge thereof		3	0
Payd to Alexander Foulsham for careinge of wood		6	0
Payd to Mr Williams and Mr Wells for theyre charges rydinge to			
Aylesham about the towne business		5	0
Payd to the clarke for wages		15	0
Payd to Porter for tylinge and mendinge the floore att the guilhowse		1	0
Payd to Esay Freeman for tyle & nayles			9
Payd to John Kinge for fyer worke att the guild		10	0
Payd to Mr Garey	3	15	0
Payd to the sparrowe ketcher		3	4
/☞/ Payd for the apparelinge of the wydowe Thowelldelles sonne to			
putt him to service as an apprentice	1	0	5

	£	s	d
Payd for a payer of indentures to bynde Gibbes an apprentice		1	4
Payd to Henry Wade for twoe thousand	1	10	0
Payd to him more for 10 roofe tyles		1	8
Payd to Maydston for carieinge the same		2	0
Payd for a chaldron of lyme & the careinge thereof		8	0
Payd to Mr Castleton[33]	3	15	0
Payd to Mr Blackborne for Cromwells rent		2	1
Payd more to the Kinges Majesties baylyff		13	9
Payd to him for a rent henn			6
Payd to the clarke		15	0
Payd to Knightes for makinge the lector in the churche		2	4
Payd to John Clere for glasinge the scholle howse		5	0
Payd to Fraunces Quayntrell for hookes and hyngens & a staple for Fosters howse			9
Payd more to him for nayles			2

Summa   £17 12s 7d

[f. 91r] /Disbursementes/

	£	s	d
Payd to Robert Bettes for lingethninge of 27 barres of iron & for three newe barres & 60 scoore wedges for the schollehowse		2	8
/☞/ Payd for fyve blockes towardes the buildinge of Foster his howse		4	9
Payd for a peece for a floore for the howse		1	0
Payd for an over sell		1	8
Payd for seaven short studdes		2	4
Payd for three longe studdes		1	6
Payd for 12 foote of board for the dores		1	0
Payd for thre planckes		2	6
Payd to Henry Kett for a loade of strawe		6	0
Payd to William Clarke for fower dayes worke		3	4
Payd to Richard Clarke for three dayes worke		3	4
Payd to John Clere for glaseinge the schoole howse	2	5	0
Payd for 80 foote of plancke for the steple		10	0
Payd for a joyce for the same			6
Payd for 16 foote of board for the steple		1	2
Payd to Maydston for careinge the same			4
Payd to the sparrowe ketcher		3	4
/☞/ Payd to Ollyett for thatchinge of Fosters howse		4	6
Payd to Lyncoln and Nealinge for dabinge of Fosters howse		4	0
Payd <more> for nayles & splent yarne			5
Payd to Knightes for makinge of three stooles & twoe doores for the steple		3	4

---

[33] Mr Castleton was the schoolmaster for a quarter in 1609.

	£	s	d
Payd to Henry Gaye for halfe a hundred of splentes		1	8
Payd for broache wandes and byndinges			6
Payd for reede			6
Payd for Henry Kett for 6 copple of sparres		3	0

Summa £5 8s 4d

[*f. 91v*] /**Disbursementes**/

	£	s	d
Payd to Mr Easton[34]	3	15	0
Payd to the clarke		15	0
Payd to Anthonye Cullender for trayninge in the towne armor		1	0
/☞/ Payd to Mr Jubbes & Frauncis Plomer which they disbursed for the towne	1	6	8
Payd for the barne to laye in the woode	1	0	0
For my fee for gatheringe the rentes		13	4
For the losse of three hundred wood sould to the poore		16	0
For the careage <of the same> & stackinge the same		13	0
Payd for a hundred and halfe of board to plancher Bettes howse		15	0
Payd for fower peces for the same howse for barferies & wyndbeames & twoe peces att the wydowe Tolies howse		3	0
Payd for careinge of them			4
Payd to Richard Clarke for mendinge of a peake wall at the wydowe Toolies howse		1	0
Payd for nayles			2
Payd to William Clarke & his sonnes for layeinge the plancher & other worke att Bettes howse		4	0
Payd more for a 100 & *dimidia* nayles			10
Payd to the sheriff for the allowinge of the charter		6	0

Summa £10 10s 4d

Summa totalis of the disbursementes £41 5s
Allowed more for rentes not payd £1 19s 3d

/**Allowance**/   Summa totalis of his allowances £43 4s 3d

/**Debet**/   & soe resteth in the accomptantes hand £7 5s 10d

Ultra

The stocke of money for the buyeinge of woode for the poore £17 17s 9d

---

[34] Nicholas Easton, schoolmaster 1609–14, had been master at King's Lynn 1593–97 and Aylsham 1601–09. He sent a large number of students to Cambridge, some younger sons from the gentry (see Williams, *The History of Wymondham Grammar School*).

£   s   d

[*f. 92r*]   **[*1609-1610*]**

The accompt of John Reynoldes collector for all the rentes & farmes of all the landes & tenementes belonginge to the towneshipp of Wymondham accomptinge from the Feast of St Michaell Tharkangell in *Anno Domini* 1609 untill the sayd feast in *Anno Domini* 1610 for one wholle yere then ended as followeth

/*Arrerages*/

	£	s	d
Inprimis in arrerages in anno presedenti	7	5	10

/*Free rentes*/

	£	s	d
Receyved of William Crane		3	0
Of Frauncys Neave		1	10
Of Alys Frosten *vidua*		2	0
Of George Mayhewe			4
Of Peter Neave			10
Of Thomas Nixon			10
Of the land holders later Edmond Cullyers			1

/*Farme rentes*/

	£	s	d
Receyved of Frauncis Plomer for Teddes Close otherwise called Tenement Brixy in Silfild & twoe acres of land therunto adjoyninge	9	0	0
Off Richard Rawlyn for three roodes of meadow att Kyddes Willowes & twoe acres of land in the North Feild		12	8
Off Stephen Wiseman for a meadow in Westwade	1	6	0
Off Agnes Flowerdewe *vidua* for a close att the Popples, three acres of meadowe att Salters Forde & thre acres of land in the North Feild	3	0	0
Off William Ovington for a close att the Clay Pyttes & three acres of land in the Northfeilde	2	16	8
Off Stephen Agas for twoe acres of land one in Bixland Feild and one att Tolyes Crosse		11	8
Off Lawrence Fletcher for a parcell of meadowe att Hockhams Carre		3	4
Off Robert Rawlyn for a pictell nere Hockhams	1	4	0
Off John Symondes senior for one acre & a halfe of land in his crafte		10	0
Off Arthure Earle for one acre of land and a parcell of land sometymes a grove		12	0

Summa   £27   11s   1d

	£	s	d
[*f. 92v*] Off William Payne for twoe acres of land in Holmfeild		12	0
Off Edmond Bucke for twoe acres of land there		12	0
Off Thomas Hobbes for a parcell of meadowe nere Wadebridge		1	0
Off Thomas Cole senior for a meadowe & thre roodes of land at			

	£	s	d
Ryvaldes, one acre att Barrowes Head & one acre in Holmefeild	2	0	0
Off Raphe Fox for one acre of lande in Claxwell Furlonge		6	0
Off Thomas Sebborne for a pictell called Howlyns <Furlonge>			
in Hungate	1	4	0
Off Abraham Hedgman for one acre & *dimidia* of land with a grove			
att thend thereof lyeinge in Claxwell Furlonge		14	0
Off Robert Wiseman senior for twoe acres & three roodes of land			
in the North Feild		14	0
Off Loy Agas for seaven acres of land in the North Feilde	2	9	0
Off John Reynoldes senior for a pictell att Hellanes end		14	0
Off Henry Kett for thre acres of land in the North Feild		15	0
Off George Norton for three acres of land in the North Feild		16	6
Off Thomas Woodcocke for three roodes of pasture lyeinge in			
Wattlefeld		7	6
Off Mr Skypp for a pictell nere his howse which he purchased of			
Mr Spendloue & twoe acres of land which heade upon the landes			
of Henry Meene	1	16	8
Off Robert Thornton *generosus* for a parcell of meadowe att			
Wadebrigge		5	0
Off Robert Agas for twoe acres of lande in the North Feild		12	0
Off Thomas Talbott gent for one acre of land lyeinge in his close			
nere the Game Place		6	8

Summa £14 5s 4d

	£	s	d
[*f. 93r*] Of William Edwardes for three roodes of land neere the			
Popples		5	0
Off Arthure Williams gent for a parcell of meadowe & pasture nere			
Mill Poole		[*blank*]	
Off Alexander Foulsham for the towne howses where he nowe			
dwelleth & the ortchard	4	12	0
Off Reynold Keene for a towne howse	3	0	0
Off Randoll Downynge for a towne shopp		12	0
Off William Burrell for one acre of land in the Park Feild		6	0
Off Robert Bettes for a towne howse	1	0	0
Off Robert Tooley for a townehowse		13	4
Off John Clere for a towne howse	1	6	8
Off John Swayne and the wydowe Cocke for a towne howse		6	8
Off the wydowe Huntley Christian Moore & Eme Crosse for a			
towne howse		6	8
Off Alys Brewer *alias* Smythe & the wydowe Beart for a towne howse		6	8
Off Thomas Alleyn & Christian Smythe *vidua* for a towne howse		6	8
Off Elizabeth Leeche & Joane Cotton for a towne howse		6	8

	£	s	d
Off Robert Cullyer for the wydowe Tooley for a howse against North Wood Common adjoyninge to Black Inham	1	13	4
Off the land holders late Thomas Leverington gent for a parcell of the schoole howse steeple to make a seller		1	0
Receyved more of Alexander Foulsham for the use of £5		7	6
Receyved more of William Gould for the use of 40s		3	0
Off the poore people for tenne hundred of brushe wood	5	0	0
Off them more for 900 & a halfe of twoe bond wood	9	10	0

Summa £29 12s 2d

Summa totalis of receiptes £71 8s 7d
Whereof to be allowed as followeth

[f. 93v] /Disbursementes/

	£	s	d
Inprimis payd to Allexander Foulsham when the 17 did meete for bread & beare		2	0
/☞/ Payd \<to Henry\> to Henry Gaye for the towne *which was about the suyt for the fynes of the Kinges mannor*[35]	5	0	0
Payd more to Allexander Foulsham att a second metinge of the 17 for bread & beare		2	0
Payd to Porter for six thowsande tyle pynn		2	5
Payd to the sparrowe ketcher		3	4
Payd to Maston for carieinge of six hundred wood \<from\> for the towne		15	0
Payd to John Appleton for makinge of twoe hundred & 3 quarters of wood		5	6
Payd to him more for makinge of one hundred & a halfe of wood		3	0
Payd to Henry Gaye for the wood aboute the Cundyett Close	6	0	0
Payd for three thowsand of fagott bondes		15	0
Payd for fortie foote of boarde for the church which John Clere had of me		3	4
Payd to Rychard Reynoldes for fellinge & makinge of fyve hundred wood		10	0
Payd to Mayston for carieinge of three hundred & one quarter of wood		8	2
Delivered to Clere 60 foote of board for the churche		5	0
Payd to Mr Easton for his quarter[36]	5	0	0
Payd to the clarke		15	0
Payd to John Dynn		10	0

[35] This dispute about the level of entry fines was to last until at least 1620–21 when Philip Cullyer went to London on several occasions to seek a reduction on behalf of the tenants of the King's manor.

[36] The schoolmaster's salary was raised to £20 per annum.

	£	s	d
Payd to Charles Wyseman for wrytinge		5	0
Payd to Steven Dey for Cromwells rent		2	0
Payd to John Appleton for makinge of 700 & a halfe a quarter of wood		14	3
Payd to Richard Reynoldes for makinge of 300 & a halfe of wood att Cakebreedes		7	0
Payd to William Payne for carieinge of 700 & a halfe of wood from Cakebreedes	1	10	0
Payd to Mayston for carieinge of 200 wood from Cakebreedes		6	8
Payd for 10 bunches of lathe for the guild howse		15	0
Payd for 2 thowsand of lathe nayles		3	4
Payd for eaves boardes		1	10
Payd for one thowsand of tyles		15	0
Payd to Porter for tylinge of the guildhowse	1	6	8

Summa £27 6s 6d

	£	s	d
[*f. 94r*] Payd to Porter for mendinge of hooles in the gable end of the chymney att the guild howse			6
Payd for one bunche of lathe		1	6
Payd for three thowsand of lathe nayles		5	0
Payd for great nayles for the eaves boardes			4
Payd for 30 <quarters> foote of quarters for eaves boardes		1	2
Payd for one thowsand of tyle att Ser Arthures kell[37]		14	0
Payd for the carieinge thereof		2	0
Payd for twoe bunches of lathe		3	0
Payd for fyve hundred of lathe nayles			10
Payd for hookes and hyngeins for ould Hammontes doore			8
Payd for nayles for the howse			4
Payd to Mr Freeman for twoe hundred of strawe		6	0
Payd for tymber for the howse		18	0
Payd to Robert Knightes for makinge of the house		6	8
Payd to Bix & his man for thatchinge of the same		5	0
Payd for reede for the same			8
Payd to Porter for twoe daies worke att the guild howse & att the scholle howse		2	8
Payd for 2 eaves boardes		1	0
Payd to Kytmere for serveinge of the mason 2 dayes		2	0
Payd for six bushells of lyme		2	0
Payd for one eaves board			6

[37] Sir Arthur Heveningham (d. 1630) seems the most likely supplier of the tiles from his estate at Ketteringham where in 1608 he supplied the bricks for the rebuilding of the church after it had been destroyed in a storm (see Smith, *County and Court*, p. 159).

	£	s	d
Payd to Foulsham for beere for Porter & his man		1	0
Payd for broache wondes & byndinges for Hamontes howse			10
Payd for one hundred of splentes		5	0
Payd for splente yarne			4
Payd for dawbinge thereof		5	0
Payd to Frauncis Quayntrell for carieing of three loades of claye to the howse		2	0
Payd to Porter for 3 thowsand of tile pynne		1	6
Payd to the wydowe Gedney for the preachers dynners		14	0
Payd to Mr Freeman for 6 hundred of strawe for Bettes & Toolies howses		12	0
Payd to Bix & his man for 3 dayes worke <of himselfe & h> thatchinge		7	0

Summa　£6　2s　6d

	£	s	d
[*f. 94v*] Payd for 4 sparres & puttinge of them up & for a peece of roofe tree		2	0
Payd for byndinges & broachewoudes for Toolyes & Bettes howses		2	0
Payd to the wydowe Toolye for splentes & for dawbinge of a peeke walle		1	4
Payd to Mr Shreeve for the allowance of the charter		10	0
Payd to Christopher Browne for a tree for the cooke stoole		5	0
Payd to Mr Easton for his quarter	5	0	0
Payd to the clarke		15	0
Payd to the sparrowe catcher		3	4
Payd for makinge of a benche in the schole howse		8	0
Payd for board for the same		8	4
Payd for planke for ytt		7	2
Payd for grounde tymber for ytt		1	8
Payd for carieinge of the stoole to the scholle howse & for nayles		1	0
Payd for quarters for ytt		2	0
Payd to Wade for a quarter of brick & for lyme & for his worke		2	4
Payd for a peece of tymber & for a planck to use att the gildhowse		3	4
Payd to Christopher Browne for makinge of the cooke stoole		3	4
Payd for tymber for the twoe postes		5	0
Payd for sawen tymber for the chayer		3	0
Payd for iron worke		4	6
Payd for a loade of claye & carieinge of it		1	0
Payd for makinge of twoe dores & hanging of them att the widdowe Toolyes howse		1	8
Payd for boardes & leadges		3	0
Payd for a dore stalle			6

	£	s	d
Payd for a hundred nayles & for 2 hyngells		1	0
Payd to Cullender *junior* for trayninge in the towne armor		1	0
Payd to the clarke		15	0
Payd to the wydowe Gedney for Mother Motley		2	0
Payd to Christopher Browne for tymber for the tayle peece of the cooke stoole		2	0
Payd to him more for settinge on of ytt		1	2
Payd to the *Kinges* baylyffe for rent		13	11
Payd to him for a rent henne			6

Summa   £11 11s 1d

	£	s	d
[f. 95r] Payd to Mr Easton for his quarter	5	0	0
Payd to Mr Blackborne for free rent for the towne land			3
Payd to Robert Englishe for dawbinge worke		2	4
Payd for splentes 2 peces of tymber nayles & a loade of claye for the church yard howse		2	4
Payd for 2 loades of strawe for Cleres house & the churche yard howse		11	6
Payd to the sparrowe catcher		3	4
Payd to Steven Dey for Cromwells rent		2	1
Payd for fower bunches of broachwondes & byndinges		2	0
Payd to Bradford & Ollyett for fower dayes worke a peece		9	4
Payd to Robert Crane for Sturmans cloathes		15	6
Payd to Clayborne		6	0
Payd to a reder towardes the redinge of the guildhowse		1	0
Payd to Mr Easton for his quarter	5	0	0
Payd to Foulsham for a shoulder of mutton & for bread & beare when the accompt was entred		1	1
Payd to the Kinges baylyff for rent for the towne land		13	8
Payd more to Henry Gaye for the wood att Cakebreedes	6	0	0
Payd for stackinge of wood		6	8
Payd for barne roame	1	0	0
Payd for gatheringe of the rent		13	4

Summa   £21 10s 5d

Summa totalis of the paymentes is   £66 10s 6d

/Rentes not payed/

He prayeth to be allowed for rentes not payd

		£	s	d
Inprimis of Frauncis Neave			1	10
Of Alys Frosten *vidua*			2	0
Of George Mayhew				4

	£	s	d
Of Petter Neave			10
Of Thomas Nickson			10
Of the land holders late Edmond Cullyers			1
Of Thomas Talbott gent		6	8
Of John Clere	1	6	8

Summa of the rentes not payd £1 19s 3d

[f. 95v] /Receipt/

Memorandum this accomptant is charged <with 57s 4d> for the admission of schollers with	2	17	4
Whereof to be allowed to make upp Mr Eastons first quarter att his comynge	1	5	0
For a booke called a callapyne		11	0
For glasinge of the schole wyndowes		2	4
For repayringe of the towne armor		6	0
And allowed him for money not receyved for schollers admitted		2	0

Summa totalis of the allowances for the wholle
payementes *out* of the receipt for schollers is   £2   6s   4d

Et sic debet in toto   £3   9s   9d

[f. 96r]   **[1610-1611]**

The accompt of John Reynoldes collector for all the rentes and farmes of all the <rentes> landes and tenementes belonginge to the towneshipp of Wymondham accomptinge from the Feast of St Michaell Tharkangell in *Anno Domini* 1610 untill the saide feast in *Anno Domini* 1611 for one wholle yere then ended as followeth

/Arrerages/

| Inprimis in arrerages in anno presedenti | 3 | 9 | 9 |

/Free rentes/

Receyved of William Crane		3	0
Of Francis Neave		1	10
Of Alice Frosten *vidua*		2	0
Of George Mayhewe			4
Of Peter Neave			10
Of Thomas Nixon			10
Of the lande holders later Edmond Cullyers			1

/Farme rentes/

| Inprimis of Frauncis Plomer for Teddes Close otherwise called Tenement Brixy in Silfild and twoe acres of lande therunto adioyninge | 9 | 0 | 0 |

Off Richard Rawlynge for three roodes of meadowe att Kyddes

	£	s	d
Willowes & twoe acres of lande in the North Feilde		12	8
Off Stephen Wiseman John Raynoldes & John Moore for three acres of lande twoe parcells of meadowe and a pightell att the Poples late in the occupacion of Agnes Flowerdewe wydowe	3	3	4
Off Stephen Wiseman more for a meadowe att Westwade	1	6	0
Off William Ovington for a cloase att the Clay Pittes & three acres of land in the North Feild	2	16	8
Off Stephen Agas for twoe acres of land one in Bixland Feilde & one att Tolies Crosse		11	8
Off Lawrence Fletcher for a parcell of meadow att Hockhams Carre		3	4
Off Robert Rawlynge for a pightell nere Hockhams	1	4	0
Off John Symondes senior for a acre & a halfe of lande lyeinge in his crafte		10	0
Off Arthure Earle for one acre of lande & a parcell of lande sometymes a grove		12	0

Summa £23 18s 4d

[f. 96v] Off William Payne for twoe acres of lande in Holmfeilde		12	0
Off Edmond Bucke for twoe acres of lande there		12	0
Off Thomas Hobbes for a parcell of meadowe Wadebrigge		1	0
Off Thomas Cole senior for a meadowe & three rodes of lande att Ryvaldes one acre att Barrowes Heade & one acre in Holmefeilde	2	0	0
Off Raphe Fox for one acre of land in Claxwell Furlonge		6	0
Off Thomas Sebborne for a pightell called Howlyns in Hungate	1	4	0
Off Abraham Hedgeman for one acre & *dimidia* of land with a grove att thend thereof lieinge in Claxwell Furlonge		14	0
Off Robert Wiseman senior for twoe acres & thre rodes of lande in the North Feild		14	0
Off Loye Agas for seaven acres of land in the North Feild	2	9	0
Off John Reynoldes senior for a pightell att Hellanes end		14	0
Off Henry Kett for thre acres of land in the North Feild		15	0
Off George Norton for three acres of land in the North Feild		16	6
Off Thomas Woodcocke for thre roodes of pasture lyeinge in Wattlefeilde		7	6
Off Mr Skypp for a pightell nere his howse which he purchased of Mr Spendloue & twoe acres of lande which heade upon the landes of Henry Meene	1	16	8
Off Robert Thornton gent for a parcell of meadowe att Wadebridge		5	0
Off Robert Agas for twoe acres of lande in the North Feild		10	0
Off Mr Doctor Talbott for one acre of land lyeinge in his close nere the Game Place		6	8

Summa £14 3s 4d

	£	s	d
[f. 97r] Off Esay Freman for thre roodes of land nere the Popples late in the occupacion of William Edwardes		5	0
Off Arthure Williams gent for a parcell of meadowe and pasture nere Mill Poole		[blank]	
Off Alexander Foulesham for the towne howses where he nowe dwelleth & the ortcharde	4	12	0
Off Reynolde Keene for a towne howse	3	0	0
Off Robert Wytherley for a towne shop late in the occupacion of Randoll Downynge		12	0
Off William Burrell for one acre of lande in the Parke Feilde		6	0
Off Robert Bettes for a towne howse	1	0	0
Off Robert Tooley for a towne howse		13	4
Off John Clere for a towne howse	1	6	8
Off John Swayne & the wydowe Cock for a towne howse		6	8
Off the wydowe Huntley Christian Moore Eme Crosse for a towne howse		6	8
Off Alice Brewer alias Smyth & the wydowe Beart for a towne howse		6	8
Off Thomas Alleyn & Christian Smyth vidua for a towne howse		6	8
Off Elizabeth Leeche & Joane Cotton for a towne howse		6	8
Off Robert <Crane> *Cullyer* for the wydowe Tooley for a howse against Northwood Common adioyninge to Black Inham	1	13	4
Off the lande holders late Thomas Leverington gent for a parcell of the schoole howse steeple to make a seller		1	0
Off George Hamont & Robert Foster for a towne howse		6	8
Off Alexander Foulsham more for the use of £5		7	6
Off William Gould more for the use of 40s		3	0

Summa   £15 8s 10d

Summa totalis of the receiptes   £53 10s 6d

Whereof prayeth to be allowed as followeth

[f. 97v] /**Rentes not paide**/

	£	s	d
Inprimis of Frauncis Neave		1	10
Of Alys Frostyn wydowe		2	0
Of George Mayhewe			4
Of Peter Neave			10
Of Thomas Nickson			10
Of the lande holders late Edmond Cullyer			1
Of Thomas Talbott gent		6	8
Of John Clere	1	6	8

/**Disbursementes**/

	£	s	d
Inprimis paid for breede and bere when the Seventeen did meete		1	9

	£	s	d
/☞/ Paid for hose and lyninges for [*blank*] Gibbes when he went unto Thomas Kett		4	4
Payd more for shirtes for him		2	6
Paid more for his doublett & lyninges for it		2	10
Paid more for a jerkyn cloathe & buttons for itt		4	3
Paid more for a payer of netherstockes & a payer of shoes for him		2	10
Paid to the sheriff for allowance of the charter		7	0
Payd to Anthonye Pile for makinge of Gibbes his doblett jerkyn hose & shirtes		4	0
Payd to Knightes & his twoe men for making of twoe dores att the Abbye steeple & hanginge of them		5	0
Payd to Thurston for 4 payer of hingles & for an iron barre & a staplet & one hundred of nayles		3	4
Paid more for the careinge of the dores & postes to churche			8
Payd for threescore and 12 foote of boarde		6	0
Payd more for 2 hartrees & ledges		2	4
Payd more for 18 foote of tymber for the postes		9	0
Payd for makinge cleane of the Abbye steple		1	0
Payd to John Clere for glasinge of the chamber att the guildhowse & for an iron barre			10
Paide for woode when the 17 did meete		1	3
Paid to Carver for a newe table for the guildhowse		11	0
/☞/ Payd to Whepdales wife for kepinge of Hadlies yongest childe		2	6

Summa £5 11s 8d

	£	s	d
[*f. 98r*] Payd to Charles Hadley for clothes for his childe		4	0
Payd to Mr Easton	5	0	0
Payd to the Kinges Majestie his baylyffe for rent		13	8
Payd to John Dey more for clothes for Hadlies childe		8	0
Payd to Raphe Fytlyn for Cromwelles rente		2	0
Payd for the preachers dynners		16	0
/☞/ Payd for Mr Chancelors dynner	3	10	0
/☞/ Payd to John Dey for kepinge of Hadlies childe	1	0	0
Payd to reeders for comynge from Norwich to take the guildhowse to reede		1	4
Payd to Robert Dixon for 8 bunches of broaches & byndinges		4	0
Paid to Mistris Hall for twoe hundred of reede	7	10	0
Paid to Mr Easton	5	0	0
Paid for three <little> formes for the little chamber att the guildhowse		4	6
Paid for *careing of* broachwondes and bindings			4
Payd for nayles for the guildhowse		1	4
Payd for sparres & other peces for the guildhowse		1	8

	£	s	d
Payd to Knightes for settinge of them upp		1	0
/☞/ Payd more for twoe bunches of lathe		3	0
Payd to the reeders for fower daies worke	1	0	0
Payd to them more for six daies worke	1	10	0
Payd to Inglishe & Bradford for makinge redye of the claye		2	4
<I paid> to John Durrant for 2 bunches of haye & for twoe loades			
of ould claye		1	8
Paid to Stephen Kett for 2 loades of claye		1	8
Paid to Stephen Agas for careinge of twoe loades of claye from			
John Durrantes		1	0
Paid to Foulsham for 2 loades of claye		1	0
Paid to Robert Dixon more for 6 bunches of broachwondes &			
bindinges		3	0
Paid for strawe & nayles & for carieinge of broachwondes &			
bindinges		1	8
Paid more to Foulsham for carieinge of reede	1	15	0
Paid to him more for a loade of reede		19	0
Paid more to the reeders for six daies worke	1	10	0
Paid for a key for the chest			6
Paid to the reders more then theire wages		3	4
Paid for fetchinge of ladders & careinge of them		1	0

Summa   £32 12s 10d

[f. 98v] /Disbursementes/

	£	s	d
Paid for 8 quartes of wyne when Mr Chauncelor came to the courte		6	0
Paid for <Clere> ashen billet for the melting of leade for the churche			
which John Clere had		2	6
Paid for thirtie foote of boarde to laye under the leade att the			
churche which he had also		2	6
Paid to Cossey for a stoppe for the towne well		1	4
Paid to Frauncis Quayntrell for makinge of the cheanes & mendinge			
of the hoopes of the stoppe		1	4
Paid more to Foulsham for a rope for the well			4
Paid to him more for halfe a chaludron of lyme		4	0
Paide to Henry Wade for bricke		4	0
Paid to Wade and his man for worke aboute the well		3	0
Paid more to Foulsham for carieinge of bricke & sande & a loade			
of claye		1	8
Paid to Durrant for a loade of ould claye to sparflewe the guildhowse		1	0
Paid to Parker & Calye for mendinge of the harthe & the backe of			
the chymney att the guildhowse			10
Paid to William Rowse for trymminge of the towne armor &			
trayninge in itt		6	0

	£	s	d
Paid more to Mr Easton	5	0	0
Paid more to the Kinges Majestes bayliff for rent		13	9
Paid unto him more for a rent henne			6
Paid to Anthonye Cullender for trayninge in the towne armor		1	0
Paid to Inglishe & Bradford for 2 dayes worke of sparflewinge of the			
guildhowse & riginge of the same		4	0
Paid to Raphe Fitlyn from Cromwelles rent		2	1
Paid to Norton for trayninge in the towne armor		1	0
Paid to Danyell Ollyett & his man for thackinge of the towne howse		2	4
Paid more to Mr Freeman for strawe		2	9
Paid more to Wade & his man for castinge of guildhowse		4	8
Paid to the wydowe Toolye for twoe sneckes			4
Paid more to Mr Easton	5	0	0
Paid for barne roame	1	0	0
Paid for gatheringe of the rent		13	4

Summma   £15   0s   3d

[*f. 99r*] /**Disbursementes**/

	£	s	d
Payde for 600 twoe bonde woode more then it was sould for to the			
poore	2	8	0
Payd for twoe hundred of twoe bond wood more then yt was sould			
for to the poore		8	0
Payd for 1400 of smalle wood more then yt was sould for to the			
poore		14	0
Payd more for stackinge of the same wood		11	0

Summa   £4   1s

Summa totalis of the allowances is   £57   5s   9d

This accomptantes disbursementes exceed his receiptes   £3   15s   9d

	£	s	d
The some for the stocke of wood for the poore	17	17	9
Whereof to satisfie and pay the accomptant his money which he			
hath layd out more then he receyved as appere in the foote of			
this last accompt	3	15	3
Payd more out of the said stocke to Thomas Weld gent which he layd			
out aboute the defence <of> for Teedes Close in the Exchequer	8	8	6
Remayninge of the stocke for wood	5	14	0

[*f. 99v*]   **[1611-1612]**

The accompt of John Reynoldes collector of all the rentes and farmes of all the landes and tenementes belonginge to the towneshipp of Wymondham accomptinge from the Feast of St Michaell Tharkangell in *Anno Domini* 1611 untill the Feast of St Michaell Tharkangell in *Anno Domini* 1612 for one wholle yere then ended as followeth

	£	s	d
/Arrerages/			
Inprimis in arrerages			nil
/Free rentes/			
Receyved of William Crane		3	0
Of Frauncis Neave		1	10
Of Alice Frosten *vidua*		2	0
Of George Mayhewe			4
Of Peter Neave			10
Of Thomas Nixon			10
Of the lande holders later Edmond Cullyer			1

/Farme rentes/

	£	s	d
Inprimis of Frauncis Plomer for Teddes Close otherwise called Tenement Brixy in Silfild and a pictell conteyninge twoe acres thereunto adioyninge	9	0	0
Of Stephen Wiseman for one meadowe att Westwade conteyninge one acre and one roode <26s and> for thre acres and a halfe late in the occupacion of William Ovington 24s 6d and for thre acres of lande late in the occupacion of Agnes Flowerdewe *vidua* 15s *in toto*	3	5	6
Of Robert Rawlyn for thre roodes of meadowe att Kydes Willowes and twoe acres of land in the North Feilde and one pightell nere Hockhams	1	16	8
Off John Moore for a pightell nere Hockhams	1	13	4
Off John Reynoldes for meadowe lyeinge in the common meadowe att Westwade 15s and for a pightell nere his howse in Suton 14s *in toto*	1	9	0
Off William Ovington for one pightell att the Claye Pittes	1	12	2
Off Stephen Agas for twoe acres of land one in Bixland Feilde & the other att Tolyes Crosse in the Northfeilde		11	8

Summa   £19 17s 3d

	£	s	d
[*f. 100r*] Off Stephen Kett for one acre and a halfe of lande lyeinge in John Symondes his crofte in Downeham		10	0
Off Arthure Earle for one acre of lande and a parcell of lande sometymes a grove		12	0
Off William Payne for twoe acres of lande in Holmefeilde		12	0
Off Edmond Bucke for twoe acres of lande in Holmefeilde		12	0
Off Thomas Hobbes for a parcell of meadow lyeinge in his meadowe att Wadebridge		1	0
Off Lawrence Fletcher for a parcell of meadowe att Hockhams Carre		3	4
Off Thomas Cole senior for a meadowe & three rodes of lande att Ryvaldes one acre att Barrowes Heade & one acre in Holmefeilde	2	0	0

	£	s	d
Off Raphe Fox for one acre of lande in Claxwell Furlonge		6	0
Off William Mappes for a pightell called Howlyns in Hungate 24s			
and for one acre & a halfe with a grove att thende thereof			
lyeinge in Claxwell Furlonge 14s *in toto*	1	18	0
Off Robert Wiseman senior for twoe acres & three rodes of lande			
lyeinge nere Beckes Deeke in the Northfeilde		14	0
Off Robert Agas for nyne acres of lande in the Northfeilde	2	19	0
Off Richard Dilham for thre acres of lande in the Northfeilde		15	0
Off George Norton for three acres of lande in the Northfeilde		16	6
Off Thomas Woodcocke for thre rodes of pasture lyeinge in Wattlefeild		7	6

Summa £12 6s 4d

	£	s	d
[*f. 100v*] Off Mr Skypp for a pightell nere his howse and twoe acres			
of lande which heade upon the landes of Henry Meene	1	16	8
Off Robert Thorneton gent for a parcell of meadowe att Wadebridge		5	0
Off Mr Doctor Talbott for one acre of land *lieinge* in his close nere			
the Game Place		6	8
Off Esaye Freman for thre rodes of land lyeinge nere the Popples late			
in the occupacion of William Edwardes		5	0
Off Arthure Williams gent for a parcell of meadowe and pasture			
nere Myll Poole		[blank]	
Off Alexander Foulesham for the towne howses where he nowe			
dwellethe & the ortchard	4	1	0
Off Reynolde Keene for a towne howse	3	0	0
Off Robert Wytherley for a towneshop late in the occupacion			
of Randoll Downinge		12	0
Off William Burrell for one acre of lande abbuttinge upon the			
Endles Waye towards the south *in the Parke Feilde*		6	0
Off Robert Bettes for a towne howse	1	0	0
Off Robert Tooley for a towne howse		13	4
Off John Clere for a towne howse	1	6	8
Off the wydowe Swayne and the wydowe Cocke for a towne howse		6	8
Off the wydowe Huntley Christian Smyth & Thomas Allen *for a			
towne howse*		6	8
Off William Chamberleyne and Dowsinge for a towne howse		6	8
Off the wydowe Breese and the wydowe Gybbes *for a towne howse*		6	8

Summa £14 19s

	£	s	d
[*f. 101r*] Off the wydowe Leeche for a towne howse		6	8
Off the wydowe Tooley for the tenement upon Northwoode			
Common adjoyninge to Black Inham	1	13	4
Off Mr Playforde for a seller made out of the schole howse steple		1	0

	£	s	d
Off George Hamond and Robert Foster for a towne howse		6	8
Off Alexander Foulesham more for the use of fyve powndes		7	6
Off William Goulde more for the use of 40s		3	0
Off Stephen Dey		5	0
Receyved by the accomptant more for one peece of tymber		4	0
Off Reynold Keene for 20 brushe fagottes		2	0

Summa £3 9s 2d

Summa totalis of the receiptes £50 11s 9d

Whereof he prayeth to be allowed as followeth

/Rentes not payde/

	£	s	d
Inprimis of Frauncis Neave		1	10
Of Alice Frosten wydowe		2	0
Of George Mayhewe			4
Of Peter Neave			10
Of Thomas Nickson			10
Of the land holders late Edmond Cullyer			1
Of Thomas Talbott gent		6	8
Of John Clere	1	6	8

Summa £1 19s 3d

[f. 101v] /Disbursementes/

	£	s	d
Inprimis payde to the accomptant not reckoned in his former accompt		17	0
Payd to Mr Horsenell for the allowance of the charter of the towne		10	0
Payd to Mr Easton	5	0	0
Payd to the Kinges bayliff for rent		13	8
Payd to the wydowe Gedney for the preachers dynners		17	0
Payde to her more for thre quartes of wyne & for horse meate		3	10
Payde to Thomas Godfrey for palinge att the tenementes and Reynold Keene his howse		6	6
Payde for a rayle & for pale nayles		1	8
Payde to John Dey for kepinge of Hadleys childe	1	0	0
Payd to Frauncis Quayntrell for iron & nayles for the cuck stoole		2	0
Payd to Christofer Browns man for a peece of tymber & settinge ytt on		1	4
Payd to Mr Easton	5	0	0
Payd for a well curbell		4	0
Payd to the souliers for trayeinge in the towne armor		3	0
Payd for a combe of lyme for the towne howse on the Common		1	4
Payd to Catchpoll for trymminge of the towne armor		2	0
Payd to Raphe Fytlyn for Cromwelles rent		2	0
Payd to Maston for carieinge of bricke and stone		1	2

	£	s	d
/☞/ Payd to the churchwardens for twoe bookes for the churche	1	5	0
Payde to Wade for thre hundred of bricke & for stone		5	0

Summa £16 16s 6d

[f. 102r] /*Disbursementes*/

Payde to Wade and his man for settinge up of the chymney att the			
wydowe Tolies howse		4	0
Payde to Raphe Jubbes for a sute fyne for Tenement Skarrells		1	0
Payd to Richard Caddywolde for breed & beere for the ringers when			
my Lord came thoroughe to towne		1	4
Payd to Mr Easton	5	0	0
Payde to Richard Bunne for twoe sparres & for fower pennyworth			
of nayles		1	0
Payd for heweinge & saweinge of groundsells		15	0
Payd for thirtie foote of tymber for groundsells		15	0
Payd for the carieinge of them to the wydowe Toolyes howse		1	0
Payd to Knightes and Farrar for groundsellinge of 80 foote & 4 at			
the wydowe Toolies howse & for settinge up of sparres there		14	6
Payd to the Kinges baylyff for rent & for a rent henn		14	3
Payd to Alexander Foulsham for lyme & carieinge of stone		7	0
Payd to Bunne & his sonne for dawbing and castinge of claye		7	6
Payd to him for fetchinge of splentes & for splent yarne & nayles		1	0
Payde to Wade and his fyve men for one daies worke of pynninge &			
makinge of a oven att Toolyes howse		7	0
Payde to him more for bricke for the oven		1	0
Payd to George Norton for carieinge of three loades of claye & for			
three burdens of strawe		1	8

Summa £8 18s 3d

[f. 102v] /*Disbursements*/

Payde to *Mr* Freman for a loade of strawe and carieinge of ytt to			
the wydowe Tolies howse		11	0
Payd for a <bundches> *burden* of broachwondes & byndinges			6
Payde to Ollyett for twoe daies worke thatchinge with his server		5	0
Payd to George Norton for twoe sparrs & settinge them upp			9
/☞/ Payd to Stephen Agas for the wydow Peirson when shee and			
all her howse laye sicke		5	0
Payd to William Payne for a loade of strawe & carieinge of ytt		11	0
Payd for twoe burdens of broachwondes and byndinges		1	0
Payd to Mr Freeman for thre loades of barlie strawe	1	2	0
Payd to him more for six hundred of winter corne strawe		18	0
Payd to Dixon for 4 bunches of broachwondes and twoe burthens			
of byndinges		4	10

	£	s	d
Payd to Mr Freeman for carieinge of twoe loades of strawe		2	0
Payd to Foulsham for carieinge three loades of strawe to the wydowe Jacksons howse		4	0
Payd to Ollyett & Bradford for 7 dayes worke att the wydowe Leeches & att the wydowe Jacksons howse		17	6
Payd for reede		3	4
Payd to Ollyett & his man for 7 daies worke		17	6
Payd to Mr Freman for halfe a hundred of rye strawe for Mother Jacksons howse		1	6
Payd to William Payne for a loade of rye strawe & carieinge of ytt		10	0
Payd to Danyell Ollyett for thatchinge		5	0

Summa £6 19s 11d

[*f. 103r*] */Disbursements/*

	£	s	d
Payd to Bradford for one burthen of broachwondes & byndinges			10
Payd to Raphe Fytlyn for Cromwelles rent		2	1
Payd to John Appleton for makinge of 20 faggottes of woode att Kinges howse & for fellinge of thornes		1	0
Payd to Freman for thre hundred of wynter corne strawe & careinge of ytt to the wydowe Toolyes howse		10	0
Payd to Ollyett for twoe daies worke to laye ytt		5	0
Payd to Mr Easton	5	0	0
/☞/ Payd to Mr Wiseman for a sheete for Osborne *to wynde him to be buried*		3	0
Payd for gatheringe of the rent		13	4
Payd for barne roame	1	0	0

/Disbursements for the wood:/

	£	s	d
Payde to Mallard & his sonne for stackinge of tenne hundred of wood saveinge tenne fagottes		5	0
Payde to him more for stackinge of 400 of wood		2	0
Payd to Frauncis Plomer for carieinge tenne hundred of wood saveinge 10 faggottes	1	10	0
Payd to him for faggot bondes		9	0
Payd to him more for makinge of wood		16	8
Payde to Richard Bunne for makinge of fortie & odd fagottes & fetchinge of <fagottes> bondes		1	4
Payd to Bradford for steweinge of wood in Teades		4	8
Payd to Frauncis Quayntrell for carieinge of twoe loades of wood out of the Northfeilde		2	0
Payd to George Norton for carieinge twoe loades of tymber		2	6

Summa £11 8s 5d

Summa totalis of the allowances £46 2s 4d

	£	s	d
			Ultra

[*f. 103v*] **/Super/**

In the handes of the wydowe Tolye of rent not payde this yere		6	4
In the handes of Robert Bettes		2	6
In the handes of William Chamberleyne		1	8
In the handes of William Randoll and Robert Foster		6	8

Summa 17s 2d

Et sic debet £3 12s 3d

[*f. 104r*]   **[1612-1613]**

The accompt of John Raynoldes collector for all the rentes and fearmes of all the landes and tenementes belonginge to the towneshipe of Wymondham accomptinge from the Feast of St Mychaell Tharkangell in *Anno Domini* 1612 untill the Feast of St Mychaell Tharkangell in *Anno Domini* 1613 for one hole yere then ended as followeth

/Arrerages/

Inprimis in arrerages *in anno precedenti*	3	12	3

/Free rentes/

Receyved of William Crane		3	0
Of Frauncis Neave		1	10
Of Alice Frosten *vidua*		2	0
Of George Mayehewe			4
Of Peter Neave			10
Of Thomas Nixon			10
Of the land houlders late Edmund Cullyer			1

/Fearme rentes/

Receyved of Frauncis Plomer for Teedes called Tenement Brixi in Silfield and a pightell conteyninge two acres theree [*sic*] unto belonginge	10	0	0
Of Stephen Wiseman for one meadowe at Salters Ford conteyninge one acre and one rod 26s and for three acres and a halfe of land late in the occupacion of William Ovington 24s 6d and for three acres of lande late in the occupacion of Agnes Flowerdewe *vidua* 15s *in toto*	3	5	6
Off John Raynoldes the elder for the parcelles of meadowe in the common meadowe att Westwade 15s and for a pightell neere his howse in Suton 14s *in toto*	1	9	0
Off Robert Rawlinge for three roodes of meadowe att Keeds Willowes and two acres of land in the Northe Feild and one pightell neere Hockehams	1	16	8
Off John Moore for a pightell nere Hockhams	1	13	4

	£	s	d
Off William Ovington for a pightell att the Clay Pittes	1	12	2
Off Stephen Agas for two acres of land one in Bixeland Field & the other at Toleys Crosse in the Northe Field		11	8

<center><<i>Summa</i> £20 8s 3d></center>
Summa £24 9s 6d

	£	s	d
[*f. 104v*] Off Stephen Kett for one acre and a halfe of lande lyinge in John Symondes his crafte in Downeham		10	0
Off Arthure Earle for one acre of land and a parcell of land somtyme a grove		12	0
Off William Payne for two acres of land lyinge in Holmefield		12	0
Off Edmunde Bucke for two acres of land lyinge in Holemfield [*sic*]		12	0
Off Thomas Hobbes for a parcell of meadowe lyinge in his meadowe att Wadebridge		1	0
Off Lawrence Fletcher for a parcell of meadowe att Hockhams Carre		3	4
Off Thomas Cole thelder for a meadowe and three roodes of land at Ryvalles, one acre *of land* att Barrowes Head and one acre of land in Holmefield	2	0	0
Off Raphe Fox for one acre of lande in Claxwell Furland		6	0
Off William Mappes for a pightell called Howlyns in Hungate 24s and for one acre and a halfe of land with a parcell of meadowe somtyme a grove at thende thereof lyinge in Claxwell Furland 14s, *in toto*	1	18	0
Off Robert Wiseman thelder for two acres three roodes of land lyinge nere Beckes Dicke in the Northe Field		14	0
Off Robert Agas for nyne acres of land in the Northe Fielde	2	19	0
Off Rychard Dilham for three acres of land in the Northe Fielde		15	0
Off George Norton for three acres of land in the Northe Fielde		16	6
Off Thomas Woodcocke for three roodes of pasture lyinge in Wattelfield		7	6
Off Mr Skippe for a pightell nere his howse and two acres of lande which abutteth uppon the landes of Henry Meene of Wickelwood	1	16	8
Off Robert Thorneton gent for a parcell of meadowe at Wadebridge		5	0

Some   £14 8s

	£	s	d
[*f. 105r*] Off Mr Docter Talbott for one acre of land in his closse neere the Game Place		6	8
Off Esaye Freman for three roodes of land lyinge in his closse late Edwardes next to a pece of land of fyve acres houlden of Sir Awsten Palgrave knight late Rycherd Rawlinge		5	0
Off Arthure Williams for a parcell of meadowe neere Mylle Poole		[*blank*]	
Off Alexander Foulsham for the towne howses where he nowe dwelleth and the ortchyard	6	1	0

	£	s	d
Off Raynold Keene for a towne howse neere the guildhowse	3	0	0
Off Robert Wetherley for a towne shoppe late in the occupacion of Randoll Downinge		12	0
Off William Burrell for one acree [sic] of land in the Parke Field abuttinge uppon the Endlesse Waye towardes the southe		6	0
Off Robert Beettes for a towne howse	1	0	0
Off Robert Toolye for a towne howse		13	4
Off John Cleere for a towne howse	1	6	8
Off the weadowe Swayne and the weadowe Cocke for a townehowse		6	8
Off the weadowe Huntley Christian Smythe & Thomas Allen for a towne howse		6	8
Off William Chamberleyne and Dowsinge for a townehowse		6	8
Off the weadowe Breece and Robert Sadler for a townehowse		6	8
Off the weadowe Leetche and the weadowe Quayntrell for a towne howse		6	8

Some   £15   4s

	£	s	d
[f. 105v] Off the weadowe Tolye for the tenement uppn Northwood Common adioyninge to Black Inham	1	13	4
Off Mr Playeford for a seller out of the schoolehowse steple		1	0
Off Robert Foster & William Randoll for the towne howse ageynst the churche yarde		6	8
Off Alexander Foulsham more for the euse of fyve poundes		7	6
Off William Gould more for the euse of fortie shillinges		3	0

Some   £2   11s   6d

	£	s	d
Off the weadowe Tolye left in *super* in the last yeres accompte		6	0
Off Robert Beettes for the like		2	0

Some total of the receiptes   £56   12s   2d

Whereof he prayeth to be allowed for rentes not payd and other disbursmentes as foloweth		[blank]	

/Rentes not payd/

	£	s	d
Imprimis of Frauncis Neave		1	10
Of Alice Frosten *vidua*		2	0
Of George Mayehewe			4
Of Peter Neave			10
Of Thomas Nixon			10
Of the land houlders late Edmonde Culyer			1
Of Mr Docter Talbott		6	8
Of John Cleere	1	6	8

Summa   £1   19s   3d

	£	s	d

[f. 106r] /***Disbursmentes***/

	£	s	d
Payd to Alexander Foulsham for bread & beere when the headborowes ded take this accompte		1	4
Payd to Olyet for thackinge at the weadowe Tolyes howse		5	0
Payd to Mr Easton	5	0	0
Payd to Raphe Fyttlyn for Cromwelles rent		2	0
Payd to the Kinges baylyff for rent		13	8
Payd to Catchepole for the vestry dore key of the churche		4	0
Payd to Knightes for makinge the churche beere		5	0
Payd for scoringe the towne armor		2	6
Payd for a daggard		1	0
Payd for fower new sckaberdes for the towne swordes		4	0
Payd for three gyrdles & hangers		2	6
Payd for flask stringes			8
Payd for souldiers wages		3	0
Payd for gonnpouder			6
Payd to the undershreve for the alowance of the charter		10	0
Payd for the preachers dynners uppon Ganne Mondaie	1	7	4
Payd for a borde that Cleere had to laye under the lead of the churche			9
Payd for twoe planckes that Knightes had for the churche		1	8
/☞/ Payd to John Deye for Handleys childes bringinge up	2	0	0
/☞/ Payd for my Lords Grace of Canterbury[38] his visitours dynners	2	0	0
/☞/ Payd to Mr Rycherdson for counsell in the towne cause	1	0	0
Payd for fower skoore & fower foote of borde for the churche		8	4
Payd to Mr Weld for learned *counsell* in the towne cause		10	0
Payd to Mr Easton	5	0	0

Some   £20 3s 3d

[f. 106v] /***Disbursmentes***/

	£	s	d
Payd to the Kinges Majesties bayliff for rent		13	9
Payd to hym for a rent henne			6
Payd to Mr Easton	5	0	0
Payd to Mr Blackborne for free rent			3
Payd to Raphe Fyttlyn for Cromwelles rent		2	1
/☞/ Payd to Mr Scottowe the preacher beinge a blinde man		10	0

/***Bartlettes Bridge discharged***/

	£	s	d
Payd to Frauncis Plomer for his charges in appearinge to an inditement found at the Sessions for Bartlettes Bridge preferred ageinst the towne discharged in open Sessions by reason yt was no common bridge for the passage of the Kinges leadge people		9	0

[38] George Abbot became archbishop of Canterbury in 1611 and died in 1633.

	£	s	d
Payd to Mr Easton	5	0	0
Payd to Rycherd Dilham for a sheete to burye Bartholmewe Boothe		3	0
Payd for the barne to laye the wood in for the poore	1	0	0
Payd for John Raynoldes fee for gatheringe the rentes		13	4
Payd and alowed for the loose in the wood provyded for the poore			
for this yere 1613	7	5	6

Some total   £20 17s 5d

Some total of allowances   £42 19s 11d   *ultra*

	s	d
Super Edmunde Bucke for one hole yere	12	0
Of John Sayer for towne shope *pro dimidio anno*	6	0
Of the weadowe Ovington *pro dimidio anno*	16	8
Of Robert Beettes *pro dimidio*	10	0
Of Robert Tooley *pro uno anno*	13	4
Of William Chamberleyne	1	8

Some total

Some total   £2 19s 8d

Et sic debet

10 12   7

ultra

£20 2s 1d remayninge in the handes of Frauncis Plomer
for the stocke to provyde the wood for the poore.

[*f. 107r*]   **[1613-1614]**

The accompt of John Raynoldes collector for all the rentes and fearmes of all the landes and tenementes belonginge to the towneshipp of Wymondham accomptinge from the Feast of St Michaell Tharkangell in *Anno Domini* 1613 untill the Feast of St Mychaell <of> Tharkangell in *Anno Domini* 1614 for one wholl yere then ended as followeth

/Arrerages/

Inprimis in arrerages *in anno precedenti*	10	12	7

/Fre rentes/

		s	d
Received of William Crane		3	0
Of Francis Neave		1	10
Of Alice Frosten *vidua*		2	0
Of George Mayhewe			4
Of Peter Neave			10
Of Thomas Nixon			10
Of the land houlders late Edmunde Cullyer			1

/Fearme rentes/

	£	s	d
Received of Frauncis Plomer for Teedes called Tenement Brixi in			
Silfild and a pightell conteyninge twoe acres thereunto			
belonginge	10	0	0

	£	s	d
Of Stephen Wiseman for one meadowe att Salters Ford conteyninge one acre and one rode 26s and for thre acres and a halfe of lande late in the occupacion of William Ovington 24s 6d and for thre acres of land late in the occupacion of Agnes Flowerdewe *vidua* 15s *in toto*	3	5	6
Of John Reynoldes thelder for thre parcells of meadowe lyeinge in the partible meadowe att Westwade nere Salters Fordes 15s and for a pightell nere his howse in Suton 14s *in toto*	1	9	0
Of Robert Rawlinge for thre roodes of meadowe att Kiddeswillowes and twoe acres of land in the North Feild, and one pightell nere Hockhams	1	16	8
Of John Moore for a pightell nere Hockhams	1	13	4

Summa   £29 6s

	£	s	d
[f. 107v] Off Richard Bunne for a pightell nere the Claypittes late in the occupacion of William Ovington	2	0	0
Off Stephen Agas for twoe acres of land *videlicet* one in Bixland Feild and the other att Tolies Crosse in the North Feilde		11	8
Off Stephen Kett for one acre and a halfe of lande lyeinge in John Symonds croft in Downeham		10	0
Off Arthure Earle for one acre of land and a parcell of lande sometyme a grove		12	0
Off William Payne for twoe acres of lande lyeinge in Holmefeilde		12	0
Off William Gibbes for twoe acres of lande lyeing in Holmefeilde		12	0
Off Thomas Hobbes for a parcell of meadowe lyeing in his meadowe att Wadebridge		1	0
Off Lawrence Fletcher for a parcell of meadowe lyeinge at Hockhams Carre		3	4
Off Thomas Cole thelder for a meadowe and three rodes of land att Ryvalles & one acre of land att Barrowes Heade and one other acre of land in Holmefeilde	2	0	0
Off John Middleton for one acre of lande in Claxwell Furland		6	0
Off William Mappes for a pightell called Howlyns in Hungate 24s and for one acre and a halfe of lande with a parcell of meadowe sometyme a grove att thend thereof lyeing in Claxwell Furland 14s *in toto*		18	0
Off Robert Wiseman thelder for twoe acres thre rodes of land lyinge nere Beckes Decke in the North Feilde		14	0
Off Robert Agas for nyne acres of land in the North Feilde	2	19	0

Summa   £12 19s

	£	s	d
[f. 108r] Off Richard Dillan for three acres of lande in the Northfeilde		15	0
Off George Norton for thre acres of land in the Northfeilde		16	6
Off the wydowe Woodcocke late the wiefe of Thomas Woodcocke deceased for thre roodes of p[a]sture lyeing in Wattlefeild		7	6
Off Mr Skipp for one pightell nere his howse and twoe acres of land which abbutteth upon the landes of Henry Meene of Wicklewood	1	16	8
Off Robert Thorneton gent for a parcell of meadowe att Wadebridge		5	0
Off Mr Doctor Talbott for one acre of lande in his close nere the Game Place		6	8
Off Esaye Freeman for thre rods of land lyinge in his closse late in the occupacion of Edwardes next to a peece of land of five acres holden of Sir Austen Palgrave knight late Richard Rawlinge		5	0
Off Arthure Williams for a parcell of meadowe nere Millpoole		[blank]	
Off Alexander Foulesham for the towne howses where he dwelleth and a little parcell of 1a [sic] yard	6	1	0
Off Reynold Keene for a towne howse nere the guildhowse	3	0	0
Off Thomas Plomer for a towne shopp nere the schole howse	3	0	0
Off William Burrell of one acre of lande lyinge in the Parkefeilde abbuttinge upon Endlesse Waie towardes the south		6	0
Off Robert Bettes for a towne howse		18	0
Off Robert Toley for a towne howse		13	4
Off John Inglish for the tenement late in the occupacion of John Clere <16s 8d>	1	6	8

Summa £17 13s 4d

	£	s	d
[f. 108v] Off the wydowe Swayne and the wydowe Cocke for a towne howse		6	8
Off the wydowe Huntley and Christian Smythe for a towne howse		6	8
Off William Chamberleyne and Dowsing for a towne howse		6	8
Off the wydowe Breece and Robert Sadler for a towne howse		6	8
Off the wydowe Leetch & the wydow Quayntrell for a towne howse		6	8
Off the wydowe Tolye for the tenement upon Northwood Common adjoyninge Black Inhams	1	13	4
Off Mr Playford for a <scholle> seller out of the schole howse steple		1	0
Off Robert Foster and William Randoll for the towne howse against the church yard		6	8
Off Alexander Foulesham more for the euse of fyve poundes		7	6
Off William Gould for the euse of fortie shillinges		3	0
Off the wydowe Crosse		3	4

Summa £4 <4s 10d> 8s 2d

	£	s	d
Received more upon the supers in the last yeres accompt of			
Robert Bettes		10	0
Of Robert Toly		13	4
Of Richard Caddywold for halfe *a* yere owing by the wydow			
Ovington		16	8

Summa received of the *super* in *anno precedenti* £2

Summa totalis of the charge   £66 6s 6d

Whereof to be allowed as followeth

[f. 109r] /Rentes not paide/

	£	s	d
Inprimis of Francis Neave		1	10
Of Alice Frosten *vidua*		2	0
Of George Mayhewe			4
Of Peter Neave			10
Of Thomas Nixon			10
Of the land holders late Edmond Cullyer			1
Of Mr Doctor Talbott		6	8
Of John Clere	1	0	0

Summa £1 12s 7d

/Disbursementes/

	£	s	d
Inprimis paid to Alexander Foulesham for the charges of the 17 att			
theire meting for the accompt of the towne revenew & other			
busines		4	0
Paid to Mr Weld for the allowance of chartre by the sheriff		10	0
Paid for halfe a hundred of board to make wyndowes and dores			
att the guildhowse		5	0
Paid for nayles and leadges		1	4
Paide to Knightes for makinge of the windoes and mendinge of a			
dore att the guildhouse & for a hundred nayles		2	8
/☞ *Apprentice/* Paid to Christofer Browne for the cloathing of			
Boothes boye being putt to him aprentice		16	0
Paide to Dillan for a sheete for the boye that dyed att Wrightes		1	8
Paid to Alexander Foulesham for charges when the survey was made			
for the towne lande		7	6
Paide for a hundred board to playncher the towne shopp and to			
make the wyndoes & doors		9	0
Paid to Knightes for layeing of the plancher & for makinge of the			
wyndowes & dooers & for a hundred nayles		4	0
/☞/ Paid to the wydowe Gedney for the charges of the justices being			
in towne in the case for the releife of the poore	2	7	0
Paid for a sheete to wynde Mother White in att hir death		2	6

	£	s	d
Paid to Mr Easton for his quarter	5	0	0
/☞/ Paid to William Buckenham for the cloathing of William Bettes			
his boye to be putt aprentice		8	0

Summa £12 11s 3d

	£	s	d
[f. 109v] Paid to the Kinges Majesties baylye for his halfe yeres rent		13	4
Paid to Dillan for a sheete for Wyllis his wife to be wound in att hir			
death		3	0
Paid to Stephen Dye for halfe a yeres rent due to the lord of			
Cromwelles		2	0
Paid to Catchpoll for mending of a k[e]ye & makinge cleane of the			
leades over the churche			6
Paide in discharge of the towne <for> the clark of the markett sittinge			
att Hingham		2	0
Paid to Gregory Cullyer & Thomas Starling for palinge att			
Keenes howse		9	4
Paide for thre loades and a halfe & thre foote of tymber for pales			
rayles postes and shoares & for 400 pale nayles	3	13	6
Paide for 200 iron nayles		1	8
Paide for thre score foote of tymber for pales rayles postes & shoers	1	10	0
Paid to Hempson for a load of clay casting & carieing		1	2
Paid to him more for carieing of fyve loades of tymber		5	0
Paid more to Gregory Cullyer & Starlinge for palinge		14	6
Paide for a plancke to Thomas Plomer for the towne shopp		1	0
Paid to the wydowe Gedney for the preachers dynners & other			
charges	1	4	8
Paid to Christofer Browne for a post for the cuckstole		2	0
Paid to him more for heweing & settinge itt upp and a cheane &			
bradds		1	8
Paide for 28 foote of board to make shopp windowes att Inglishes		2	0
Paid <to younge> for binding out of yonge Stacies daughter		4	0
Paid to Mr Easton	5	0	0
/☞/ Paide for cloathes for Hollowaies boye to binde him apprentice		10	0
/☞/ Paid for the bindinge forth of Ruddes childe		10	0
Paide for 8 boardes to part the howse att Inglishes & for a dore		5	0
Paid more for a groundsell & a thrashall			10
Paid to Francis Plomer when the towne was indicted att the Sessions		8	0
Paid for a sheete to bury ould Whiting		2	8

Summa £16 7s 10d

	£	s	d
[f. 110r] Paid for 80 & 10 foote of tymber to groundsell the towne			
howses	1	6	8

	£	s	d
Paid to Knightes for layeing in of the groundsells & mendinge the stayers		15	0
Paid to Inglish and Warner for thre dayes worke for dabinge		6	0
Paid to William Martyn for splentes			10
Paid to Goold for splent yarne & nayles			10
Paid to Mr Freman for a loade of claye		1	0
Paid to him more for splentes			4
Paid to ould Sadler for splentes			6
Paid to Mistris Pleasance for sande			8
Paid to Robert Jacobb & his man for pynninge of the towne howse		5	0
Payd to William Hawes for carieinge of the groundsells			10
Paid to Foulesham for lyme		5	0
Paid to him more for twoe loades of clay castinge & carieinge		1	8
Paid to John Thorne for mending of the grisinges			4
Paid for 7 raftes to undersett the howses		2	0
/☞/ Paid to Dillon for a sheete for John Brewer his wife		3	0
Paid to Stephen Dey for Cromwells rent		2	1
Paid to Mr Easton	5	0	0
Paid to the Kinges Majesties baylyff for rent		13	9
Paid more to him for a rent henn			6
Paid to Mr Freman for binding forth of Cockes boye	3	0	0
Paid to him more for binding out of Bloomes boye to Quayntrell		13	4
/☞/ Paid to Robert Carre for cloathes for the boye which came from London		6	8
Paid for a table plancke inche board & halfe inch board & quarters & tables feete for the comunion table & seates for the comysarie	1	4	4

Summa £14 10s 4d

[f. 110v] Paid for trayninge and for tryminge of the towne armor and for powder		12	0
Paid for a head peace		2	0
Paid for dawbinge of Thomas Plomers shopp		2	0
Paid to Edward Rydnall for the ringers		4	0
Paid to Mr Woodes the preacher		4	0
Paid to Roger Carver for making of a newe stocke for the towne muskett		2	6
Paid for planckes to make fyve studdes for Inglishe his howse		2	0
Paid for 100 foote of plancke for Dam Bridge		16	0
/☞/ Paid \<for\> to laborers stone gatherers & for a cart to carye the stones gravell & planckes		11	0
Paid to Mr Easton	5	0	0
For the collectinge of the towne rent		13	4

	£	s	d
Paid for the barne to laye in the towne wood	1	6	8

Summa £9 15s 6d

To be allowed for money lost in the sale of the wood for the poore	2	19	0

Summa totalis of allowances £56 3s 11d   ultra

Super the wydowe Swayne		6	8
Of William Chamberleyne		3	4
<Of ould Randoll		3	4>
Of Robert Foster		3	4

Summa 13s 4d

Et sic debet

Memorandum that the accomptant John Reynoldes did by his
  assigne paye this debet of £9 9s 4d to the headborowes *in*
  the yere 1614 which saide som was delivered into the handes
  of Stephen Deye   9 9 3

ultra

Remayninge in the handes of Francis Plomer for the stocke to
  provide wood for the poore   20 16 1

[f. 111r] </**Raynoldes his debett**/

For the arrerage of £9 9s 3d which is sett downe to be in the
  handes of John Raynoldes as a debett to the towne: we can not
  finde howe yt is dischardged: butt desyer better satisfaccion from
  John Raynoldes howe the same is answered to the towne.>

/**Plomer**/

For the stock in woode mencioned to remayne in the handes of
  Frauncis Plomer amountinge unto   20 16 1
  with the woode burned at the fyer & with certaine okes bought
  of Fynderne to the use of the towne for the rebuildinge of the
  schoole & for other paymentes: & with 5s 4d payd by the said
  Frauncis Plomer upon his accounte into the handes of Arthure
  Earle we   fynde the whole accounte satisfyed & paid.

[1614-1615]

/**Arthure Earle**/

The accompte of Arthure Earle collector of all the rentes and fearmes of all the
landes & tennementes belonginge to the towneshippe of Wymondham
accomptinge from the Feaste of Sanct Michaell the Archangell in Anno Domini
1614 untill the Feaste of Sanct Michaell the Archangell 1615 for one whole yere
then ended as followethe:

Inprimis of John Moore for the pightell at the Poples	2	0	0

	£	s	d
Richard Cadawaoulde for three acres & a halfe of land late in the occupacion of Anne Flowerdewe wydowe & for a pightell by the Clay Pyttes	3	4	0
Of him & John Myddleton for the partable meadowe at Westwade	1	10	0
Of Robert Rawlinge for the pightell next the pightell in the possession of John Moore	1	10	0
Of Stephen Wyseman for three acres & a halfe of land late in the occupacionof William Ovington & the medowe at Salters Ford <& two acres of land late in the occupacon of Robert Wy> & for the arrerage of two acres of land late in the possession of Robert Wyseman & three roodes	3	18	0
Stephen Agas for two acres of land		15	0
Stephen Kett for one acre & a halfe in Stephenes Crofte		12	0
Arthure Earle for an acre and a grove within his close		12	0
William Gybbs for two acres in Holmefelde		16	0
William Payne for two acres in the same feld		16	0
Thomas Cole for the close at Ryvalls & 3 roodes of land without and for two acres of land more	2	16	0
John Myddleton for an acre of land in Claxewell Furlonge		8	0
William Mapes for two acres of land by Stephenes Medowes & one pightell called St Thomas Pightell in Downeham in Hungatte	2	0	0
[f. 111v] Robert Agas for 9 acres & one roode of land	3	13	0
John Raynoldes for a pightell at Hell Lane	1	6	8
Richard Dyllan for three acres of land	1	1	0
George Norton for three acres of land in fower peeces & one acre late in the occupacion of Robert Rawlinge	1	12	0
Thomas Woodcock for two <acres> peeces of pasture lyeinge within his groundes in Suton		8	0
Mr Skypp for two acres of land & a pightell adjoyninge to his howse	2	0	0
Mr Thorneton for a parcell of medowe at Wattbrigg		6	8
Esay Freeman for three roodes of land within his close abuttinge upon Beck Lane		6	0
Thomas Plomer for the shopp		16	0
William Burrell for one acre of land in Sylfilde		8	0
Robert Rawlinge for an acre of land & a medowe in the Dryftes		14	8
Larrence Flecher for the medowe at Hockhams Carr		4	0
Francis Plomer for Teddes	11	0	0
The 6 tennementes in Townegrene & one tennemente in Vicar Street & no rent taken for them this yeere & two also in Markettsteade decayed		[blank]	
Mr Playford for the schoolehowse celler		3	4

	£	s	d
The wydowe Toolye for a tennemente against Norwoode Common	1	13	4
Thomas Hobbs for a parcell of medowe at Watbrigge		1	0

Some of the chardge £46 11s 8d

Out of which he crave to be alowed as followethe:
For rent not receaved in the yere 1615:
/Some <29s 4d> 21s 4d/

For Stephen Kett which he deteynethe		12	0
From Robert Agas		4	0
From Playford		3	4
<From William Burrell		[?8 0]	>
From Geordge Norton		2	0

/Disbursementes/

Payd to Mr Browne[39] the schoolemaster the 14 day of July 1615	5	0	0
Payd to a butcher for wethers to present unto the Honorable the Lord Hubbertt	5	8	0
Paid at the Sessions for a default for sufficient brydges at Westwade Chappell		7	9
Paid for wyne suger cakes & other thinges bestowed of the Lord Hubbert[40]	1	3	0
Paid to John Machyne for the armor scoringe		1	0
Paid <to Robert for> unto three menn trayning in the towne armor		3	0
Payd for amending the <fier> towne water tanckardes		4	0
Paid unto two men for caringe of broken tymber from the howse of John Kett to the schoolehowse			4
Paid to the hayward of Crowmewells for the whole yeres rent		4	1
Paid for the chardges of the meetinge of the justices at Norwche concerning the relief of the poore at Wymondham		18	6
[f. 112r] Payd for the preacher *his* chardge upon Gan Monday		10	0
Payd for a payne lost in the shrieffes turne		6	8
Paid to the Kynges bayliffe for the halfe yere <of Our Lady> *rent* due at Michelmas in anno 1615		14	5
Paid to Mr Browne for his quarter ended at Sanct Michaell 1615	3	15	0

[39] Mr Brown, schoolmaster 1615–?18.
[40] Sir Henry Hobart of Blickling (c. 1554–1625) was born of a distinguished Suffolk legal family whose seat was at Intwood, south of Norwich. He accumulated a series of major legal posts culminating in his appointment as Lord Chief Justice of the Common Pleas 1613. A protégé of Robert Cecil, first Earl of Salisbury, he bought up a large number of estates in Norfolk, including Blickling and property in Wymondham from the widow of the improvident Sir Edward Clere. His influence in Wymondham was based in part upon his lordship of the manors of Grishaugh, Cromwells and Rustens of which Grishaugh was the most important. This included control of the town's market and the leet court which served the whole township.

	£	s	d
Paid to Francis Plomer for the gates amending at Teddes		4	0
Paid to diverse pore men for workynge at the guildhowse for the digging & laying up of the stones	1	12	7
Payd to the shrieffe for the alowance of the charter		10	0
Payd to Robert Agas which he paid to the clarck of the markett		4	0
The some of the disbursementes as aperethe in the particulars	21	6	2
besides the alowance of rent not received that yere, as apereth in the begining of the alowances particularly expressed before the disbursementes	1	1	4
And so ther remaynethe in the handes of the said Arthure Earle accomptante for the towne to the use of the towne	24	4	2

[1615-1616]

/Arthure Earle/

The accompte of Arthure Earle collector of all the rentes and fearmes of all the landes & tennementes belonginge to the towneshippe of Wymondham accomptinge from the Feaste of Sanct Mychaell the Archaungell in *anno* 1615 untill the Feaste of Sanct Mychaell the Archaungell 1616 for one whole yere then ended as followethe:

/Arrerages/

	£	s	d
Inprimis in arrerage in <his handes> the accomptantes hande as aperethe in the former accomte by him made	24	4	2

/Rentes/

	£	s	d
Item of John Moore for the pightell at the Poples	2	0	0
Richard Cadawaoulde for three acres <& a halfe> of land late in the occupacion of Anne Flowerdewe wydowe & for a pightell by the Clay Pyttes	3	4	0
Of him & John Myddleton for the partable medowe at Westwade	1	10	0
Of Robert Rawlinge for the pightell next the pightell in the possession of John Moore	1	10	0
Of him for an acre of land & a medowe in the Dryftes		14	8
Of Stephen Wyseman for three acres & a halfe of land late in the occupacion of William Ovyngton & the medowe at Salters Fordd & two acres of land late in the occupacion of Robert Wyseman	3	14	0
Stephen Agas for two acres of land		15	0
John Symondes for one acre & a halfe in Stephenes Crofte		12	0
[f. 112v] Arthure Earle for an acre & a grove within his close		12	0
William Gybbs for two acres in Holmefelde		16	0
William Payne for two acres in the same felde		16	0
Thomas <Close> Cole for the close at Ryvalls & 3 roodes of land without & for two acres of land more	2	16	0

	£	s	d
John Myddleton for an acre of land in Claxewell Furlong		8	0
William Mapes for two acres of land by Stephenes Medowes & one pightell called Sanct Thomas Pightell in Downegham in Hungatt	2	0	0
Robert Agas for 9 acres & one roode of land	3	14	0
John Myddleton for a pightell at Hell Lane	1	6	8
Richard Dyllan for three acres of land in the Northe Feld & three roodes more late in the occupacion of Robert Wyseman	1	7	0
Geordge Norton for three acres of land in fower peeces & one acre late in the occupacion of Robert Rawlinge	1	12	0
John Osborne for two peeces of pasture lyeng within his groundes in Suton late Thomas Woodcockes		8	0
Mr Skypp for two acres of land & a pightell adjoyninge to his howse	2	0	0
Mr Thorneton for a parcell of medowe at Wattbrigg		6	8
Esay Freeman for three roodes of land within his close abutting upon Beck Lane		6	0
Thomas Plomer for the shop		16	0
William Burrell for one acre of land in <the Dryftes> Sylfelde		8	0
Robert Tungwoode for the yardd wher Raynold Kene dwelled	1	6	8
Larrence Flecher for the medowe at Hockhams Carr		4	0
Frannces Plomer for Teddes	11	0	0
The sixe tennementes in Towngreene & two tennementes in Markettsteade decayed & no rent taken for them		[blank]	
Mr Playfordd for the schoulehowse celler		3	4
The wydowe Tooly for a tennemente against Norwoode Common	1	13	4
Thomas Hobbs for a parcell of medowe at Wattbrigge		1	0

Some totall of the chardge   £72 4s 6d

/Disbursementes/

	£	s	d
Inprimis paid to the wydowe Gedney for beere & cakes at the meetynge of the townsemen in takyng the accomptes		4	0
Paid to Robert Crane for the preacher *his* chardges upon Gan Munday		9	3
Paid to the Kynges bayliffe for the rent due for one whole yere being the yere 1616	1	7	11
Payd to the hayward of the mannor of Cromewells for a yeres rent		4	1
Paid to the schoolemaster for his quarter at the purification of the blessed Lady the Virgine Mary	5	0	0
Paid to the schoolemaster for his quarter ended at Crouchmas	5	0	0
[*f. 113r*] Paid to Richard Male for cariing of the shrubbery out of the schoolehowse			6
Paid for mattes for Mr Serjont Richardsons sones which were decayed by the schollers		1	0

	£	s	d
Paid to the schoolemaster for his quarter ended at Lammas	5	0	0
Paid to John Quayntrell for amendinge the stockes		4	0
Paid to Nathaniell Brewer for the trayned mens wages, the armour mendinge, for gunpowder & bandoleres		16	8
Paid to William Hamonde in his necessity towards the building of his howse		8	0
Paid to the schoolemaster for his quarter ended at All Saints	5	0	0
Paid to Grigory Cullyer for amendinge the bridges at Westwade		2	4
Paid for strawe to thack Nevells howse & carpenders work		6	0
Paid to Richard Bunn for dawbing of Nevells howse		3	4
Paid to John Locke for thatchinge of Nevells howse		3	8
Paid <to Robert> for the chardges of the burying of the wydowe Mayden		2	6
Paid to Thomas Plummer for dawbying of the towneshop			6
Paid to Thomas Byshopp for a corslett	1	2	0
Paid to Whytinge for ryvinge of sixtenne hundred of harthe lathe & twelve hundred of sapp lathe		10	6
Paid to him for ryving for 2 d[ozen] pales & for bondes for to bynde up the lathe			5
Paid to Johnson & Edwardes for helpinge to loade the board stockes in Teddes		1	6
Paid for caringe of the same to the sawing pytt		2	6
Paid to Johnson for saweinge of 13 hundred board for the schoolehowse	1	8	2
Paid to Johnson for castinge of bord into the water			10
Paid to John Cole for the like			4
Paid to Johnson & Edwardes for helpinge to loade the boardstockes		1	9
Paid for caring of them to the pytt		2	6
Paid to Johnson for sawinge of six hundred & 20 foot of board more for the schoole		13	4
Paid for taking the board out of the water & perkynge them		1	8
Paid to Geordge Norton for his ropes & stayses to loade the boarde at Fyndernes		2	0
Paid for the carters dynners & for beere		5	3
Paid for caring of fyve loades of planck from Coles to the schoolehowse		5	0
Paid for caringe of the same into the schoole & setting them up			10
[f. 113v] Paid to Ryder for helpinge to loade the tymber at Fyndernes		1	0

Some of the disbursementes   £29 13s 5d

Besides he prayethe alowance for rent not recyved as followethe

Of Robert Agas		4	0
Of Playfordd		3	4

	£	s	d
Of Geordge Norton		2	0

Some of the disbursementes & alowances *ut supra* £30 <[*two numbers*]> 2s 9d

And so ther remaynethe in the handes of Arthure Earle this

accomptant £42 1s 9d

[1616-1617]

/Arthure Earle/

The accompte of Arthure Earle collector of all the rentes and fearmes of all the landes and tennementes belonginge to the towneship of Wymondham accomptinge from the Feaste of Sanct Michaell the Archangell in *anno* 1616 untill the Feaste of Sanct Michaell the Archangell 1617 for one whole yere then ended as followethe: which accompte was made & yelded up the 30 of January 1617.

/Arrerages/

	£	s	d
Inprimis in arrerages as aperethe in his former account	42	1	9
John Moore for the pightell at the Poples *per annum*	2	0	0
Richard Cadawould for 3 acres <& a halfe> of land & one pightell at the Clay Pyttes	3	4	0
John Myddleton & Richard Cadawould for the medowe lyeing in the partable medowe at Saltersford	1	10	0
Stephen Wyseman for the medowe at Saltersford & fyve acres & a halfe of land	3	14	0
[*f. 114r*] Steven Agas for two acres of land one in the North Felde & one in Bretlond Feild *per annum*		16	0
John Symondes for one acre & a halfe in Stephenes Crofte		12	0
Arthure Earle for one acre & a grove within his close at Kyddsfalgate		12	0
Thomas Moore for two acres in Holmefelde		16	0
William Payne for two acres in the same feld		16	0
John Cole for the close at Ryvalls & three roodes without & one acre at Barroughe Head	2	8	0
Humfry Murrell for one acre in Holmefelde		8	0
John Myddleton for one acre in Claxwell Furlong & one pightell at Hellanes end	1	13	8
William Mapes for two acres at Stephenes Medowes & a pightell <upon Downegham Common> in Hungate	2	1	0
Robert Agas for nyne acres of land in the Northe Feld	3	10	0
Memorandum he is abated 2s for a pece therof deteyned by Richard Kett & abated more 2s for one roode more not expressed he clayminge yt for his owne & so referred tyll further viewe & better satisfaccion be geven: his charge was £3 14s & now but £3 10s *ut supra* besides the reservations aforesaide		[*blank*]	
William Rowse for three acres of land nere Wyndemyll Hill	1	1	0

	£	s	d
Richard Dyllan for 3 roodes *nere* Beckes Dyke		6	0
Richard Osborne for two \<acres\> peces of pasture within the ground late Thomas Woodcock called Wellcrofte in Suton		8	0
Mr Skyppe for two acres of land lyeng in Crownethorpe nere Crownsell Woode & for one pightell nere his howse	2	0	0
Mr Thornetonn for a parcell medowe at Wattbrig		6	8
Esay Freeman for three roodes of land abuttinge upon Bekes Lane	\<7	0\>	
& for 3 roodes of medowe late in the occupacion of \<Westwad\> Robert Rawling nere Kyddes Willowes		12	8
Robert Tungwoode for the tennement yard in the Vicarstret	1	6	8
John Herbert sadler \<for\> and Mr Harmon of Norwich for the towneshopp *per annum*		16	0
William Burrell for one acre of land in the Parkfelde		8	0
The wydowe Tooly for the tennement against the Common	1	13	4
Robert Rawling for a pightell nere the Poples & one acre of land	\<2	4	8\>
38s[*arabic numerals*]	1	18	0
Larrence Flecher for a medowe in Hockhams Carr		4	0
Thomas Hobbs for a parcell of medowe at Wattbrig		1	0
Robert Cullyer for Teddes *per annum*	13	0	0
Item for the celler in the schoolehouse		[*blank*]	
Thomas Talbott *legum doctor* for one acre of land within his close	\<1	3\>	
at the Game Place, deteyned by him		6	8

[*f. 114v*] /**Fre rentes respyted as followethe not comprehended in his account**/

Wylliam Crane *per annum* for free rent going out of his howse *per annum*		3	0
John Cadawould for fre rent going out of his howse *per annum*, sometyme John Wysemans		1	10
Nycholas Page for fre rent going out of his howse *per annum*, sometymes Frostens		2	0
Frannces Mayhewe for free rent going out of his howse *per annum*, sometyme Porters			4
Item of the wydowe Cook for a tennement late Peter Neaves for fre rent *per annum*			5
William Greene for fre rent *per annum* for his tennement late Neaves			5
Edmund Cullyer for free rent *per annum* going out of a parcell of land			1

/**Respyted not being comprehended in his accounte**/

Item the rent of the sixe tennementes builded by Philipp Cullyer, at 6s 8d a pece	2	0	0

/**Some of the fre rentes & the other sixe tennementes 48s 1d**/

Some totall of his charge £92 18s 6d

	£	s	d
/Alowances of rentes/			
Whereof prayethe to be alowed for rentes not received as followeth			
Of Mr Doctor Talbott		6	8
For the free rentes aforesaid		8	1
For the sixe tennementes	2	0	0

Some to be alowed for the rentes not paid   £2 14s 9d

/Paymentes/

He prayethe further to be alowed for money paid as followethe

	£	s	d
Inprimis deteyned by Stephen Agas of his rent		1	0
Item deteyned by George Norton for his rent		2	0
Item paid to Robert Crane baker for that he layd out when he was churche warden		3	0
Item paid to Richard Cadawould for beere, cakes & cheese when the townesmen did meete about the takinge of the towne accomptes		4	8
[*f. 115r*] Item paid to Johnsonn master of the howse at Moadlinge Gates[41] for Wylliam Mappes daughter having the fallinge sickenes	3	10	0
Item paid to the shrieffe for the alowance of the charter		11	0
Item paid for the markets bushell		4	0
Item paid to the schoolemaster for his quarter ended at Candlemas	5	0	0
Item payd for thackinge, strawe, & splent yarne for Garrades howse	1	0	0
Item paid to William Quayntrell for iron plates for the markett bushell		2	0
Item paid to Philippe Lynes upon his accompte when he was churche warden	1	4	0
Item paid to William Burrell that he layd out about the clarck of the markett for the towne		4	0
Item payd to the Kynges baylie for the halfe yere rent		13	6
Item paid to William Grene for the sealinge & sizinge of the markets bushell			8
Item paid to the schoolemaster for his quarter wages ended at Crouchmas	5	0	0
Item paid for the preachers charges & the company with him when he came from Cambridge upon Gan Munday		16	0
Item payd to <Edward> Adam Bettes for levilinge the ground wherupon the markets crosse do stand		1	0
Item paid to the schoolemaster for his quarter wages ended at Lammas 1617	5	0	0

---

[41] Magdalen Gate, Norwich.

	£	s	d
Item paid to the carpenders & other workemen for amending of Damme Bridge against the judges comming over yt, the same being much decayed		10	0
Item paid for fyeng of the towne well		1	6
Item paid for amendinge the towne corslettes, for blackinge of them, for scoringe the swordes & daggardes, for fringinge & scoringe the pykes, for the wages of three trayned men, for gunpowder and towardes the offycers charge		13	4
/☞x/ Item payd to Philipp Cullyer towardes the buildinge of the schoolehowse	30	0	0
Item paid to the heyward of Crownewells for the towne rent		4	1
Item paid for the *towne* pumpe[42] in the Markettsteade	1	10	0
[f. 115v] Item paid to the schoolemaster for his quarter ended at Hallowmas 1617	5	0	0
Item payd to John Shore of Besthorpe in parte for bringing up of a towne child chardged upon the towne	2	0	0
/x/ Item paid for the charges of Mr Chauncelor & his men when he came to Wymondham to examine the differences ther in respect he should not call any out of the towne	1	0	0
Item payd to <he> *diverse pore* men that laboured to quenche the fyer happened at Damm Bridge & for watchinge the same all the next night for the safty of the towne		16	0
Item payd for the towne pumpe in Towngreene belonging to the towne tennementes ther	1	10	8
Item paid to the Kynges bayliff for the halfe yere rent for the towne landes due at Michelmas 1617		13	11
Item paid to him for a rent henn			6
Item payd for the repayringe of the towneshoppe		10	3

Some totall of his disbursementes & alowances   £71 1s 10d

So ther remaynethe in the handes of Arthure Earle this accomptante

£21 16s 8d

[f. 116r]   **[1617-1618]**

/*Arthure Earle*/

The accompte of Arthure Earle collector of all the rentes and fearmes of all the landes & tennementes belonginge to the towneshipp of Wymondham from the Feaste of Sanct Mychaell the Archangell in *anno* 1617 untill the Feaste of Sanct Michaell the Archangell 1618 for one whole yere then ended as followethe taken the 20 day of July 1619

---

42 The first mention of a town pump in the Town Book.

Wymondham in the 17th century

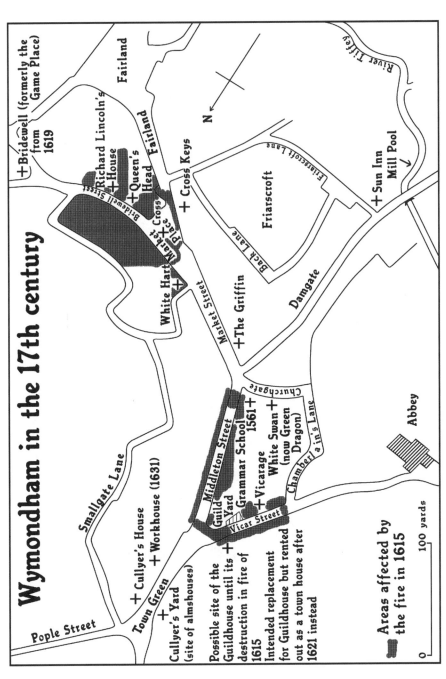

Bridewell (formerly the Game Place) from 1619

Fairland

Richard Lincoln's House

Queen's Head

Fairland

Cross Keys

Market Place

Cross

Bridewell Street

White Hart

Market Street

The Griffin

Back Lane

Friarscroft

Friarscroft Lane

Damgate

Sun Inn

Mill Pool

River Tiffey

N

Smallgate Lane

Cullyer's House

Workhouse (1631)

Town Green

Pople Street

Cullyer's Yard (site of almshouses)

Possible site of the Guildhouse until its destruction in fire of 1615

Intended replacement for Guildhouse but rented out as a town house after 1621 instead

Middleton Street

Guild Yard

Grammar School

Vicarage

Vicar Street

White Swan (now Green Dragon)

1561

Churchgate

Chamberlain's Lane

Abbey

Areas affected by the fire in 1615

0   100 yards

Map 2

	£	s	d
/*Arrerages*/			
Inprimis in arrerage as aperethe in his former accounte	21	16	8
/*Free rentes*/			
Wylliam Crane for free rent goinge out of his howse *per annum*		3	0
John Cadawoulde for free rent goinge out of his howse *per annum*		1	10
Nycholas Page for free rent goinge out of his howse by yere		2	0
Frances Mayhewe for free rent goinge out of his howse *per annum*			4
The wydowe Cooke for free rent goinge out of her howse *per annum*			5
William Greene for free rent goinge out of his howse *per annum*			5
Edmund Cullyer for fre rent going out of a parcell of land *per annum*			1
/*Farme rentes*/			
Mr Thomas Talbott *legum doctor* for one acre of land within his close at the Game Place deteyned by him		6	8
Item for the rent of the sixe tennementes builded by Philipp Cullyer at 6s 8d a pece	2	0	0
John Moore for the pightell at the Poples *per annum*	2	0	0
Richard Cadawould for three acres of land & one pightell at the Clay Pittes	3	4	0
John Myddleton & Richard Cadawould for the medowe at Saltersford lyeng in the partable medowe	1	10	0
Stephen Wyseman for the medowe at Saltersford & fyve acres and a halfe of land	3	14	0
Steven Agas for two acres of land one in the Northefeld & one in Bretland Feld *per annum*		16	0
John Symondes for one acre & a halfe in Stephenes Crofte		12	0
Arthure Earle for one acre & a grove within his close at Kydesfalgate		12	0
[*f. 116v*] Thomas Moore for two acres in Holmefeld		16	0
William Payne for two acres in the same feld		16	0
John Cole for the close at Ryvalls & thre roodes nye unto the close & one acre at Barrouhe Heade	2	8	0
Humfry Murrells for one acre in Holmefelde		8	0
John Myddleton for one acre in Claxewell Furlonge & one pightell at Hellanes end	1	13	8
William Mapes for two acres at Stephenes Meadowes & a pightell in Hungate	2	1	0
<Robert> Agas for nyne acres of land in the Northefeld	3	10	0
And he is abated 2s for a pece therof deteyned by Richard Kett and abated more 2s for one roode more not expressed he clayminge yt for his owne & so referred till further viewe & better satisfaccion be geven, his charge was £3 14s & nowe butt £3 10s *ut supra* besides the reservation of the tytle & right of the rest		[*blank*]	

	£	s	d
William Rowse for three acres of land nere Wyndemyllhill	1	1	0
Richard Dyllan for three roodes neere Beckes Dyke		6	0
Richard Osborne for two peeces of pasture within the ground late			
Thomas Woodcockes called Wellcrofte in Suton		8	0
Mr Skyppe for two acres of land lyeing in Crownethorpe nere			
Crownsell Wood & for one pightell neere his howse	2	0	0
Mr Thornetonn for a parcell of medowe at Wattbridge		6	8
Esay Freeman for 3 roodes of land abuttinge upon Beckes Dyke and			
3 roodes of medowe late in the occupacion of Robert Rawlinge			
neere Kyddes Willowes		12	8
Robert Tungwood for the tennemente yard in the Vicarstreete	1	6	8
John Herbert sadler & Mr Harman of Norwich for the towneshoppe		16	0
William Burrell for one acre of land in the Parkefelde		8	0
Widowe Tooly for the tennemente against the Common	1	13	4
Robert Rawlinge for a pightell neere the Poples & one acre of land	1	18	0
Larrence Flecher for a medowe at Hockhams Carr		4	0
Thomas Hobbs for a parcell of medowe at Watbrig		1	0
Robert Cullyer for Teddes *per annum*	13	0	0
Item for the celler in the schoolehowse		[*blank*]	
Some totall of the charge accomptable by the said Arthure Earle	£72	13s	5d

[*f. 117r*] /**Alowances of rentes**/

Wherof he prayethe to be alowed for rentes not received as followethe

Of Mr Doctor Talbott		6	8
Item for the free rentes		8	1
Item for the sixe tennementes	2	0	0
Item deteyned by Geordge Norton		2	0

He prayethe further to be alowed for money paid as followethe

/**Paymentes**/

Item payd to Richard Cadawould for beere cakes & cheese when the			
townsemen did meete		5	0
Item paid to the shreiffe for alowinge the charter		11	0
Item paid for the caringe of the planck boordes & coyners from the			
Abby yard to the schoolehowse & for tyle from the crosse to the			
schoole		2	6
Item paid to John Shoo the remaynder behinde for takinge of a			
towne childe so he is paid all for the same	2	0	0
Item paid to Richard Dyllan for clothe to make a sheete to bury			
Fuller in yt		3	0
Item payd to the Kynges bayliffe for the towne rent		13	6

/**x**/ Item paid the 27 of Aprill 1618 for the charge of Mr Chauncelor
at the visitation for the Lordes Grace of Canterbury for Mr Doctor

	£	s	d
Norrys a commyssioner with him for the preacher the register servauntes & clarckes dynners	1	7	6
Item payd for Mr Chauncelors breakefast		4	10
Item for wyne for them		2	4
Item for hay & oates for ther horses		5	0
Item paid to Rushebrooke & his man for amending of the churche & for lyme		2	0
Item payd to William Crane for the caringe of pore people			8
Item payd for the preachers charges in Gan Weeke & the preachers with him		12	2
Item payd to the schoolemaster for a Greeke lexicon to contynue in the schoole		18	0
Item paid to Mr Fyrmurie[43] for teaching of the schollers from Candlemas to Lent or ther about	2	13	4
Item paid to the schoolemaster for his quarter ended at Mydesommer 1618	3	15	0
Item layd out to John Ovington being a pore townesman towardes the apparelling of him when he was sent for to be in service for his better mainetenance		10	0
[f. 117v] Item paid to Machen for <scoking> scoringe of the towne armor		3	0
Item payd to Mr Wylliam Wells for the cuttinge of Lemondes legg which the surgeons had	3	6	8
Item paid to the kynges bayliffe for rent		14	5
Item paid to the schoolmaster for his quarter ended at Myhelmas 1618	5	0	0
Item paid for the byndinge up of the lathe & layinge itt into the celler			6
Item paid to the Lady Cleres bayliff for rent for the whole yere		4	1
Item layd out for clothe to make Lyncolnes sonne two shirtes		4	0
Item paid to the schoolemaster for his quarter ended at Christmas 1618	5	0	0

Some totall of the alowances & disbursementes   £31   15s   3d

Rentes which remayne still unpaid for the same yere as followethe over & besides the some of £31   15s   3d above wrytten

	£	s	d
John Myddleton		15	0
Steven Agas		16	0
Thomas Moore		16	0
John Myddleton againe	1	14	8

[43] Mr Firmurie, usher for part of 1617–18.

	£	s	d
Richard Osborne		8	0
Robert Rawlinge	1	2	4

Some   £5 12s

So the some aforesaid alowed ther remaynethe in the accomptantes

handes   £35 6s 2d

ultra

/Memorandum that Arthure Earle ys to be charged with 5s 4d receyved of Francis Plomer for the remainder of the stocke of wood not accompted./

	£	s	d
For 200 hundred of two bond wood felled in Teddes & 400 & a quarter of brushe woode of which 29 faggottes stolne of the two bond wood & 70 faggottes of the brushe woode, the 2 bond wood sold at 22s the hundred & the brush at 10s 6d which over & besides the wood stolne or misrekoned amountethe to	3	15	11
Payd for the felling of the same 3s 6d for bondes 4s 6d & for making of the wood 10s *in toto*		18	0
The remaynder of the woode	2	17	11

[*f. 118r*]   **[1618-1619]**

The accompt of Arthure Earle collector of all the rentes and farmes of all the landes and tenementes belonginge to the towneshipp of Wymondham from the Feaste of St. Michaell Tharkangell in *anno* 1618 untill the Feaste of St. Michaell Tharkangell 1619 for one wholle yere then ended as followeth

/Arrerages/

	£	s	d
Inprimis in arrerages as apeareth in his former accompt	35	6	2

/Free rentes/

	£	s	d
Of William Crane for free rent goeinge out of his tenementes *per annum*		3	0
Of John Cadawold for rent goienge out of his tenement *per annum*		1	10
Of Nicholas Page for rent goeinge out of his tenement *per annum*		2	0
Of Francis Mayhewe for rent goienge out of a parcell of grounde in his yard *per annum*			4
Of the wydowe Cooke for rent goeinge out of her tenement *per annum*			10
Of William Grene for rent goeinge out of his tenement *per annum*			10
Of the land holders sometime Edmund Cullyer for fre rent goeinge out of a parcell of land *per annum*			1

/Farme rentes/

	£	s	d
Off Mr Doctor Talbott for one acre of land within his close nere the Game Place nowe Bridewell deteyned by him		6	8
For the tenementes lately builded by Phillip Cullyer att his owne charge, the headboroughes & other the inhabitantes of			

	£	s	d
Wymondham abovesaide, in consideracion of the buildinge, have left the dispose of the profittes of them to the discretion of the saide Phillip Cullyer, to be imployed to such charitable uses duringe his life as he shall thinke good		[*blank*]	
Of John Moore for the pictell att the Popples *per annum*	2	0	0
Of Richard Bunne for a pictell att the Claye Pittes *per annum*	2	0	0
[*f. 118v*] Off Richard Cadywold for thre acres of land in the North Feilde *per annum*	1	4	0
Of John Middleton & Richard Cadywold for the meadowe lyeinge in the partible meadowe att Westwade *per annum*	1	10	0
Of Stephen Wyseman for the meadowe att Salters Ford & fyve acres & a halfe of lande in the North Feilde *per annum*	3	14	0
Of Stephen Agas for twoe acres of lande whereof one lyeth att Tolies Crosse & the other in Bixland Feilde *per annum*		15	0
Of John Symondes senior for one acre & a halfe in Stephens Croft *per annum*		12	0
Of Arthure Earle for one acre of land & a grove att Kyddes Falgate within his close there *per annum*		12	0
Of Thomas Moore for twoe acres of land in Homefeilde *per annum*		16	0
Of William Payne for twoe acres of land in the same feilde *per annum*		16	0
Of John Cole for the close att Ryvalles & three roodes of land without & one acre in Bixland Feilde *per annum*	2	8	0
Of Humfry Murrell for one acre of land in Homefeilde *per annum*		8	0
Of John Middleton for one acre of land in Claxwell and one pictell in Hell Lane *per annum*	1	14	8
Of William Mapes for two acres of land att Stevens Meadowes and one pictell in Hungate *per annum*	2	1	0
Of Robert Agas for nyne acres of land in the Northfeilde *per annum*	3	10	0
Of Richard Dyllan for three roodes of land *per annum*		6	0
Of William Rowse for three acres of land nere Mill Hill *per annum*	1	1	0
Of George Norton for three acres of land in the Northfeild in fower peces & for one acre late in the occupacion of Robert Rawlinge *per annum*	1	10	0
[*f. 119r*] Off Richard Osborne for twoe peeces of pasture within the groundes late Thomas Woodcocke *per annum*		8	0
Of Mr Skypp for twoe acres of land lyeinge in Woodfeilde & for one pictell nere his howse in Digbecke *per annum*	2	0	0
Of Esay Freman for three roodes of land abbuttinge upon Beckes Lane *per annum*		6	0
Of Robert Tungood for the tenement in Viccar Streete *per annum*	1	6	8
Of Mr Harman & the sadler for the towne shopp *per annum*		16	0
Of William Burrell for one acre of land in the Parke Feilde *per annum*		8	0

	£	s	d
Of the wydowe Tooley for the tenement next Black Inhams *per annum*	1	13	4
Of Robert Rawlinge for three roodes of meadowe att Kyddes Willowes and one pictell nere to the Poppelles & one acre of land in the North Feilde *per annum*	2	4	8
Of Lawrence Fletcher for the meadowe att Hockhams Carre *per annum*		4	0
Of Thomas Hobbes for a parcell of meadowe att Wade Bridge *per annum*		1	0
Of Mr Thorneton for a parcell of meadowe att Wade Bridge *per annum*		6	8
Of Robert Cullyer butcher for Teddes Close *per annum*	12	0	0

Summa totalis of the arrerages and the farme rentes received
this yere is   £83 18s 2d

Whereof this accomptant praieth to be allowed for disbursements and payementes as followethe

[*f. 119v*] /**Paymentes**/

	£	s	d
Inprimis gyven to the sheriff for the allowinge of the charter		11	0
Paide to John Machyn for scouringe of the towne armor		4	8
Paide to the schole master for his quarter ended att Our Ladie	5	0	0
Paide to the Kinges Majesties bayliff for the rent due att Our Ladie 1619		13	6
Paide to the hayward of the mannor of Cromwelles for rent		2	0
Paide for the preachers charge in Gan Weeke		13	1
/**x**/ Paide att the visitacion of the late Lord Bishopp of Norwich[44] deceased for his charges	5	11	2
Paide for the schole master for his quarter ended att Midsomer	5	0	0
Paide to Richard Cadywold for beere cakes & cheese for the townesmen when they mett		2	8
Paide for wynne sugar beere and cakes when my Lord Hobart came to towne	1	2	0
Paide to John Thorne for mendinge the pumpe in Townegrene		1	6
/**x**/ Paide to Phillip Cullyer by consent of the townesmen which he laide out about the buildinge of the crosse	25	7	0
Paide to Robert Crane for the visitors charges there		11	0
Paide to Mr Peacham[45] for his quarter att Michaellmas att his goeinge from the schole	5	0	0

[44] That is John Jegon who died in 1618.

[45] Henry Peacham, schoolmaster 1618–19, a well-known educationalist, was the author of works on drawing and poetry. Several of his epigrams make reference to Wymondham and local people. The Earl of Arundel, Lord Lieutenant of Norfolk, placed the education of one of his younger sons in Peacham's hands (see Williams, *The History of Wymondham Grammar School*).

	£	s	d
Paide to the Kinges Majesties bayliff for rent due att Michaelmas 1619		14	5
Paide to the hayward of the mannor of Cromwelles for rent due att Michaelmas 1619		2	1
[*f. 120r*] Paid for makinge cleane of the schole howse chamber			4
Paide to Garrardes sonne for carieinge of the speetes for the towne			2
Paide to Stephen Agas for the repayring of Dam Brigg		3	4
Paide to John Middleton upon his accompt which he had laid out more then he had received beinge church warden	2	7	2
Paide to John Machyn for makinge of a k[e]ye for a schole howse dore			8
Paide more for mendinge of Dame Brigg		1	4
Paide to Mr Cudworth[46] the schole master for his quarter ended att Christmas 1619	5	0	0
Paide to John Middleton when he was constable about the trayned men & other thinges	1	3	8
Paide to Bettes for mendinge of the water tankardes		5	6
Paide for strawe to thatche the wydowe Swaynes howse in the church yarde		7	0

Summa totalis of the allowances £60 5s 3d *ultra*
The free rentes not accompted nor the rent for one acre of land
in the handes of Mr Doctor Talbott senior
And so there remayneth in the accomptantes hand

Summa £23 12s 11d *ultra*
Some of £6 18s received of Stephen Deye et *sic* debet £30 10s 11d

[*f. 120v*]   **[1619-1620]**

The accompt of Arthure Earle collector of all the rentes and farmes of all the landes and tenementes belonginge to the townshipp of Wymondham from the Feaste of St. Michaell Tharkangell in *Anno Domini* 1619 untill the Feaste of St. Michaell Tharkangell in *anno* 1620 for *one* wholle yere then ended as followeth

Inprimis in arrerages as appeareth by his former accompt	30	10	11

/Free rentes/

	£	s	d
Of William Crane for free rent goeinge out of his tenememtes *per annum*		3	0
Of John Cadywold for rent goeinge out of his tenement *per annum*		1	10
Of Nicholas Page for rent goeinge out of his tenement *per annum*		2	0
Of Frances Mayhew for rent goeinge out of a parcell of grounde in his yarde nowe Stephen Kett grocer *per annum*			4

---

46 Mr Cudworth schoolmaster 1619–21.

	£	s	d
Of the wydowe Cooke for rent goeinge out of her tenement *per annum*			10
Of William Greene for rent goeinge out of his tenement *per annum*			10
Of the land holders sometyme Edmond Cullyer for fre rent goeinge out of a parcell of land *per annum*			1

/Farme rentes/

	£	s	d
Of Mr Doctor Talbott for one acre of land within his closse nere the Game Place nowe Bridwell[47] deteyned by him		6	8
Of John Moore for the pictell att the Popples *per annum*	2	0	0
Of Richard Bunne for a pictell att the Claye Pittes *per annum*	2	0	0
Of Richard Cadywold for *3* acres of lande in the North Feilde *per annum*	1	4	0
Of John Middleton and Richard Cadywold for the meadowe lyeinge in the partible meadowe att Westwade *per annum*	1	10	0
[f. 121r] Off Stephen Wiseman for the meadowe att Salters Forde & fyve acres and a halfe of land in the North Feilde *per annum*	3	14	0
Off Stephen Agas for twoe acres of land whereoft one lyeth att Toolies Crosse & the other in Bixland Feild *per annum*		15	0
Off John Symondes senior for one acre & a halfe in Stephens Crofte *per annum*		12	0
Off Arthure Earle for one acre of land & a grove att Kyddes Falgate within his close there *per annum*		12	0
Off Thomas Moore for twoe acres of land in Homefeilde *per annum*		16	0
Off William Payne for twoe acres of land in the same feilde *per annum*		16	0
Off John Cole for the close att Ryvalles and three roodes *of land* without and one acre in Bixland Feild *per annum*	2	8	0
Off Humfry Murrell for one acre of land in Homefeild *per annum*		8	0
Off John Middleton for one acre of land in Claxwell and one pictell in Hell Lane *per annum*	1	14	8
Off William Mapes for twoe acres of land att Stevens Meadowes and one pictell in Hungate *per annum*	2	1	0
Off Robert Agas for nyne acres of land in the North Feilde *per annum*	3	10	0
Off Richard Dillan for three roodes of land *per annum*		6	0
Off William Rowse for three acres of land nere Mill Hill *per annum*	1	1	0
Off George Norton for three acres of land in the North Feild in fower peeces and for one acre late in the occupation of Robert Rawlinge *per annum*	1	10	0
Off Richard Osborne for twoe peeces of pasture within the groundes late Thomas Woodcocke *per annum*		8	0

[47] This makes it clear that the Bridewell was established from at least as early as 1619 on its present site. While it was ordered to be set up in 1598 (see Smith, *County and Court*, p.104), there is no reference to it in the Town Book until 1618–19.

	£	s	d
Off Mr Skippe for twoe acres land lyeinge in Wood Feild and for one pictell nere his howse in Digbecke *per annum*	2	0	0
Off Esay Freeman for three roodes of land abbuttinge upon Beckes Lane *per annum*		6	0
[*f. 121v*] Off Robert Tungood for the tenement in Viccar Streete *per annum*	1	6	8
Off Mr Harman and the sadler for the towne shopp *per annum*		16	0
Off William Burrell for one acre of land in the <North> Parke Feilde *per annum*		8	0
Off the wydowe Tooley for the tenement next Black Inhams *per annum*	1	13	4
Off Robert Rawlinge for three roodes of meadowe att Kyddes Willowes and one pictell nere to the Poppelles and one acre of lande in the North Feild *per annum*	2	4	8
Off Lawrence Fletcher for the meadowe att Hockhams Carre *per annum*		4	0
Off Thomas Hobbes for a parcell of meadowe att Wade Brigge *per annum*		1	0
Off Mr Thornton for a parcell of meadowe att Wade Brigg *per annum*		6	8
Off Robert Cullyer butcher for Teddes Close *per annum*	12	0	0

Summa totalis of the arrerages & rentes   £79 9s 7d

Whereof this accomptant praieth to be allowed for disbursementes and payementes as followeth

[*f. 122r*] /**Disbursementes**/

	£	s	d
Inprimis paide for the allowinge of the charter for the towne		11	0
Paide to John Machyn for mending of the vault dore		2	0
Paid to Richard Cadywold for beere cakes & cheese & fyringe when the townesmen mett att the scole howse		4	0
Paide to Thomas Dymer towardes the bell frames in the steeple	10	0	0
Paide to the scole master for his quarters exhibicion due att Our Lady 1620	5	0	0
Paide to the Kinges bailiff for rent due att Our Ladye 1620		13	6
Paide to Richard Male for mendinge the towne howse against Norwood Common		12	0
Paid for 8 cuppell of sparres att 10d the cuppell		6	8
Paide for a payer of belferies & for a pesse to lay over quart att the howse end		2	0
Paide in charges att my Lord Bishops beinge [48] att Wymondham	6	10	9

---

[48] This could have been either John Overall 1618–19 or his successor, Samuel Harsnett 1619–28.

	£	s	d
Payd in charges for the preacher came to towne	1	1	6
Paide to Brewer to releeve poore women to laye in		10	0
Paide to the heyward of Cromwelles for rent due for the towne land		2	0
Paide to Manser for servinge in the towne armor att the muster		1	0
Paide to the scole master for his quarters exhibicion due at			
Midsomer 1620	5	0	0
Paide more to the Kinges baylyff for the rent due for the towne land			
att Michaelmas 1620		14	5
Paide to John Machyn for scowringe the towne armor		3	9
Paide to Robert Baxter for cakes wyne & sugar att my Lord Hobartes			
beinge in towne		18	6
[f. 122v] Item paid to Mr Heyward for a fyne for the towne land			
holden of the mannor of Cromwelles	1	0	0
Paide to him more for the entery & for a copie		6	1
Paide more to the heyward of Cromwelles for rent for the towne land		2	1
Paid to David Kinge for servinge in the towne armor 2 daies & for			
halfe a pounde of powder		2	6
Paide to William Colman for one daie servinge in the towne armor		1	0
Paid to the schole master for his quarters exhibicion due att			
Michaelmas 1620	5	0	0
Paide in charges when the justices were in towne	1	12	0
Paid to the schoole master for his quarters exhibicion due att			
Christmas 1620	5	0	0
Paide towardes the charge of establishing of the fynes belonging to			
the Prince	1	0	0
Paide to Robert Agas which he laide out beinge church warden	1	0	2
Paide to him more for strawe & carriage of claye for the wydowe			
Swayne		9	8

Summa totalis of his allowances for his disbursementes   £48 4s 9d

Et sic debet

£31 4s 10d

Whereof to be allowed 6s 8d for one acre of land in the handes
of Mr Doctor Talbott senior *et sic debet*   £30 18s 2d

Memorandum the accomptant is not charged with the free rentes.

GLOSSARY

OED, *The Oxford English Dictionary* (1933, second edition 1989)

W. Rye, *A Glossary of Words used in East Anglia* (English Dialect Society, 75, 1895)

R. A. Salaman, *Dictionary of Woodworking Tools c. 1700–1970 and Tools of Allied Trades* (1975)

L.F.Salzman, *Building in England down to 1540* (Oxford 1967)

J. Wright, *The English Dialect Dictionary* (1898-1904)

D. Yaxley, *A Researcher's Glossary of Words found in Historical Documents of East Anglia* (Larks Press, Guist, Norf. 2003)

abuttell to abuttal or survey land to re-establish abuttals or shared boundaries

allowing acknowledging, i.e. of the Wymondham market charter

All Saints 1st November

amending repairing

amercement fine imposed for an offence

anker anchor, an iron clamp much used in the construction of the hood or mantel of a fireplace

archeyerd *See* **orteyard**

arm (a pike) to prepare it for use, e.g. by fitting a hand grip of material

arrerage(s) that which remains unpaid; balance carried forward in accounts

assumpcion assumption, taking a task, duty, responsibility upon oneself

baly bailiff, lower representative of the lord of the manor than a steward

bandoleres bandolier, a shoulder belt for ammunition

barfraye, barfrey wooden shed to shelter cattle, protect carts and agricultural implements or produce; a penthouse; a specific building timber of unknown purpose, perhaps a lower purlin

bars of iron to which the glazing of windows was wired and soldered

beere stoole stand for a barrel of beer

belfery belfry; possibly some kind of roof member similar to a barfraye

billet a thick piece of wood cut to a suitable length for fuel, possibly *c.* 3 ft. 6 ins. in length and 15 ins. in girth

bindinges hemp cord to tie thatch to laths or wattling which lay across the rafters; used to secure thatch at gable ends

board *See* **timber**

blacking (armour) polishing armour with plumbago or graphite to turn it black

bond (financial) formal document securing repayment of a loan

bonds (ties) hazel or willow withes, used to tie up bundles of laths or firewood. Faggots and other firewood were often referred to as **one bond** or **two**

bond. *c*.1550 one bond wood was *c*. ¾ yard long. The Norfolk wages assessment for 1633 (*NRO, Norfolk and Norwich Archaeological Society Collection C3/1/9*) gives 5 ft. and 6 ft. lengths for two bond faggots.

bord stock *See* **timber**

bradds *See* **nail**

breaking splitting tree trunks from the side using wedges as opposed to riving from the end; not an alternative term for sawing

brick used extensively for both piers and chimneys, average size 9 ins. × 4½ ins. × 2 ins.; several Wymondham kilns, e.g. off Pople Street, supplied local needs

brief A royal mandate under letters patent addressed to the minister and churchwardens authorising a collection for a supposedly deserving cause, e.g. relief of a disaster

broaches split lengths of hazel sharpened at both ends, twisted into the shape of **broachwondes** great hairpins and used to peg down thatch

bunch bundle, as of reeds; precise dimensions not given in the Town Book

burden, burhen load of undefined size

bushel dry measure of varying quantity, typically 8 gallons, used for materials such as grain, hair and lime; tub-shaped vessel of one bushel capacity

byllett *See billet*

callapyne calepine, foremost 16th century Latin dictionary; first published in 1502

Candlemas 2nd February

carr clump of trees, typically alders, on moist or boggy ground

casting term seemingly used for a variety of operations involving digging and throwing motions; the digging out of sand and clay; the covering of house walls with daub *(see also dabing)*

chalder measure of 32 bushels (36 from 1664–65) used locally for lime

Chancellor, Mr i.e. chancellor of the diocese

charter possibly a charter awarding exemption from ancient demesne, which had to be renewed annually

church beer beer brewed on special occasions to raise funds for church maintenance

churchwardens by the 1580s leading parish officials with major ecclesiastical and civil duties under the law. Wymondham had four

claptree post against which a gate shuts

clarke (parish) appointed by the incumbent: rang the bell for services, laid out the Prayer Book and Bible for the vicar, made preparations for christenings and communion services, wore a surplice in church and led the congregation in the responses to prayers.

clarck (market) one of the most important lesser officials in Wymondham of manorial origin. Responsible for the observation of market rules: opened and closed trading by ringing his bell, inspected weights and measures, collected

market tolls and stallholders' fees, presided over the weekly market court
which punished trading offenders

clerk (spiritual) clergyman; one in holy orders

collector collector of the rents of town lands and houses

comb, coomb measure of capacity (4 bushels) for cereals and dry materials,
e.g. lime

comysarie commissary, an officer representing the bishop

constable unpaid parish or petty constable responsible for local law-keeping
and the collection of local and national taxes

corslett corslet, an iron breastplate worn by pikemen at the muster

coulder rubbish as produced by building operations

coyner corner post for a timber-framed house

craft croft

crampitte crampit, an iron bar with a hook at either end to bind masonry or
wood together

Crouchmas the Festival of the Invention (i.e finding) of the Holy Cross, 3rd
May

crownacyon coronation, i.e. of James I

crowning removing the main branches from the trunk of a felled tree

cuckstole cucking stool, an instrument of punishment, especially for common
scolds or dishonest traders; consisted of a chair at the end of a long boom in
which an offender could be exposed to verbal abuse outside his front door or
wheeled to a pond or river to be ducked

cundyt money conduct money, travelling expenses for the conduct of soldiers
from their hundred to the coast to join the King's army

curble, curbyll capping of stone, wood or brick round the mouth of a well

currier dresser and colourer of tanned leather

dabing daubing, putting daub into place which involved a slapping action

dawb daub, a mixture of clay, straw or hay, dung and sometimes hair used to
cover laths or wattle between the main upright timbers of a house

debet he owes (Latin)

decayed in disrepair, or worn out

dimidia half, a half (Latin)

discharge to free or relieve a person from a charge or responsibility

dore stalle strip of wood within a door-frame against which the door closes

dormant horizontal beam; a dormer

doublett doublet, a kind of close-fitting, sleeveless jacket

dresser a plank of great size; a plank or bench for dressing or preparing food,
especially meat; a shelved item of furniture acting as a display unit

dryftes drifts, roads or lanes along which cattle are driven; lands subject to
drove rights

dyete living allowance for servants when their master was away from home

dystrane distrain, to seize goods or animals for non-payment of debt or other-money owed, or as a punishment

entry fine a money payment made by a tenant to his lord on the transfer to him of property held by leasehold or copyhold

et sic debet and thus he owes (Latin)

fadome of reed fathom, 6 bundles of reed each a foot in diameter

falgate gate giving entrance to a field or fold; here incorporated in a place name

falling sickness epilepsy

feoffee one of the trustees who administered the endowments of the charity for the support of Wymondham's poor and its free Grammar School

ferme farm, block letting for fixed payment for a number of years; applied not only to land, but also, for example, to tithes, rents and fines

fine sum of money paid to the lord by a tenant on entry to manorial property

free rent ?contemporary bookeeping term for rent free; ?a rent charged upon freehold property

fringing (pike) pikes were decorated with a fringe below the head

fudder of lead fodder, 20 cwt of lead

furlong rectangular block of strips in the open field

fyeng clearing, cleaning out

Game Place place where pageants and religious plays were performed and games played. By 1619 the name had changed to 'Bridewell', when the house of correction opened there

Gan Munday on Gang or Rogation Monday the Master or a fellow of Corpus Christi College, Cambridge preached a sermon. During this week the bounds of the parish were beaten: 'gang' is Old English for 'procession'

gard guard, looking after; bind or trim, e.g. with an ornamental border

gemowe hinge with pin-plate and hanging-plate of identical size

generosus gentleman (Latin)

gyrdle belt from which a weapon could be hung

grisinges gresings, a staircase or flight of steps

groundsell groundsill, the horizontal timber at the base of a framed house into which vertical posts and studs are tenoned

grove, grovet small wood

hanger short sword

harthe lath *See lath*

harthtree beam supporting the hood over a fireplace; ? a wooden jamb, a pair of which gave vertical support to the mantletree or bressumer over the fireplace opening

headborowghe headborough, in Wymondham a senior citizen who represented one of the divisions of the town or the outlying hamlets in the select vestry which acted much like a town council; a member of the 'Seventeen' chosen from the holders of certain ancient manorial tenements

hede pece headpiece, a helmet

heare hair, very often from cows, used as a binding agent in daub and plaster

hemp used to make yarn, commonly to link closely packed vertical splints within the timber frame to take daub and/or plaster

hether hither, nearer

hewing roughly shaping felled timber before it went to the saw-pit was broken or riven; the smoothing of planks or boards with an adse

heyward hayward, a manorial officer responsible for regulating open-field cultivation and the use of the common

hooke and hingle commonest type of hinge consisting of the hook, an iron wedge driven into the door-frame from the broader end of which a round iron pin rises vertically to carry the hingle, an eyed piece of iron attached to the door

horsemeat feed for horses

hose long stockings, thigh length, usually of wool, worn by men

houses used sometimes in the plural to mean buildings, not necessarily implying multiple dwelling houses

hundred one hundredweight; one hundred but also the long hundred of 120

hyngle *See* **hooke and hingle**

inckle inkle, a kind of broad linen tape

indenture pair of contracts or title deeds written on the same piece of parchment and separated by means of a tooth-like cut to avoid forgery, e.g. apprenticeship agreements

indytted indicted, charged before justices of the peace in quarter sessions

inprimis, imprimis in primis, first (Latin)

issue legal dispute

jerkyn man's close-fitting jacket, usually of leather

joyce joist, horizontal timber laid across from wall to wall, or to an intermediate axial beam, to support a floor above or a ceiling below

kell *See* **kill**

key (of a well) ? timber curble strengthened by pegs or keys driven through the joints

kill kiln

lading *See* **leadinge**

Lammas Lammas Day: August 1st until 1752; marked the end of the hay harvest after which meadowland was commonable

laths thin strips of riven wood, usually oak, nailed across rafters to take thatch or tiles or across upright timbers to take plaster

sapp lath lath riven from the outer sappy wood of an oak log

lath nails *See* **nails**

leades leads, roof covered with lead sheets

leadges ledges or battens, wooden members set horizontally or diagonally across the back of doors or shutters with a planked outer face

leadinge load; the act of loading

legum doctor doctor of law (Latin)

lime used in mortar and for whitewash

load five quarters or 40 bushels or 320 gallons by volume; about 19½ cwt by weight dependent on the material (also known as a 'cart-load')

lynsey wollsey linsey-woolsey, a thin coarse cloth made of linen and wool

making (of wood) i.e. cutting; 'making' often used as an imprecise term in 16th and 17th centuries

mandyltre mantletree, the lintel over a fireplace

match hemp rope impregnated with saltpetre to ignite charge in matchlock muskets

matt mattress

Michaelmas feast of St Michael the Archangel, 29th September, a quarter day

Midsomer Midsummer, 24th June, the feast of St John the Baptist

minister clergyman

muster meeting of the local companies of infantry with a troop of horse for training under the general supervision of a county deputy lieutenant

nails many different varieties; often named according to their use, shape, or price. The following types appear to have been used in 16th and 17th century Wymondham:

bradds brads, nails without heads, wedge-shaped but not necessarily short

great nails large nails whose precise shape is unclear

lath nail small wedge-shaped nail with the thick end squeezed to form slight 'lips' and a blunt thin end to punch through lath without splitting it

nails by price many nails were classified by their price per hundred: in Wymondham 'thre peny' and 'fower penye' nails were priced by the hundred

nails by use board, pale or plank nails

pale nail nail used when erecting paling

tacks short nails with broad, flat heads for nailing down cloth or matting

netherstocks stockings

nihil nothing (Latin)

obligacion obligation, a bond containing a penalty against failure

orteyard orchard

Our Lady Lady Day, 25th March, New Year's day until 1752 and, together with Michaelmas, a half yearly day for paying rent.

over quart probably 'overthwart' meaning across

over sill ? lintel, a horizontal member above a door or window

pale riven wood or stakes for fencing; a fence composed of pales

pale nayle *See* **nails**

pammont pamment, a floor tile

parcell quantity; part of

part (a house) to partition

partable owned by more than one person

payne pain, a legal penalty or fine

peak, peek (wall) gable end wall

pentise penthouse, a roof sloping out from the side of a building; a single slope roof; covered way between buildings

perkyng perking, stacking up on end wigwam fashion

pesse piece, as in a piece of timber

pewter pewter vessels and plates hired out by the township for special occasions

pictell, pightell a small angular enclosed field

pinning joining timbers at joints with heart of oak pegs. *See also wedges*

plancher floor of wood in most cases; to lay a wooden floor

plank *See* **timber**

plate a horizontal timber bar or beam, e.g. rung of a ladder

post vertical timber carrying a load, e.g. principal post

pottell a measure containing 2 quarts; a large container made of pottery, leather or metal

Purification of the Blessed Virgin Mary 2nd of February

quarter short stud, i.e. one not running from groundsill to bressumer, or from bressumer to somer or wallplate. Crossquarters were horizontal members running between studs or between principal posts and studs. The term was also used of quartered board used for eaves.*See also timber.* A measure of dry volume equal to 8 bushels or 2 combs.

raft a rafter

rayle a rail, a bar of wood employed in a horizontal position, e.g. in a fence or door, or timber framing between studs

rayling fitting with rails; making rails as in 'rayling a tree'

reed *See* **thatch**

register registrar

removed moved house

rent henn old feudal payment in kind, here commuted for money payment

riging unclear; may relate to finishing roof ridge with a layer of sedge or to pargetting, creating patterns in relief, i.e. with ridges

rod 5½ yards or 16½ feet

rolls, searching of examining records (e.g. manorial) kept on rolls of parchment

rood quarter of an acre

roof tree ridge piece in a roof

ryngle ring, used to raise a simple sneck or latch

ryving riving, splitting timber along the grain to retain its maximum strength; laths, pales and some boards were riven

sapp lath *See* **lath**

sawing pytt a saw-pit

scorsletts *See* **corslett**

seller cellar, or storeroom at ground level, e.g. in the 'steple' of Becket's Chapel

server (thatcher's) thatcher's helper who took materials up to the thatcher on the roof

setting up erecting building members; assembling of prepared timber framing on site and the raising of that framework

Seaventenn, the Wymondham select vestry, nominally of seventeen headboroughs. *See Introduction, pp.3, 10*

shoare shore, prop of timber used to support part of a building during construction or repair

shooting casting of metal, e.g. in making bells or lead cames for window glass

show (of soldiers) muster or parade of soldiers

shredes twigs or flexible ends of branches perhaps used to form the horizontal members pieces of a 'wattle', or to cover rafters as a cheap alternative to laths or proper wattles before thatching; small pieces of wood to extend rafters to carry a roof edge beyond the line of a wall

shredinge removal of twigs from the ends of branches after felling a tree

sizinge in context probably trimming to an exact measure - here one bushel

skalde scald, scabby; suffering a disease of the scalp

skoringe scouring, cleaning and/or polishing, e.g. armour

sneck a latch – the simplest way of closing a door or window

soweger soldier

sparr *See* **timber**

sparflew to 'spar fill', to plaster between spars or common rafters; to daub wattles in a timber framework

sparrow ketcher sparrow catcher

splentes splints, or staves, slender pieces of wood (usually hazel or oak) riven or left in the round. Cut to a point at one end and a square at the other, they were fitted vertically into holes in the underside of the bressumer or intermediate rail and a slot in the groundsill to form the uprights of wattling onto which daub was worked. Also used as part of wattling laid across rafters to take thatch, or in the construction of internal partitions

splent yarne twine made of hemp used to tie splints to studwork or rafters. In general used where ties were needed in building operations

spyles spills, riven flexible pieces of thin branches, usually of hazel, employed as the horizontals in wattling; ? a type of nail

staging scaffolding made of poles lashed together with ropes of hemp or withies to carry a working platform of hurdles

staplet a staple, a fastening made of U-shaped wire or iron bar with sharpened ends driven into a post to take a bolt or hasp

stelynge steeling, welding a piece of steel on to the edge of an iron tool; re-steeling: reworking a blunted edge on a tool

steple steeple, refers in this context to the tower of Becket's Chapel, or to the west tower of Wymondham Abbey

stewinge *See 'timber'*

stock (materials) stock of 'wool, hemp, flax, iron, or other stuff as the country is most meet for' (*Poor Relief Act, 18 Eliz.I c. 3, 1576*) to be kept by the overseers for the poor to work into goods in return for poor relief; the firewood which is sold to the poor at below market price or the money with which to purchase it

stocke (musket) wooden piece to which the barrel and firing mechanism of the musket is attached

stockes instrument of punishment consisting of a framework with holes for the ankles (and the wrists in some cases) in which an offender could be exposed to public derision

stothe *See* **stud**

stoppe stop, or a well bucket

stoyle stile, a vertical member in a panel, panelled door, or other piece of framing; a stud

stud vertical timber in a timber-frame intermediate between principal posts

summa totalis sum total, total (Latin)

super, supra above (Latin)

sute suit, a legal action

tanckard (water) large bucket kept in churches for fighting fires in the parish

tenement property holding; rented land and/or a building; part of a house

tacks *See* **nails**

taske tax or rate

thack, thacking thatch, thatching

thatch the commonest form of roofing material: various types of straw – barley, rye and winter corn straw are mentioned in the Town Book – and reed, the most durable and expensive of thatching materials

thrashall threshold.

tiles (floor) floor tiles seem to have been used in the most important buildings in the town

tiles (roofing) plain clay pin tiles were in fairly common use in Wymondham by *c.* 1600 on the more important buildings such as the guildhouse, school and market cross. Even the guildhouse had a mixture of roofing material – part thatch, albeit reed, part tiles.

tyle pynnes tile pins of oak used to hang tiles on laths

timber a term used to describe the more substantial, shaped, pieces of wood used in the construction of houses. Oak was the preferred for building, but elm and ash were also used at times, e.g. parts of the market cross are made of elm. The different types of timbers need some explanation:-

board the thickest was termed a **plank** and was used where strength was important. **Board** was used for flooring and making doors and shutters. Both planks and boards were sawn(rather than riven) at the saw-pit. It is difficult to tell how far standard dimensions were used locally for boards. Where it was particularly important to avoid warping, quartered boards (called 'quarters') were used. These were cut from trunks that had been divided length-wise into four by medial cuts at right angles.

spar common rafter

stewing may mean the same as water seasoning, soaking timber in water

stocks trunk of a tree that has been roughly hewn ready for the saw-pit - hence 'board stocks' from which boards are to be cut

water while most timber was erected 'green' or unseasoned, and fully seasoned

seasoning oak was very expensive, a half-way house was water seasoning. Boards were placed in running water to wash out some of the natural sap and then 'perked' or stood upright to dry off, a fairly quick process. While such timber was less likely to warp, it lost some of its natural resilience.

towne hall guildhouse used by the vestry as its meeting place

town, townshipp the same area as the parish in Wymondham's case

trencher a wooden plate, often with a hollow at the edge for salt

trussell trestle

tryminge trimming, repairing; putting right in the building sense

ultra besides, over and above (Latin)

undersett to set under, as of a replacement groundsill

ut supra as above (Latin)

vault a privy; a cellar; an undercroft

vessell appears to refer to the town's stock of pewter, a curious use of the singular when a plural would have been appropriate *See* **pewter**

videlicet that is (Latin)

vidua widow (Latin)

visitation bishop's visitation (and that of the archbishop when the see was vacant): held in major centres at three-yearly intervals to maintain order and obedience to Church Law in the diocese, generally by the bishop's principal legal official, the **chancellor**, or by a **commissary** deputed to visit a single archdeaconry. Churchwardens were required to make a **presentment** of things wrong in the parish.

vyce vice, a newel stair turning round a central post

wedges little iron wedges that were driven in where the vertical iron bars passed through the horizontal ones used to support glazing

wether castrated ram

whyte to whitewash with lime or lime and ground chalk mixed in water

wood 'wood' usually refers to firewood or slender pieces used as broaches or shreds, while major wooden elements in building were called 'timber'

wyndbeames brace in the plane of the roof usually linking a principal rafter and a purlin to stiffen the roof structure

yarn (splent) *See* **splent yarne**

Ordinances of the
Norwich Carpenters' Company

EDITED BY PHILIP HOWARD

Introduction

Three sets of ordinances, or byelaws, were issued between 1594 and 1684 by the Norwich City Council. Two dated 1594 and 1684 were specifically for the governance of the Norwich carpenters' guild. Other city trade guilds would have had similar series of ordinances drafted from time to time to meet their particular circumstances. There is also a more general ordinance dated March 1618 relating to penalties of which copies would have been distributed to all the city craft guilds. Its full text has not been included, but the relevant matters are noted.

These ordinances form part of a collection of ten legal documents, dated between 1594 and 1747, originally held by the carpenters' company which finally disbanded about 1740.[1] This collection went on the antiquarian market in the later eighteenth century and passed through the hands of a London bookseller who bound them into one volume. There is a note written inside the front cover 'Bought of Mr. Lowe, Bookseller, High Holborn, August 20, 1801, £1. 11s. 6d.' There is also a bookplate of John Towneley, Esq. with arms and a motto 'TENES LE VRAYE' and the numbers 16. 4. 5. Subsequently this volume passed to Walter Rye and it now forms part of the Rye Collection of manuscripts in the Norfolk Record Office.[2]

These ordinances are valuable sources of information about guild organisation, the appointment and duties of officers, the problems they faced, and very significantly the relationship between the guild and the city authorities. Guild officials were subject to city jurisdiction and required to

---

[1] This entire series of documents has been transcribed – Philip Howard, 'Norwich Craftsmen in Wood 1550–1750: A Study of Communities', (unpublished M. Phil. dissertation, University of East Anglia, 2000), 3, pp. 5.1 – 5.25. It should be noted, however, that these initial transcripts were completed only a few weeks before the Norwich Library fire in 1994 and could not be compared again with the originals before the dissertation was finally submitted. The writer is indebted to Paul Rutledge for checking the transcriptions published here.

[2] Norfolk Record Office, Rye MS 31, Ordinances of the Carpenters' Company.

swear allegiance to the incoming mayor. This collection of documents also
includes the oath sworn by these officers before the mayor. A transcript is
included here as it is further evidence of the relationship between the city
authority and the local guilds.

City and Guild

Occupational guilds held significant positions in mediaeval and early
modem towns and cities. Around 1450 there were thirty-one such guilds in
Norwich; by 1622 this number had increased to seventy-seven. Carpenters
were listed on both occasions. In reply to a national inquiry into the activities of craft guilds, initiated by the King's Council in 1389, the Norwich
carpenters' company stated that they were founded in 1349.[3]

Guilds' control over occupations could be perceived as a potential
economic threat which raised concerns at both national and local levels. In
the mid-thirteenth century Norwich city authority had begun to impose an
oversight on trade guilds. The third city charter of Henry III, 1256, which
dealt with many matters concerning the self-government of the City,
contained a short and important clause 'Et quod nulla Gilda decetero
teneatur in ciuitate predicta ad detrimentum eiusdem ciuitatis...'. 'And
that no guild is henceforth to be held in the City to the detriment of the
said City...'.[4]

By the early fifteenth century the city authorities were again concerned
about the influence guilds might gain in local political life. They began to
tighten their supervision of these bodies in 1414, after disputes between the
City and the guilds. The following year they found it necessary to pass a
number of ordinances for crafts.[5] Crafts chose their own officers: a
headman, wardens and searchers, who had then to be presented to the
mayor. Their duties included searching for faulty work and when it was
found they were to assess fines. In 1449 they were placed under a compre-
hensive piece of legislation, the 'Ordinances for Crafts'. The reason given
was for the good governance of the guilds. Their regulations 'before this
tyme hath ben unknowen to the said wardeynes ... to gret hurte of the said
crafts. Therefore that beter forme correction and rewle shulde be had
herafter...'. The ordinances of 1449 set out in detail instructions covering
many aspects of conduct and business from dress to the training of apprentices, along with religious observances.[6]

[3] J.Toulmin Smith, ed., *Returns made to the King and Council by Order of Parliament as to the Ordinances, Usages, Properties etc. of English Gilds in the Twelfth Year of Richard II, An. 1389*, Early English Text Society (1870), pp. 37–39. It is reproduced in Howard, 3, p. 5.1.

[4] W.Hudson and J.C.Tingey, *The Records of the City of Norwich* (1906), i, pp. 17–18.

[5] Hudson and Tingey, i, p. 105.

[6] Hudson and Tingey, ii, pp. 278–96.

Craft guilds were many-sided organisations whose functions included furthering members' business interests, a religious dimension (which ceased at the Reformation), social responsibilities towards sick members and, as instruments of civic authority, monitoring standards of craftsmanship. This breadth could lead to conflicts of interest and probably an unwillingness to serve as guild officers by some masters. The officers of the carpenters' guild were usually a headman, two wardens and up to six searchers. There was also a more minor official, a beadle, whose duty was to inform members of guild meetings. These officers served for one year. The officers of the joiners' guild frequently served for two years and made do with one searcher.[7]

Ordinances of 1594

The significance of the year 1594 becomes clearer when related to the records of guild officers who swore their allegiance to the incoming mayor. The names of the officers of the carpenters' company do not appear in the mayoral court records between 1532 and 1593, some sixty years, except for 1554 in Mary's reign. This is far more than clerical oversight, but this absence remains unexplained. The ordinances of 1594 may have formally marked a restoration of relationships between the guild and the City.

Turning to the 1594 ordinances,[8] the preliminary paragraph [1] states these ordinances were approved by the Common Council at a meeting on 11th December 1594. The first section [1 a] summoned the guild to call a meeting of members within the following two months in Newhall (Blackfriars' Hall) or another suitable venue. The beadle of the Carpenters' Company was instructed to inform all members that they were required to attend this meeting. Non-attendance without a good reason was punishable, defamatory language was not to be permitted, and no one was to leave the meeting before it concluded without permission. The meeting's main purpose was to appoint guild officers [2] – a headman, two wardens and six searchers – for the year. The fact that the beadle was already in office is evidence of the prior existence of this guild. The headman, wardens and searchers appointed were to be city freemen and within a month of the meeting had to swear their allegiance to the mayor. Their

[7] The names of guild officers appear in the Mayor's Court Books when they swore their allegiance to the new mayor. The names of officers of the carpenters' guild from 1511 to 1734, when this guild ceased the practice, have been transcribed and are in Howard, 3, pp. 4.1–4.9. The names of officers of the joiners' guild have also been transcribed, Howard, 3, pp. 4.9–4.12.

[8] The paragraphs in both the 1594 and the 1684 ordinances have been numbered consecutively in square brackets for ease of reference. A table of contents that prefaces the 1684 ordinances has not been transcribed.

duties were to inspect work regularly and impose fines for defective work-manship and if necessary distrain, 'levying of distresses'. These guild officers were also to appoint a beadle each year.

The responsibilities of the headman and wardens are well summarised in the oath which they had to swear before the mayor. A seventeenth-century copy of this oath is among the documents in this collection, a transcript of which is given below. These officers were charged to keep 'peace, rest and tranquility ... and all manner of good governance and ordinances within your craft'. Secondly, 'ye shall make good and true search in your craft', and serious defaults were to be reported to the mayor. Finally, any further ordinances had to be approved by the Common Council before they could be put into effect.

After these paragraphs calling the 1594 assembly, the following section laid down that a similar meeting was to be called annually for the election of officers for the ensuing year [4]. Once more all guild members were to attend unless there was good reason for their absence and they could not leave before the meeting ended without the agreement of the majority of those present. Members were required to share in the group responsibility for the annual election. Elections could raise strong feelings, but defamatory speakers risked being fined twelve pence, a day's wage for a craftsman.[9]

A significant part of these ordinances deals with poor workmanship. If work was '...defective or insufficient either in workmanship or stuffe the same shalbe viewed by the said hedman and wardens and serchers or the morer parte of them ...' [6]. Searches were to be made quarterly [8]. Additionally, guild officials had to be ready to inspect work at other times if required [9]. Failure to allow inspection of work was also a punishable offence [10]. Men had to be responsible for the quality of their work; it was an offence to correct another's defective workmanship [7]. For defective work fines were assessed by the headman, wardens and searchers, but were collected by one of the mayor's officers [1c]. The fine was divided, a third to the mayor, a third to the guild headman and wardens, no doubt for guild funds, and the remainder to 'the poore men of the saide occupation'. If the craftsman did not pay the fine he could be committed to prison until it was paid.

Defence of the client against unsatisfactory workmanship through regular inspection was a feature of these ordinances. In addition he could appeal to the headman and wardens if dissatisfied with the quality of the work [8]. He could also claim part of the fine as recompense [6]. The headman and wardens along with a number of searchers always had to be available at reasonable notice [8–9]. If urgent repair work had to be under-

[9] H.Phelps Brown and S.V.Hopkins, *A Perspective of Wages and Prices* (1981), pp. 28–30.

taken a citizen could call on the headman or wardens to find a suitable carpenter within three days. If a craftsman was not found the citizen had the right to call on a 'foreigner', that is a craftsman who was not trained within the City or a member of the city guild [14].

A major concern of trade guilds was to defend and further the interests of its members. It was forbidden to train anyone who had not been formally apprenticed [12]. This offence could lead to a fine of twenty shillings. Craftsmen trained outside the City, 'foreigners', who wished to work in the City were required to obtain a licence from the mayor [13]. There was an exception for those with special skills which local craftsmen did not possess. This could have been significant for men trained in London or immigrants from the Low Countries and France where techniques may have been more advanced. A provision in this clause provides evidence of other craft guilds in Norwich for members of these immigrant communities, '... provided all wayes, that the carpenters alians shall and maye make there lawes and other there owne workes belonginge to their companye for their countryemen onlye ...'. Provision was also made for timber-framed houses prefabricated outside the City. These out-of-town craftsmen had to pay a fee to the city guild – for houses up to twenty feet in length two shillings and over this size three shillings and four pence. Guild members had the monopoly of buying and selling timber in the City [15]. Timber could not be bought or sold by members before two in the afternoon [16]. This may have been designed to prevent unwanted competition between guild members.

Though these ordinances were issued by the City Council they are informative about guild organisation and the difficulties faced by guild officials. Their responsibilities extended from inspections of workmanship, which maintained the reputation of city craftsmen and benefited clients, to furthering the interests of members. As it is issued by the city authority inevitably the emphasis is on standard of work and discipline rather than the defence of members' interests, which may have occupied a greater proportion of the headman and wardens' time and effort than indicated by this document.

Guild Officers' Oath

In this collection of guild legal documents are seventeenth-century copies of two oaths – one taken by those who were to be made a city freeman and a second sworn by newly-elected guild officers before the mayor.[10] The

---

[10] The names of officers of the various city trade guilds are recorded in the Mayor's Court Books when they swore their allegiance to the new mayor usually at his first session. Those between 1630 and 1635 have been published: W.L.Sachse, ed., *Minutes of the Norwich Court of Mayoralty 1630–1631*, Norfolk Record Societ xv (1942), pp. 57–8, 167–8; W.L.Sachse, ed.,

freemen's oath has been published,[11] but it is relevant to include the guild officers' oath further illustrating the relationship between city authority and trade guilds. It summarizes numerous matters covered in the discussion of the 1594 ordinances.

> Ye shall sweare that ye shall with all your power kepe peace rest & tranquility within your craft and all manner of good governance & ordinances within your craft ye shall hold and kepe, and ye shall make good and true search in your craft during your continuance in your offices, and all manner notable defalts that ye find in your craft well and truly ye shall present them up unto Mr Maiore, and that ye conceale no defaults sparing no man for love, hate ne dreade, and if ye make any ordinances within your craft ye shall not put them in execution till they be confirmed by the Common Counsell of the Citty, but that ye shall so governe your craft in all thinges that it may be to the encrease, profit and worshipp unto all the Citty, and well and truly you shall endeavour yourselves in all things that belongeth to your severall offices for to doe. So helpe you God.

General Ordinance Relating to Craft Penalties, 1618

In this collection there is a further ordinance for city craft guilds concerning the collection of fines on poor workmanship. It was passed by the Common Council on 16 March 1618. Poor workmanship would appear to have been a problem across numerous city crafts and provisions for the collection of fines inadequate. This ordinance gave the mayor's officer powers to seize craftsmen's property

> ... goods of any such offender by the officer of the maior of that Citty for the tyme beinge and sale of the offender's goods, sendinge the overplus yf any be so to the party distreyned... .

Imprisonment until the fine was paid may no longer have been a satisfactory deterrent. This is also evidence that the city authority had issued similar series of ordinances for other city craft guilds each tailored to their particular circumstances.

Minutes of the Norwich Court of Mayoralty 1632–1635, NRS xxxvi (1967), pp. 11–12, 79–80, 147–8. The names of officers of the carpenter's company, when recorded, between 1511 and 1735 and the joiners' company between 1554 and 1700 have been transcribed; Howard iii, pp. 4.1–4.12.

[11] P.Millican, *The Register of the Freemen of Norwich 1549–1713* (Norwich, 1934), pp. xi-xii; E.Griffiths and A.Hassell Smith, 'Buxom to the Mayor', *A History of the Norwich Freemen and the Town Close Estate* (Norwich, 1987), p. 8.

1684 Byelaws

An initial reading gives the impression these byelaws covered the same ground as the 1594 ordinances though phrased in more expansive legal terminology. Why was a new series issued ninety years later? This question is addressed in the preamble. Some provisions had become obsolete while '... many new fraudes deceipts and inconveniences are of late discovered to be practised by and used by the said carpenters ...' [19b]. Faulty workmanship was being produced which could not be punished because of inadequate legislation. Additionally, with increased wage levels existing fines were proving to be less of a deterrent. In 1594 a craftsman's daily pay was 12d. but by 1684 it had risen to 1s. 6d.[12], an increase of 50 per cent.

Rather than repeating matters already discussed in the 1594 ordinances only significant changes in the 1684 byelaws will be noted. At quarterly meetings they were '... to consult about matters of the good and benefit of the said trade and occupation and well ordering of the same ...' [21]. There was no reference made to separate guilds for the immigrant communities. The level of fines had increased: absence from the guild assembly without good reason could now carry a penalty of 10s. 6d. [22] from 12d., a tenfold increase. The appropriate level of fines for poor workmanship was again left to the discretion of the examining officials, but there was now a ceiling of five pounds [26].

Some craftsmen must have been preventing guild officers from examining their work because of inadequacies in the wording of previous legislation. It may have only allowed searchers to enter workshops and even this could have been blocked by people other than the master, such as members of his family. Inspection could now take place 'at all times in the day convenient to enter any shop house yard ground or other place whatsoever of any carpenter' [40]. The clause that property could be seized to cover the non-payment of fines sanctioned in the 1618 general legislation was now incorporated in these ordinances [45]. Imprisonment may have created more problems than it solved.

Difficulties appear to have arisen due to members being unwilling to undertake guild responsibilities. It may be thought the reason was because this could make inroads into masters' working time as well as embitter relationships with fellow masters. This apparent unwillingness will be considered further in the concluding paragraphs. If no appointments were made the mayor could ' ... elect and choose a headman and two fitt persons of the said company such as to him shall seem most fitt to be wardens of the said company of carpenters and six fitt persons to be searchers for the yeare then next ensueing ...'. If these people refused to serve they could be fined forty shillings [24].

[12] Phelps Brown and Hopkins, pp. 28–30.

Again, like the 1594 ordinances, privileges were also conferred on members. Guild subscriptions were lower for those who were freemen or local men. They paid two pence, but 'foreiners' working in the city had to pay sixpence quarterly [28]. Masters who were not freemen after Christmas 1684 could not take on any apprentice or employ a journeyman. The work they undertook was also restricted [30]. This pressured masters to become freemen and be admitted to the guild [34]. Those who offended against these orders could be fined severely. It could appear that towards the end of the seventeenth century the guild with the approval of the city government had a tight grip on the local craft community. However, there were reservations. There were workers trained outside the city, probably from London or the Continent, with skills local men did not possess. Craftsmen who were not freemen could undertake work which local men 'cannot artificially make and finish' [29]. Their superior abilities would place them in a very advantageous position. It is interesting that their existence was so significant it had to be acknowledged.

City Government and the Carpenters' Guild

It might appear that the relationship of the city authorities towards the carpenters' guild remained much the same during the seventeenth century between the ordinances of 1594 and 1684. However, evidence from other sources suggests this was not so. Over time the three areas of concern – defending the interests of the City against potential threats, defending townspeople from defective workmanship, and defending the interests of the craft membership – varied at differing times. Trade guilds came to be seen as less of a political threat. In 1622 the City tried to rationalise guilds into twelve grand companies. Unfortunately they tried to link disparate trades, each grouping under one of the more affluent occupations. The group with which the carpenters were associated was headed by apothecaries and included upholsterers, tanners, stationers, painters and basket makers. Each grand company was to be headed by two masters who were aldermen. No carpenter had ever risen to that status. These masters were to exercise disciplinary powers for the punishment of offences against rules of the respective crafts.[13] Such proposals would have met little favour with carpenters and the idea was doomed to failure.

A further example of the declining authority the City held over occupational groups is the numbers of apprenticeships registered in the seventeenth century. In the decade 1631–1640 eight carpentry apprenticeships were registered but this had declined to one between 1691 and 1700.[14]

---

[13] Millican, p. xx.
[14] Howard, ii, p. 2a.1.

The entry for the last carpenter was 1691 while those for a turner were 1660 and a joiner 1667. [15]

The City's defence of the interests of the craftsmen lay in placing the authority to work locally largely in the hands of the guild. Closer reading however shows that there were exceptions. The 1594 ordinances exclude 'the carpenters alians ... belonginge to their companye'; the refugee community had their own guilds [13]. Secondly, there were also highly skilled craftsmen trained outside the City, such as in London, whose abilities were of value. Some decided to conform with local practice and became freemen; they were registered as 'Not Apprenticed' meaning not apprenticed in Norwich. Others who knew they had marketable skills did not bother, but their existence is recognized [13]. Curbs on these men were included in the 1594 legislation, ' .... no carpenter in the same Cittie or liberties thereof (not being a freeman of the same Cittie) shall after Christmas next comynge kepe anye apprentice, or sett any journye man on worke...' [17].

Changes were also taking place in working practices particularly after the Commonwealth period – a few workshops may have been getting larger, employing more journeymen under one master. These masters would have become more powerful, increasingly in a position to ignore guild supervision and city rulings. Guild practices had not adapted to changing conditions. These still suited the more traditional workshop masters. The 1684 ordinances appear at first to be a restatement of those of 1594, but could the fact that the mayor had to take powers to appoint guild officers, when necessary, be evidence not of an unwillingness by masters to undertake these duties because of inroads into time spent on workshop management, but be an indication of protest? Protest because these craftsmen felt the City Council was not providing sufficient pressure to curb changes in workshop development? This was undermining the interests of traditional local craftsmen. Instead of seeing the 1684 ordinances as a continuance of tradition was it really an indication of change? These changes may have impacted on the guild officers' ability to gain access to inspect the quality of craftsmanship and materials in the larger ateliers. This in turn would reduce the City Council's ability to defend townspeople against poor workmanship in spite of the powers written into the 1684 ordinances.

Were links between the city authority and the craft guilds slowly being severed? The last year the joiners' guild officers swore allegiance to the mayor was 1700,[16] but the carpenters continued to do so until 1734.[17]

---

[15] Howard, i, p. 35.
[16] Howard, iii, p. 4.12.
[17] Howard, iii, p. 5.9.

After 1700 the joiners' company appears to have broken its ties with the city government, but this did not stop workshops continuing to develop in Norwich providing such items as furnishings to a growing consumer market.

The consequences of the final severance between the carpenters' company and the City Council can be seen in the last document of this collection, the 1742 Deed of Accord signed by thirty Norwich master carpenters.[18] By that time the carpenters' company had officially ceased to exist, but its former members must have felt the guild should be replaced by a similar body with authority now based in its membership. These carpenters who put their names to this document still required an outside body or figure of authority to replace that of the City Council. They chose the city chamberlain and undertook that '... one for another or the heires executors or administrators of the other covenant grant and agree to and with the chamberlain of the said city for the time being in manner and form following ...'. In 'manner and form following' an association was formed on the lines of the previous company, its continuity envisaged by the inclusion of their heirs and successors in the oath initiating the venture. This body must have only had a relatively short existence for its legal documentation, along with that of the former guild, appeared by 1801 on the antiquarian market eventually to find its way into the Rye Collection now in the Norfolk Record Office.

[18] Howard, iii, pp. 5.20–23.

Guild Ordinances 1594

RULES FOR THE GOVERNANCE OF THE CARPENTERS' COMPANY OF NORWICH AS SETTLED AT AN ASSEMBLY HELD IN THE GUILDHALL IN 1594

[*1*] **1594 At Assembly** in the Guyldhall of the Cittie of Norwich uppon Frydaye beinge the 11th daye of December in the 37th yeare of the raigne of our Souvereigne Ladye Queene Elizabethe &c. yt was enacted as hereafter ynsuthe for the occupacion or trade of carpenters, Mr. Christofer Soame beinge the thirde tyme then maior.

/ For setting of assemblies/

[*1a*] **Inprimis** that the companye of carpenters maye within twoo monthes next after thende of this assemblye (beinge thereunto warned by the bedell) assemble them selves together at the Newhall, or at anye other open and convenyent place where the mayour of Norwich for the tyme beinge shall appoynt. Wheare yf any soe beinge warned shall make defaulte of appearance without a juste or reasonable excuse to be allowed by the sayde mayour for the tyme beinge, or being present shall depart thence before thende of there assemblye without the assent of the morer parte of the company then there present

[*1b*] */ For unsemely quarellous/*

or shall give or use anye unsemely, quarellous, malicious or slanderous speeches to or againste any of the same companye

[*1c*] */ For the levieng of destresses/*

he or they soe offendinge shall forfeytt and loose for every suche defaulte twelve pence to be levyed by distresse of the goodes of the parties offendinge by one of the mayors offycers or sergeauntes. And to be devyded into three parttes, one part thereof to Mr. Mayor, an other parte to the hedman and wardens and the thirde parte to the use of the poore men of the saide occupation, and for wantt of a sufficient distresse to commytt the partye offendinge to prison by commaundement of Mr Mayor for the tyme beinge there to remayne untill the same payne or forfyture be satisffyed.

[*2*] */ An Act for chosinge of hedman and wardens and serchers/*

Item that at the saide assemblye as above saide the company aforesaide, or the morer parte of them being freemen of the saide Cittie then being present, shall choose one hedman and twoo wardens of the same company (being freemen) to remayne untyll an other hedman and twoo wardens shalbe chosen and sworne in suche manner as hereafter is declared whiche saide hedman and wardens soe chosen with the morer parte of the same companye (beinge freemen) shall immediatlie choose to themselves sixe persons out of the same companye which saide six persons shalbe serchers for the yeare followinge, and shalbe within one monethe next after the ende of the saide present assemblye sworne before the mayor for the tyme beinge. That they or the morer part of them shall trewlie veiwe present and sett reasonable fynes of all suche defaultes or anye of them as shalbe presented unto them as they or anye of them shall understand of concerninge or belonginge to the same occupation and the same to be levyedd and devyded as is abovesayd.

[3] / For choosing of a bedel/

Item that the saide hedman and twoe wardens and searchers shall yearlie name and choose at the same assembly out of the same companye to be a bedell to serve the saide wardens and companye who shall truelye doe his offyce in warnynge assemblies and other meetinges uppon payne of twelve pence for everye defaulte to be levyed and devyded as is aforesaide.

[4] / An Act for devyding of the fynes and the levyeing of them/

Item that the companye of carpenters maye once everie yeare within one monethe after the mayour shall have taken his oathe (beinge thereunto warned by the bedell) assemble them selves together at the New Hall or at any other open and convenyent place where the hedman and wardens for the tyme beinge shall appointe where (if anye being soe warned) shall make default of appearance without a reasonable excuse to be allowed by the wardens for the tyme beinge, or being present shall departe thence before thende of there assemblye without the assent of the morer parte of the companye then there present, or shall give or use anye unsemely, quarelous, malicious or slanderous speeches to or againste anye of the same companye there, they soe offendinge shall forfeit & loose for every suche defaulte twelve pence to be levyed by distresse[19] of the goodes of the partye or partyes offendinge by one of the mayors officers or sergauntes and to be devyded into three partes, one part thereof to be to the mayor, and thother part to the hedman and wardens, & the third parte to the use of the poor men of the sayde occupation. And for wantt of a sufficient distresse to commytt the partie soe offendinge to pryson by commande-ment of Mr Mayor for the tyme beinge, there to remayne untill the same payne or forfiture be satisfyed.

---

[19] distresse – distraint, seizure of goods to the value of an unpaid fine or debt.

[5] /An Actt for the hedman and wardens and searchers for setting of fynes/

Item that at the sayde assemblye soe to be holden yearlie within one monethe after the mayor shall have taken his othe, the sayde companye or the morer part of them beinge freemen of the saide Cittie then beinge present shall choose one hedman and twoo wardens of the same companye (beinge free men) to remayne for a yeare then to come to be sworne before Mr Mayor, as other wardens been, whiche sayde hedman and twoo wardens soe chosen with the morer parte of the same companye (being freemen) shall immediatlie choose to them selves sixe persons out of the same companye, which sayde sixe persons shalbe serchers for the yeare followinge and shalbe sworne before Mr Mayor for the tyme beinge, that they or the morer parte of them shall truely veiwe presente and sett reasonable fynes of all suche defaultes or eny of them as shalbe presented to them or as they or anye of them shall understande of concernynge or belonginge to the same occupacion and that the same to be levyed and devyded as is aforesayde.

[6] /An Actt for evill workmanship or evill stuffe/

Item that if anye carpenter take uppon him to worke anye worke within the saide Cittie or liberties thereof whiche shalbe defective or insufficient either in workmanship or stuffe the same shalbe veiwed by the said hedman and wardens and serchers or the morer parte of them and by them or the morer part of them fyned according to the quantitye and qualletye of the offence, whiche fyne shalbe levyed by distresse or by commyttinge the partye offendinge to pryson as is abovesayde. And thone moytie[20] to be payde over to the owner of the worke demandinge the same, in recompence of the faulte; and the other moytie thereof to the mayor hedman, wardens and serchers for the tyme beinge, equallie to be devyded amongest them.

[7] /An Act for amending of other mens worke/

Item that no person of the same occupacion shall take uppon him to amende anye other mans worke defective or insufficient, soe as the saide defaulte shalbe veiwed as is aforesaide within three dayes next after notyce thereof given to the saide hedman or wardens or one of them before the same be veiwed as aforesaide uppon payne of sixe shillinges eight pence to be levyed and devyded as is laste above sayde.

[8] /An Actt for searching/

Item that the hedman and wardens shall make there searche quarterlie at the least besydes all other tymes when they shall be by the owner requyred

---

[20] moytie – a half part.

and shall cause the serchers (or the morer part of them) soe sworne to veiwe all defective worke uppon payne of tenn shillings yf they the said hedman and wardens shall neglect the same, to be levyed as is aforesaide, the one halfe thereof to be to Mr Mayor for the tyme beinge and the other half to the use of the poore of the same occupation.

[9] /An Act for the searchers to be alwaies redye/

Item that the said searchers, or the morer part of them shalbe redye to veiwe all suche defaultes uppon reasonable warnynge thereof to them to be given by the hedman wardens or bedell uppon payne of three shillings fower pence to be levyed and devyded as before in the fyrste article.

[10] /An Act for resisting the serchers/

Item yf any person shall willfullye resiste withstande or denye either the saide hedman or wardens or the said serchers or anye of them to serch and veiwe anie workmanshipp or defaulte, that then the partie soe offendinge shall forfeitte and loose for every suche defaulte fyve shillinges to be levyed and devyded as afore in the firste article.

[11] /An Act for taking of quarterlie mony/

Item that the hedman and wardens of the said occupation shall yearlie at the quarter serches take and gather of every one man being of the saide occupation of carpenters workinge for himself towardes there paynes taking of the saide sixe searchers 2d. And that every one making default of payment thereof after reasonable request thereof to paye for everye default six pence to be levyed as aforesaide in the firste article.

[12] /An Act for teaching of anye other then apprentices/

Item that noe carpenter in the same Cittie or liberties thereof shall will-ingly teache anie person (other then his apprentice) or suche as shall serve as an apprenticeship in the same occupation by anye pretence or colour of servys for anye composition, covenaunte or other devyse directlie or indi-rectlye upon payne of twentie shillinges to be levyed and devyded as above-saide in the firste article.

[13] /An Act against forreyners/

Item that no person being a forryner shall worke in the saide occupation within the saide Cittie or liberties of the same without the lycence of the mayor of the said Cittie for the tyme beinge except it be in suche workes as the artificers of the same occupation dwellinge in the said Cittie or liberties of the same cannot artificiallye make and fynishe. So as the person or persons that shall have suche worke to doe maye gett artificers of the same trade freemen of the same Cittie to worke the same worke by greate or by the daye as he or they shall thincke good for suche wages as is or shalbe established by the lawes of this lande, uppon payne of forfiture for every defaulte twentye shillinges to be levyed and devyded as aforesaide in the firste article. **Provided** all wayes, that the carpenters alians shall and maye make there lawes and other there owne workes belonginge to their companye for their countryemen onlye as before they have accustomed to doe (any thing before to the contrary notwythstandinge) **all so provided** that the carpenters inhabiting without the sayde Citie and liberties thereof maye dwell and sett upp within the saide Cittie or lyberties thereof souche howse or howses as have been firste framed in the country soe as they doe paye unto the hedman and wardens of the sayde companye for the tyme being for and in the name of a knowedge or fyne for every suche howse or howses at the raysinge thereof suche summes of money as are hereafter mencioned vidz for every of the saide howse or howses of the length of twentie foote or under two shillinges six pence and for every of the same above the lengthe aforesaide three shillinges and fower pence.

[14] /An Act for the wardens to commaunde the carpenters to worke/

Item That yf anye person within this Cittye or libertyes thereof have anye carpenters worke to doe and resorte to the hedman or wardens to have anye of sayde occupation to worke with him, then yf the hedman or wardens shall not within three dayes next after notyce to them givyn or presentlie after (yf the same worke shalbe in anye present perill or dispayre) appointe and sende him suche a sufficientt workeman as for whome he will answere for then it shalbe lawfull for anye suche person to sett anye foreyner to worke the same without anye penaltie, fyne or forfeyture to be loste or payde for the same by the said forryner, anye thinge herein conteyned to the contrarie notwithstandinge.

[15] /An Act for buying and selling of timber beinge noe carpenters/

Item that noe person or persons <beinge noe carpenters> *not being a carpenter*[21] shall buye anye timber to breake into borde, plankes, sparres, joyces or other peeces to sell the same by retayle nor shall buye any borde, plankes, sparres, joyces or other broken tymber to thentent to retayle the same under an hundred foote of borde or plancke or sixe couple of sparres or six couple of joyces to any one person at anye one tyme uppon payne of forfeyture of the saide tymber, borde, and plancke soe soulde and retayled or the value thereof, to be levyed and devyded as is aforesaide in the first article.

---

[21] This alteration is made in a late seventeenth-century hand.

[16] /An Act for buyeing of timber in the markett before an howre prefixed/

Item that noe carpenter shall buye or cause to be boughte or chepe[22] to buye contractt or take promys for directlye or indirectlye anye tymber whole or broken, bordes or planckes in the markett of the same Cittie, or comynge into the same, to be there solde before twoo of the clocke in the after noone uppon payne of tenn shillinges for everye suche defaulte to be levyed & devyded as is abovesaide in the firste article.

[17] /An Act for keping of apprentises being no free man/

Item that no carpenter in the same Cittie or liberties thereof (not being a freeman of the same Cittie) shall after Christmas next comynge kepe anye apprentice, or sett any journye man on worke, or take anye worke to doe by the greate uppon payne of twentie shillinges for everye suche defaulte, to be levyed and devyded as in the saide firste article.

---

[22] chepe – to bargain.

BYELAWS OF THE COMPANY OF CARPENTERS 1684

[*18*] **Norwich By-Lawes** ordinances and constitutions made ordained and appointed att an assembly of the maior sheriffs citizens and commonalty of the said City held for the same City within the Guildhall there the tenth day of April[23] in the yeare of our Lord one thousand six hundred eighty and <three> *foure* and in the <five> *sixth* and thirtieth yeare of the reigne of our Sovereigne Lord Charles the Second by the grace of God of England, Scotland, France, and Ireland King Defender of the Faith in the tyme of William Helwys Esq. his maioralty, for the better regulateing the art and manuell occupacion of a carpenter within the said City and County thereof as followeth.

/*Preamble*/

[*19a*] **Forasmuch** as divers kings of this nation in former times by severall letters patents under the great seal of England have granted unto the citizens of the City of Norwich being an ancient City that if any customes or ordinances in the said City obteined and used shalbe in any part hard or defective soe that for any thing in the said City newly happening where a fit remedy not being clearely ordained there shalbe need of amendment that then the maior and sheriffs of the said City for the time being and aldermen of the said City or the greater number of them shall have full power and authority to appoint and order a fitt remedy in that behalfe such as shalbe conformant to good faith and reason and for the common profit of the citizens of the said City and of other persons thither resorting the same to be done with the consent of the sixtie citizens of the Common Council of the said City yearely to be chosen or the greater number of them and that when and soe often as need shall require and to them shall seeme convenient soe as allwaies such ordinances shalbe profitable to the king and his faithfull subjects and agreeable to good faith and reason as is aforesaid as by the charters aforesaid may more plainly appear.

[*19b*] **And whereas** the makeing of such lawes and ordinances is not onely warranted by the charters of this City but alsoe by the use and custome of the said City tyme out of mind used and approved which usages and customes are alsoe confirmed to the citizens of the same City by divers grants to them made by severall kings heretofore as also by His Majesties most gracious charter that now is as by the same may

---

[23] tenth and April are inserted in the same hand into spaces previously left blank.

alsoe appeare. And whereas the carpenters inhabiting in the said City and liberties of the same anciently and tyme whereof the memory of man have not beene to the contrary have beene a company of artificers of that craft by them selves and have beene freemen of the said City and have used to contribute to the public charges and beare publique offices in the said City as other freemen of like rank and quality within the same have used to doe and have used to be governed regulated and ordered by certaine by-lawes orders and constitutions made within the said City by the maior and sheriffs of the said City and greater part of the aldermen of the same with the consent of the greater number of the sixty citizens of the Comon Council of the said City and according to the charters usages and customs of the said City and according to the same during all the said tyme have yearely chosen and have had a headman, wardens and searchers in the said company who have usually every yeare been sworne before the maior of the said City for the time being for the faithfull execution of the severall offices in the governeing and ordering of the said company in the said craft according to the charters, usages and customs of the said City and according to the said by-laws orders and constitucions and for the finding out and presenting of offenders against the same or any of them, yet in regard many of the same by-lawes orders and constitucions are very ancient and almost become obsolete for want of use, others of them are defective for want of well penning and frameing the same and many new fraudes deceipts and inconveniences are of late discovered to be practiced by and used by the said carpenters in frameing repaireing and building houses and other edifices within the City and liberties of the same and in useing and putting in therein insufficient and defective timber and other materialls and stuffe by them deceiptfully used in theire said trade and occupation and many deceipts aswell in workmanship as otherwise have beene daily found out and discovered for which a fitt remedy by the said former by-lawes and ordinances is not provided, to the great prejudice and damage not only to the honest dealeing carpenters of the said company but also to all good people of this kingdome who imploy such carpenters as use such deceipts as aforesaid which deceipts and inconveniences for want of good lawes and ordinances to punish and reforme them doe daily increase more and more and others take incouragement to offend in the like kind in hope to escape through impunity, for prevencion whereof and for the better ordering and regulateing the said company of carpenters in the said City and liberties thereof and others of that craft who resorte to the same to exercize theire said trades and upholding of just dealeing in the same and for the better punishing of such abuses and practices for the future as have beene found to be hurtfull to the same and to the said company and all others within the said City and liberties of the same who make use and employ any of the said trade in building or otherwise.

[*20*] **It is** enacted ordered constituted and ordained and be it hereby enacted ordered constituted and ordained at the present court of assembly holden by the maior sheriffs and greater number of aldermen of the said City with the consent of the greater number of the sixty persons of the Common Council of the said City in manner and forme following (that is to say) that the headman wardens and searchers of the said company already sworne shall continue in theire said offices untill theire yeare be out unlesse new officers be before that time chosen and sworne in theire places and shall execute all such power and authority for the putting in execution of all such by-lawes orders rules and constitutions as heretofore have been now are and hereafter shalbe made touching and concening the regulating of the said trade & company.

[*21*] **And** that the headman and warders of the said company for the time being and at all times hereafter for the time being shall cause an assembly of the said carpenters inhabiting in the said City being freemen of the same once every quarter of the yeare to be warned and holden for the said company at the Newhall of the said City or some other publick or convenient place in the said City as usually hath beene to consult about matters of the good and benefit of the said trade and occupacion and well ordering of the same.

[*22*] **And** that if any carpenter who is an inhabitant and a master carpenter who use the said trade within the said City or liberties thereof and a freeman of the same being warned by the beadle appointed by the headman wardens and searchers for the said company shall not appeare at such an assembly at the time and place appointed for the same and fairely and civilly demeane himselfe and continue there during the time of such assembly unless there be just cause of his absence or for his departure by reason of sickness or other necessary occasion for the same from such an assembly before the end thereof shall forteite and pay to the use of the said maiore sheriffs citizens and cominalty of the said City for every such absence or departure contrary to the meaning hereof ten shillings and six pence.

[*23*] **And** that the headman, one warden, two searchers and six other carpenters being freemen of the said City soe mett shall make such an assembly and what they shall act or doe shalbe taken and accounted as the act of such an assembly of the said company and that no meeting of any person of the said company under that number shalbe holden or deemed for any assembly sufficient according to the intent and meaneing of any of the lawes or ordinances heretofore made or hereafter herein following mencioned to be made touching the said company of carpenters.

[*24*] **And** that at some assembly to be holden for the said company at or
before the foure and twentieth day of June now next ensueing there shalbe
a headman two new wardens and six new searchers chosen for the said
company of the same carpenters for the yeare then next ensueing which
said persons so to be chosen shall within one month next after the foure
and twentieth day of June now next ensueing be presented to the maior of
the said City for the time being as usually hath been to take an oath before
him to such effect & purpose as other wardens of other companies in the
said City usually doe for regulacion of theire offices, and that in case no
such headman wardens or searchers shalbe chosen and presented to the
maior within the time aforesaid, that then it shalbe in the power of the
maior of the said City for the time being as use hath beene to elect and
choose a headman and two fitt persons of the said company such as to him
shall seeme most fitt to be wardens of the said company of carpenters and
six fitt persons to be searchers for the yeare then next ensueing and shall
give them theire oaths for the due performance of the same offices, and
that the like course for electing and choosing of headman wardens and
searchers for the said company before every foure and twentieth day of
June yearely and presenting them before the maior of this City for the
time being from time to time within one month after to be sworne and for
the chooseing and swearing of headman wardens and searchers for the
said company by the said maior for the time being in case there be no
such eleccion made and presented to him within the time aforesaid as be
herin before limitted by the said company shall allwaies hereafter yearely
from time to time be holden observed and kept, which said officer or officers so sworne shalbe headman wardens and searchers to all intents and
purposes within the meaning of this by-law and that if any headman
warden or searcher so chosen by the assembly for the said company or
appointed as aforesaid by the said maior for the time being shall refuse or
neglect to take upon him or them the office he or they shalbe chosen or
appointed unto as aforesaid, every one soe refuseing or neglecting shall
forteite to the chamberleine of the said City for the time being to the use
of the said maior, sheriffs citizens and cominalty for such offence forty
shillings.

[*25*] **And** that the headman and two wardens and six searchers for the
time being shall yearely name and choose at the same assembly out of the
said company one to be beadle to serve the said headman wardens and
company who shall well and faithfully doe his office in warneing assemblies
and other meetings soe often as he shalbe required thereunto by the said
headman upon paine of forteiture of twenty shillings for every default in
not doeing his office when required.

[26] **And** that if any carpenter take upon him to worke any worke within the said City or liberties thereof which shalbe defective or insufficient either in workmanship or stuffe if the same shalbe viewed by the headman wardens and searchers of the said company for the time being or the major part of them soe judged to be defective by them or the major part of them so judges to be defective then to be fined according to the quantity and the quality of the offence soe as the said summe so sett for fine exceed not five pounds.

[27] **And** that no person of the same occupacion of carpenters whatsoever shall take upon him to amend any other mens worke defective or insufficient soe as the said default shalbe viewed as is aforesaid within three daies next after notice thereof given to the said headman or wardens or one of them before the same be viewed as aforesaid upon paine of forty shillings for every such offence.

[28] **And** that the headman and wardens of the said occupacion for the tyme being shall yearly att one of the quarter searches take and gather of every one man being of the said occupacion of carpenters haveing served an apprenticeship or be freeman of the said City working for himself towards theire pains taking of the said six searchers two pence and that every one makeing default thereof after reasonable request thereof to pay for every default two shillings. And shall take of forreiners working in the said City six pence quarterly and every quarter of a yeare for search and upon refuseal to pay the same to forfeite two shillings and six pence.

[29] **And** that every person being no freeman of the said City that shall as a master carpenter worke in the said occupacion within the said City or liberties of the same except it be in such work as the freeman artificers of the same occupacion dwelling in the said City or liberties of the same cannot artificially make and finish and soe as the person or persons that shall have such worke to doe may gett artificers of the same trade freemen of the said City to worke the same work by great or by the day as reasonably as he or they shall thinck good for such wages as is or shalbe established by the lawes of this land upon payment of forteiture for every default twenty shillings.

[30] **And** that no carpenter in the said City or liberties thereof not being a freeeman of the said City shall after Christmas now next comeing keep any apprentice or sett any journeyman on work or take any sort of worke belonging to a carpenters craft or trade to doe by the great upon payne to forteite for every time doeing the contrarie forty shillings.

[*31*] **And** that no person or persons not being a carpenter and a freeman
of the said City shall at any time hereafter buy any timber to breake into
board, planck, sparrs, joysts, laths, or other pieces to sell the same by
retaile, nor shall buy any board plancks sparrs joysts or other broken
tymber to the intent to retaile the same under an hundred foot of board or
planke or six couple of sparrs or six couple of joysts or one load of laths to
any person or persons at any tyme upon payne to forfeite the said timber
board and planke so sold and retailed or the value thereof to the chamberlain of the said City for the time being for the use of the said maior, sheriffs
citizens and cominalty and theire successours.

[32] **And** that no carpenter within the said City or County thereof shall at
any time hereafter take unto him any person under pretence to become his
servant or other pretence whatoever or directly or indirectly to learne the
said trade and occupacion of a carpenter for any summe or summes of
money or other composicion or aggreement whatsoever other then such
person as shalbe bound and serve as an apprentice to the same occupacion
ought to doe by the space of seaven yeares or haveing beene an apprentice
and served seaven yeares to serve as a journeyman upon payne that every
carpenter doeing the contrary to fortfeite for every time soe offending to
the use aforesaid forty shillings.

[*33*] **And** that no person of the said trade of a carpenter within the said
City or liberties thereof shall at any time hereafter keepe any boy or boys
at worke with him or them above one monthe at the most before such boy
or boys be bound an apprentice (by indenture for the space of seaven
yeares) with such person as shall so keepe him or them at worke upon
paine to forfeite for every day soe keeping or setting him or them at worke
more than one month as aforesaid three shillings.

[*34*] **And** that no person or persons of the occupacion of carpenters craft
which at any time hereafter shall come to the chamberlains council of this
City for the time being or the major part of them to be made free of the said
City by redempcion or purchase shalbe admitted to his or theire freedom
unless he or they have served as an apprentice to the same occupacion by
the space of seaven years at the least within the City with a freeman of the
same City under the sume of twelve pounds of lawfull English money first
paid to the maior sheriffs citizens and cominalty of the said City of Norwich
and their successours for the time being or theire receivers thereof in theire
behalfe. And the headman and wardens of the said company for the time
being after such person or persons shalbe admitted to his or theire freedomes
as aforesaid shall admitt them into theire company and not take for the same
of any one person above the summe of three shillings and four pence.

[35] **And** that no person or persons of the said occupacion within the said City or County thereof shall at any time after the feast of St Michael the Archangell[24] now next ensueing publickly use or occupy the same ocupacion in the said City or County thereof before he or they have obtained his or theire allowance from the headman and wardens of the said company for the time being or any two of them to be admitted into the said company and have first paid for such his or theire admittance three shillings and foure pence to the said headman or wardens uppon payne of forefeite for every day useing or ocupying his or theire trade contrary to this article twelve pence.

[36] **And** that no person or persons of the said occupacion within the said City or County thereof shall directly or indirectly by himselfe or servants or otherwise use or exercise the said occupacion or doe any sort of worke belonging to a carpenters craft upon the Lords day commonly called Sunday at any time in the said day (works of necessity only excepted) upon payne to forteite for every time offending herein five shillings.

[37] **And** if any person of the said trade and occupacion within the said City or liberties thereof shall maliciously upbraid defame or discredit or by any other way or meanes miscall or misuse by word or deed the headman or wardens of the said company for the time being or any other officer belonging to the said company in theire place and office at any assembly of the said company or else where for and concerneing the execucion of theire office in any part thereof to them apperteineing or shall use any uncivill or undecent language to any person or persons of the said company in or at any assembly of the said company or shall not keepe silence there he being thereunto required by the headman or wardens of the said company for the tyme being that then every one doeing the contrary in any part of this article shall forfeite for every offence two shillings and six pence.

[38] **And** that the headman and wardens of the said company for the time being shall from time to time upon or before the first day of October every yeare yield and give up a true and perfect accompt of all such monyes as they or any of them have received for fines forfeitures or otherwise or disbursed or laid out touching the said company unto them who shall then be the headman and wardens for the yeare then following. And if there shalbe none then chosen then to them who were headman and wardens the yeare before upon payne that every such headman or warden who shall neglect or refuse to yield up such accompt aforesaid

---

[24] the 29th of September.

within the time aforesaid shall forfeite for every such neglect tenne
pounds.

[*39*] **And** that the same headman and wardens and every of them shall pay
into the hands of suceeding headman and wardens before the twentieth
day of the same month of October all such monyes as shalbe found upon
such accompt to be remaineing in his or theire hands together with all
books and other writings as to the said company belongeth upon paine that
every such headman or warden not paying the monyes which upon such
accompt shalbe found to be in his or theire hands as aforesaide or not
delivering the said books and other writings within the time aforesaid shall
forfeite forty shillings for every weeke which he or they shall detaine the
monyes books or writings aforesaid in theire hands after the said day
contrary to the true meaneing of this article.

[*40*] **And** that it shall and may be lawfull to and for the headman wardens
and searchers of the said company for the time being or the major part of
them from time to time and at all times in the day convenient to enter any
shop house yard ground or other place whatsoever of any carpenter or
other person whosoever within the said City or liberties thereof there to
viewe and search at their will and pleasure for all manner of defective
stuffe or workmanship by them or any of them the said headman wardens
or searchers suspected to be, as also to view and search whether any person
of the said company of carpenters have offended against any of the articles
aforesaid to the end that such persons as shalbe found to offend against any
of them may be presented and punished for the same accordingly. And
that the said searchers or the major part of them shall make such search
quarterly and every quarter of the yeare at the least besides all other times
when they or any of them shalbe credibly informed (by any person grieved)
or by the headman wardens or beadle of the said company for the time
being of any offence against any of the aforesaid articles upon payne that
every such person who shall refuse to make such search shall forfeite for
every default five shillings.

[*41*] **And** if any carpenter or other person whatsoever his or theire wives
children servants or assignes shall wilfully resist withstand or disturbe in the
day time the said headman wardens or searchers or any of them or refuse
to lett them or any of them search as aforesaid that then everyone
offending therein shall forfeite for every such offence tenne shillings.

[*42*] **And** if any headman warden or searcher of the said company shalbe
remisse or negligent in the execucion of his office or shall conceale connive
at or spare the presenting of any person or persons who they shall find to

offend against any of the articles aforesaid and shall not present them to be brought to punishment shall for every such offence forteite the summe of twenty shillings.

[*43*] **Provided** that the carpenters forreiner inhabiting without the said City and liberties thereof may erect and sett up within the said City or liberties thereof such house or houses as have been first framed in the countrey so as they doe pay unto the headman and wardens of the said company for the time being for and in the name of an acknowledgement for viewing and searching the stuffe and workmanship and fine for every such house or houses of the length of twenty foote or under five shilling and for every of the same above the length aforesaid tenne shillings.

[*44*] **And** if any person within this City or liberties thereof have any carpenters worke to doe and resort to the headman or wardens of the said company for the time being to have any of the same occupation to worke with him then if the said headman and wardens shall not within three daies next after notice to them given or presently after if the same worke shalbe in any present perill or despaire appoint and send him such a sufficient workman as for whome he will answer for and at the usuall wages that it shalbe lawfull for any such a person to sett any forreiner to work the same without any penalty fine or forfeiture to be lost or paid for the same by the forreiner, any thing herein conteined to the contrary notwithstanding.

[*45*] **And** it is further ordained constituted and established by the said maior sheriffs and greater number of aldermen of the said City with the consent of the greater number of the sixty persons of the Common Council of the said City that all fines forfeitures and sumes of money hereafter to be forfeited and payable by or upon any of the articles aforesaid by any offender or offenders contrary to any of the said articles shall from hence-forth be levyed recovered and disposed of in such sort as hereafter ensueth and not otherwise or in any other manner (that is to say) by distresse and sale of goods and chattells of every such offender to be taken by the officer or officers of the maior of the said City for the time being by warrantt under the hand and seale of the said maior, rendring the overplus to the party distrained or otherwise if not paid without suite, that then the same shalbe recovered by accion or accions of debt, bill or playnt to be brought or prosecuted in the name of the chamberlaine of the said City for the time being before the sheriffs of the said City for the time being in the Guildhall Court. And that the chamberlaine of the said City for the time being shall in all sutes against any offender or offenders upon any of the said lawes ordinanaces or constitutions by force of this act or ordinance recover his ordinary costs of suite to be expended in or about the prosecucion thereof.

And that all such summe and summes of money soe to be recovered as aforesaide (the ordinary costs of suite to be expended being deducted) and all other summes of money which shalbe paide without suite by any delinquent for or in respect of any offence in the afore mencioned ordinances or constitucions expressed by submission or composition shalbe divided into three equall parts, one part thereof shalbe paid to the maior of the said City for the time being to be putt into the hamper to and for the use & benefitt of the poore of the said City and the other third part thereof shalbe paid to the headman and wardens of the said company for the time being to and for the use of the said company. And the other third part thereof to be paid to such person or persons as shall first give notice of the offence for which such forfeiture shall become due and shall prosecute such suite with effect in the name of the chamberlaine of the said City for the time being or shall procure payment of any summe of money to be forfeited and payable for such offence or offences by submission or composicion.

[*46*] **In Witness** whereof the said maior sheriffs citizens and cominalty of the said City of Norwich have to these present by-lawes ordinances and constitutions putt and affixed theire common seale of the said City the day and yeare first in these presents mencioned and written.

John Aldrich of Eaton
Farm Accounts 1663–1667

EDITED BY ANDREW HICKLEY

Introduction

These accounts[1] permit a narrow but detailed examination of the business of farming in Norfolk as managed by an innovative farmer in the 1660s, a period round which there is currently much debate as to the origins of agricultural innovation and change. They also give some insight into the landscape of Eaton, a Norwich hamlet, in the second half of the seventeenth century.

Tax lists and rentals in his hand show Aldrich acting as bailiff or agent at Eaton for his kinsman John Hobart of Weybread, Suffolk, from 1655 to 1680.[2] Hobart himself was tenant by leases of 1642 and 1662 from the Dean and Chapter of Norwich Cathedral of both the manor and the rectory of Eaton.[3] During these years Aldrich hired land from him in slightly fluctuating but increasing amounts from 1655, when he paid £3.15s.0d. half-yearly rent for meadowland only, until the peak was reached in 1674 with the half-year's rent of £148.5s.0d. Acreages are seldom noted, but in 1657 he took on ten closes measuring just over 97 acres.[4] The accounts published here cover his own farming operations, not his activities as Hobart's agent. Personal details of John Aldrich, other than what is shown in his account book, are sparse. He was buried neither at Eaton nor in St Giles parish, Norwich, where he had a house[5] and he does not seem to have left a will.

The account book must have been retained by the Cathedral at the expiration of Hobart's tenancy and it has remained among the Cathedral's archives. It takes the form of a small booklet measuring approximately

[1] Norfolk Record Office, DCN 59/12/1.
[2] NRO, DCN 51/21 and DCN 59/12/6-14.
[3] NRO, DCN 47/4, ff. 61r., 112v., 185r., 316v. and 318v.
[4] NRO, DCN 51/21.
[5] NRO, DCN 59/12/7 and p. 221, below.

4 x 2½ inches (10 x 6 centimetres) in which are recorded expenditure at one end and income at the other. The first expenditure accounts are for 6th October 1663 and the last for 25th May 1667. The first income entry is for 23rd October 1663 and the last for 22nd April 1667. There is a total of just under 1,050 entries. The pages are unnumbered. Page numbers have been added in this edition, A for expenditure and B for receipts (which are entered at the reverse end of the book).

The present-day parish of Eaton forms the southernmost suburb of Norwich, approximately two miles south of the city centre. The original settlement grew adjacent to a bridge carrying the main road to London over the River Yare which forms the southern boundary of the parish. This proximity to Norwich, in the seventeenth century still one of England's most important and populous commercial centres, has undoubtedly had a major influence on its development and the pattern of land-use in the area. Eaton sits on the border between what is generally described as the 'wood-pasture' region of south-east Norfolk, characterised by heavy clays, and the lighter, sandier heathlands of north Norfolk which extend into the area immediately north of Norwich. The soils are alluvial in the valley bottom, which remains liable to winter flooding today, and are formed by light loamy clays away from the low-lying valley bottom, classified by the Soil Survey of England and Wales as part of the Burlingham Association.

There are no seventeenth-century maps of Eaton to identify the area that Aldrich farmed. A map dated 1806 may well be a reasonable representation of the parish more than a hundred years earlier.[6] There are two large farms. They are separated by what is now the modern A11 Newmarket Road and the Unthank Road. To the west is an area of just over 316 acres which is probably the Eaton Hall Farm. Aldrich's payment in July 1665 'For nayles at Eaton Hall' (p. 217), his reference to his West Field ditches (p. 215) and the fact that the map shows meadowland only in this western area, to which the accounts also refer, indicate that at least its nucleus may be Aldrich's farm. The amount of open-field land that the rentals mention under his name is negligible,[7] and his use of innovative crops, including turnips and clover, together with the reference (above) to ten closes, suggest that much of the holding was in individually managed, enclosed fields not in communally managed open fields. Payments for fencing, new ditching and 'layer' (saplings for hedging) (pp. 213, 223, 233–4) may infer that he was himself engaged in a process of enclosure during the period covered by the accounts. References in the Hobart lease of 1662 and in an estate particular of 1670[8] to a foldcourse and to furlongs in the West Field imply that nevertheless elements of the medieval landscape still survived. But 'The

---

[6] NRO, DCN 127/10.

[7] And that he enclosed – NRO, DCN 51/21, Lady Day 1663.

[8] NRO, DCN 49/14/28.

ditch on the south syde of the late Aldercarre', the 'new wood of Eaton' and what was evidently an oak tree nursery hint at recent innovation in the shape of improvement of meadow land and, intriguingly, extension of woodland.

The book gives a good picture of farming activities, but it has its limitations. Although there are many references to quantities of barley threshed and numbers of fattened steers sold or of sheep shorn, there is little that can be evaluated in terms of yield, vital in determining agricultural output or productivity. Again, though the most frequent entries are wage payments, there is seldom a description of the work undertaken. We are left with the framework of Aldrich's farming year with occasional glimpses of its detail.

Fattening beef cattle was the heart of Aldrich's enterprise and its scale of operation is large; all the expenditure over £20 consists of beef cattle purchases, including the biggest single outgoing of £60 for thirty steers to over-winter in October 1666 (p. 241). Bearing in mind that the yearly wage for the farm labourers appearing in these accounts was around £15, the scale of these purchases becomes apparent. The accounts highlight the importance of St Faith's fair and Magdalen fair, both just to the north of Norwich, the one held at Horsham and the other at Sprowston in October and July respectively. In 1727 Daniel Defoe described St Faith's Fair as 'after the Falkirk Tryst, the largest and best known fair attended by Scottish drovers'.[9] Aldrich also bought cattle at the more distant Harleston fair.

The use of turnips as cattle fodder has become identified as an indicator of one of the changes that produced the 'agricultural revolution'. These innovations have become central to the debate amongst agrarian and economic historians on the nature and timing of the 'revolution'. Current thinking favours the view that the field-scale planting and hoeing of turnips is an eighteenth-century phenomenon, but these accounts make it clear Aldrich is using turnips as an integrated and significant part of his business. Mark Overton's estimates based on probate inventories show that the average farm in Norfolk and Suffolk was growing less than one acre of turnips in the 1660s,[10] although turnips were certainly being introduced on the great Norfolk estates of Blickling in the 1660s and Felbrigg in the 1670s.[11] Aldrich's accounts include payments for weeding twenty and twenty-one acres of turnips (pp. 215, 224), identifying him as an early innovator in this respect.

Another interesting innovation is the method of selling fattened beef cattle as 'futures' to be collected by the purchaser in some cases over

[9] D.Dymond, *The Norfolk Landscape* (Bury St Edmunds, 1990), p. 165

[10] M. Overton, *Agricultural Revolution in England: the transformation of the agrarian economy 1500-1850* (Cambridge, 1996), fig. 3, p. 100.

[11] E.Griffiths ed., *William Windham's Green Book 1673-1688* (Norfolk Record Society LXVI, 2002, p. 19).

several months. Sometimes, sales are made but payment is not demanded at the time the cattle are taken (although 'earnest money' often changes hands), indicating that a credit system had been established, implying regular trade, careful record keeping and an acute knowledge of the market on both sides of the contract.

In summary, the beef trade illuminated by these accounts shows a trading network crossing national boundaries and covering hundreds of miles, a sophisticated marketing operation driven by the economic power-house which Norwich represented in the seventeenth century, and an innovative system of animal husbandry which conventional thought has identified as a distinctly eighteenth-century phenomenon.

Although the proximity of Norwich makes Aldrich's livestock – sheep as well as cattle; 334 sheep were sheared in June 1666 (p. 227) – the leading part of his farming enterprise, there is no doubt that the arable part of the business is also important. There are numerous references to cart horses and plough horses, to the buying of seeds including wheat, barley, oats, clover, nonsuch (like clover an innovative crop), flax and peas, and to a variety of other purchases from new plough wheels to fans for winnowing. Arable farming, then, is not a mere adjunct to a cattle-fattening business but an integral part of a mixed farming operation.

An important aspect where the accounts provide an insight is, of course, the income derived from the sale of arable produce. Of the five corn crops that are mentioned in the income section – barley, rye, wheat, mixtlin and oats – the first two account for nearly 92 per cent in terms of volume, 1,332 coombs, and 88 per cent of value, £518 17s 4d. Barley is the distinctly dominant crop, accounting for 67 per cent of output by volume. Holderness's analysis of tithe collection accounts, probate inventories and other sources shows that between 1640 and 1680 on the north-west Norfolk heathlands barley accounted for 48 per cent of 'crop preferences'; in east Norfolk it accounted for 42 per cent, and on the High Suffolk Woodland (which extended into the South Norfolk clay plateau) the proportion of barley was 26 per cent[12]. Eaton sits between these areas but can perhaps best be compared with the north-west Norfolk heathlands. The dominance of barley on Aldrich's farm may reflect the importance of the brewing industry in Norwich, though it is not certain that he was growing malting barley. Barley also fits well with livestock farming enterprise; the crop can be used as animal feed once crush in a mill. It matures quickly spring-sown on light soil as on this farm, allowing the possibility of using the land more flexibly, for example for winter grazing. than would be the case with autumn of winter sown crops. Norwich's need for beef may help to explain

---

[12] B.A.Holderness, 'East Anglia and the Fens' in J.Thirsk ed., *Agrarian History of England and Wales*, vol. 5 (Cambridge, 1975), pp. 218-19.

Aldrich's innovatory approach. His accounts, despite their limitations, present a valuable insight into farming in seventeenth-century Norfolk and the beginnings of the agricultural revolution.

Acknowledgements

I should like to thank the staff of the Norfolk Record Office, especially in drawing my attention to the document in the first place, and to Dr Tom Williamson for his inspiration and encouragement.

Note on the analysis of the farm accounts

Following transcription, the contents of the accounts were categorised and entered into a database so that they could be analysed and manipulated. In order to facilitate further study and analysis, the editor would be happy to provide electronic copies of this database on request.

Conventions

Contractions have been expanded, but words suspended by a colon have been left as in the original except where the meaning is unclear. Dates within the text and £ s d have been standardised. Otherwise conventions have been followed as stated on p. (viii).

Aldrich of Eaton
Farm Accounts 1663–1667

[EXPENDITURE ACCOUNT]

	£ s d
[A1 October 1663]	
Oct. 6th at St Fayths fayre	
For 20 Irish steeres	37.00.00
For 20 Scottish steeres	28.00.00
Spent by Turner at the fayre	00.02.00
For 10 steeres	36.00.00
For tolls & tarring for bullocks	00.01.00
For a plough horse	02.10.00
To the droveres men	00.01.03
9th to Pightlin his quarters wages	04.10.00
For a fanne	00.04.00
10th to Tho. Banks 12 dayes	00.16.00
To John Herd	00.10.00
To George Robinson 12 dayes	00.12.00
To John Young for 5 days	00.05.00
To John Cotton 12 dayes	00.12.00
To George Goddard 12 dayes	00.10.00
To Tho: Lombe part of his wages	00.07.08
To [blank] for a fortnight	00.05.00
To [blank] Fox the carpenter 1 day	00.01.08
For a peck of turnep seed	00.05.04
For 6 stotts at 6s 4d a peice	01.18.00
23rd to Tho: Bankes a fortnight	00.12.00
To John Cotton a fortnight	00.10.00
To George Goddard a fortnight	00.10.00
To Tho: Lombe part of his wages	00.11.06
For greasing lambes	00.16.00
To John Heard a fortnight	00.13.00
For drinks for the horses	00.03.00
	108.06.11
[A2 October 1663]	
30th to John Cotton for a week	00.05.00
To George Goddard for a week	00.05.00
To Thomas Bankes for a week	00.06.00
To John Heard for a week	00.06.00

	£ s d
To George Robinson for a month	01.04.00
To John Frank for 9 weekes	01.16.00
For harvest gloves payre	00.03.00
To knacker for worke &c.	00.07.04
For an old pike for a swanhooke	00.01.00
To [blank] Churchman for 2 shotts	00.18.06
Nov. 27th to Tho: Bankes a month	01.04.00
To John Heard a month	01.04.00
To John Cotton a month	01.00.00
To George Goddard a month	01.00.00
To John Young for 13 dayes	00.13.00
To him for five flayles	00.01.00
To Tho: Lombe part of his wages	00.11.06
To Sizers boy 3 weekes	00.09.00
To George Robinson a fortnight	00.12.00
To Sam Banks for drawing of bricks	00.04.00
Dec. 5th to Tho: Banks 6 days	00.06.00
To John Heard 6 dayes	00.06.00
To Tho: Budd 6 dayes	00.05.00
To John Cotton & Geo: Goddard each 6 dayes	00.10.00
To Tho: Budd 6 dayes	00.05.00
To the boy	00.02.00
To John Frank a month	00.16.00
For cutting the River Mr Waddsworth	00.06.00
To Rich: Pightlins bill	00.03.00
To Sam: Banks for casting brickearth	01.00.00

[A3 December 1663]

For a pound of sope	00.00.04
To Tho: Lombe part of his wages	00.03.10
To Richard Cole for worke	00.03.06
Dec. 16th to Alderman Tooke for six coombs 2	
bs seed oates upon accompt	02.10.00
To him for 1 coomb of seed wheat	01.08.00
21st to George Robinson for threshing one and twenty coombs	
of barley	00.13.00
To Tho: Banks for a fortnight	00.12.00
To John Herd the like	00.12.00
To Cotton & Goddard each a fortnight	01.00.00
To [blank] a fortnight	00.08.00
To Richard Coke	00.10.00
To Tho: Budd for a fortnight	00.10.00

	£ s d
To Tho: Lombe part of his wages	00.07.08
To [blank] for earnest	00.01.00
For a new plough & 2 mending	00.08.06
For spring layre	00.04.00
For a lanthorne	00.01.06
For 10 sackes	01.05.00
For mending a fanne	00.01.00
For 13 baskets	00.06.02
For mending of baskets	00.01.04
26th to R Fox for 12 days ½	00.18.09
To George Robinson threshing 29½ co. of barley	00.18.08
To Tho: Banks & Joh. Herd each a week	00.12.00

[A4 December 1663]

To Cotton & Goddard each a weeke	00.10.00
To Tho: Budd & the boy each 6 dayes	00.08.00
To Tho: Lombe in part of his wages	00.03.10
Jan. 4th to Rich Pightlin his quarteres wages ending at Xmas last	04.10.00
8th To Tho: Bankes a fortnight	00.12.00
To John Heard the like	00.12.00
To Cotton & Goddard each a fortnight	01.00.00
To the boy a fortnight	00.08.00
To Tho: Lombe in part of his wages	00.03.10
To Tho: Budd	00.09.00
To Robinson parish clark of Eaton	00.01.00
16th to Tho: Bankes & John Heard 6 dayes	00.12.00
To Cotton & Goddard each a week	00.10.00
To the boy a week	00.04.00
To Tho: Budd a weeke	00.05.00
To John Fox & his youth a week	00.14.00
To George Robinson for threshing of 24 coombs of barley	00.15.00
For spring layre	00.04.00
To Ri: Cole for felling 10 trees	00.06.00
To the knacker for collars & harness	00.10.00
For a fann mending	00.00.08
For two carthorses	10.16.00
For a coomb of seed wheat Tho: How	01.04.00
24th to Rich: Conley in part of sawing	01.00.00

[A5 January 1664]

To John Fox & his youth 5 dayes	00.11 08
To John Frank 5 weekes	01.00.00

	£ s d
To Tho. Bankes & J. Heard each a week	00.12.00
To Cotton & Goddard each a week	00.10.00
To the boy a week	00.04.00
To Tho. Budd a week	00.05.00
To George Robinson for threshing of 32 coombes of oates	00.09.00
Feb. 13th to Sam Bankes in full for scouring all of my fen ditches	
from my fishouss to Cringleford Bridge	01.05.00
March 22nd to a rate for repayre of Eaton church &c.	10.16.00
April 1st 1664 to Richard Pightlin his quartirs wages due at	
Our Lady [25th March]	04.10.00
To Sam: Bankes for drawing the ditches above the fishouse 100 rods	00.12.00
30th to Winter in full of howghing my turneps last year. viz 16 acr	
& of 4 acr ½ peas twice over	01.03.04
To him for houghing 4 acres ½ once	00.16.04
To him for three dayes worke removing of plumme trees out of	
the garden	00.01.06
May 7th to Sam Bankes for drawing the ditch between	
Mr Greene & me	00.07.00
June 6th to another rate for Eaton Church	02.03.02
Payd as by Edw: Turners bills from Jan: 29th to Feb. 26th	33.18.10

[A6 June 1664]

Payd as by Edw: Turners bills from <Aprill 8th to Ma> March 11th	
to Aprill 8th 1664	24.03.03
June 18th payd as by Edw: Turners bills from Apr: 23 to June 17	28.05.06
28th towardes my sheepshearers	00.10.00
July 7th payd to Edward Turners bills from 17th June till 1st July	
whereof three pounds eleven shillings for household occasions	
crossed	22.16.11
9th to Pightlin in full of his wages	03.10.00
15th payd to Edwd Turner his bill	05.04.00
22nd payd for 20 Irish steeres at Magdalen fayre	46.10.00
To Edward Turner 2 bills	05.14.07
29th to Edward Turner a bill	02.14.08
Aug. 6th To Edwd Turner a bill	04.17.04
To Edwd Turner a bill	06.00.02
15th to months rate	01.11.08
To a fourth part of a months rate	00.07.11
To a rate for Kings Bench Marshalsea maymed Souldiers &[?c.]	
in the late warrs for a year ordered at Midsomer last	00.16.06
22nd to Edward Turner a bill	05.11.06
27th to my Sister Aldrich for a boare	01.00.00

	£ s d
29th for 10 Cumberland steeres for [*to feed on*] turnips bought at	
Harlston fayre	30.00.00
Sept 10th to Edward Turner a bill	10.10.06
16th for 15 shotts at 7s. 6d a peice	05.12.06

[*A7 September 1664*]

23rd for 20 hogg ewes one sheare	06.10.00
For 40 ewes two sheares	14.00.00
For 4 rammes	01.08.00
To Edwd Turner a bill besides the sayd sheep & shotts	02.09.04
30th to Edwd Turner a bill	10.11.06
Oct. 6th for 10 bullocks at St Fayths fayre for the stake	31.00.00
7th for 20 bullocks for winterstalls	46.00.00
For 4 bullocks of a lesser sort	07.04.00
22nd to Edward Turner a bill besydes the severall summes	
crosst in it	08.01.09
29th to Edward Turner his bill uncrosst	02.09.00
Nov. 6th to Edward Turner his bill	01.17.00
19th to Edward Turner his bill	04.08.00
25th to Edward Turner his bill	03.01.03
Dec. 2nd to Edward Turner his bill	02.05.04
23rd to Edward Turner his bill	07.15.10
Jan. 13th To Edward Turner his bill	28.00.06
20th to Edward Turner his bill	30.04.06
Feb. 17th To Edward Turner his bill	06.19.02
For a steere to stake with turneps	04.00.00
Feb. 3rd to Wm Winter for houghing of one and twenty acres of	
turneps twice	07.00.00
29th for 11 shotts at 12s 6d a peice & three at 10s 6d a peice	01.11.06
To Turner upon his bill	01.18.07
March 7th to Turner upon his bill	01.15.08

[*A8 March 1665*]

March 31st 1665 to Turner his bill	20.15.04
April 25th to Mrs Joane Briggs for a halfe yeares rent for hir meddow	01.10.00
May 20th to Sam: Banks for drawing all my West Feld ditches &	
the Poundmead	01.05.00

[*Rest of page and pages A9 and A10 blank*]

[*A11 June 1665*]

June 23rd 1665

Payd to Thomas Banks a week	00.06.00

	£ s d
To John Cotton a weeke	00.06.00
To George Goddard a weeke	00.06.00
To the boy a weeke	00.04.00
To John Frank five dayes ½ weeding	00.02.09
To Elizabeth Mileson 5 dayes weeding	00.02.06
To Hen: Feakes for making 400 furrz faggotts for my brickkilne	00.05.04
27th to Tho: Hopkins the shepheard in partof his quarters wages	
due at Midsomer	01.00.00
30th to Tho: Bankes a weeke	00.06.00
To George Cotton a weeke	00.06.00
To George Goddard 5 dayes ½	00.05.06
To the boy a weeke	00.04.00
To Eliz: Mileson 5 dayes weeding	00.02.06
To John Frank 5 dayes weeding	00.02.06
To John Young 3 dayes ½	00.03.06
To John Carre 3 dayes ½	00.03.06
To Henry Feakes for making 600 furres	00.08.00
July 1st to Richard Pightlin his quarters wages due at Midsomer last	04.10.00
3rd to Budde for washing and clipping my sheep at 6s per 100,	
meat & drink	01.00.00
To the Newton shepheard & his wife who helped to wind the fleeces	00.02.00
	10.06.01

[A12 July 1665]

	£ s d
To Rich: Cole who helped	00.01.00
To Cobb who helped	00.01.00
7th to Tho: Bankes 6 dayes	00.06.00
To George Goddard 6 dayes	00.06.00
To John Young 1day	00.01.00
To John Carre	
To the boy Thomas Woods a week	00.04.00
To Goddards daughter at the sheepshearing	00.00.06
To Robert Cormett 1day ½	00.01.06
To John Frank 6 dayes weeding	00.03.00
To Eliz: Mileson 6 dayes weeding	00.03.00
To George Robinson 6 dayes	00.06.00
To Henry Feakes for making 400 furrs	00.05.04
To Cobb & his wife 2 dayes each haymaking	00.02.00
To Goodwife Woods 1 day haymaking	00.00.06
For drink to the sheepwashers	00.02.06
For 2 stone of tarre	00.04.08
For a stone of pitch	00.02.04

	£ s d
To Tho: Hopkins my shepheard in further part of his quarters wages	00.10.00
14th to George Goddard 6 dayes	00.06.00
To Thomas Woods 6 dayes	00.04.00
To Cobbs wife and hir daughter 5 dayes a peece haymaking	00.05.00
To Goodwife Fenn 5 dayes haymaking	00.02.06
To Goodwife Woods 5 dayes haymaking	00.02.06
	04.06.00

[*A13 July 1665*]

15th for loading 2 chaldirs of lyme	00.01.04
For 2 stone of oker	00.02.04
For a hay rake	00.00.06
To John Frank 4 dayes	
To Eliz: Mileson 6 dayes	
To Mary Barten 3 dayes [*blank*] haymaking	00.08.06
To Jane Pightlin 4 dayes	
To Thomas Bankes 6 dayes	00.06.00
To George Robinson 5 dayes	00.05.00
To Hen: Feakes making 6 hundred furs	00.08.00
To John Cotton 2 dayes	00.02.00
18th to Tho: Hopkins in full of his quarters wages ending at	
Midsommer last	01.10.00
21st to John Cotton 6 dayes	00.06.00
To George Goddard 6 dayes	00.06.00
To Thomas Woods a week	00.04.00
22nd to John Johnsons	
For 26 Irish Steeres at Magdalen fayre at £1 19s a peice	50.14.00
For custom of them 5d for tarre 5d	00.00.10
To Goodwife Cobb and hir daughter each 4 dayes haymaking	00.02.00
To Goodwife Fenn for the like	00.02.00
24th for a peck of turnepseed	00.08.00
To my mowers in part	01.10.00
For nayles at Eaton Hall	00.01.07
To Tho: Bankes 6 dayes	00.06.00
To George Robinson 5 dayes	00.05.00
To Hen: Feakes for making 6 hundred furrs	00.08.00
	58.00.07

[*A14 July 1665*]

To John Frank, Eliz: Mileson, Jane Pightlin each 4 dayes haymaking	00.06.00
To Mary Barton 3 dayes haymaking	00.01.00
25th for 2 pitchfork staves	00.02.00

	£ s d
29th to John Cotton 6 dayes	00.06.00
To George Goddard 6 dayes	00.06.00
To Tho: Woods a weeke	00.04.00
To Tho: Bankes 6 dayes	00.06.00
To George Robinson 4 dayes	00.04.00
To Richard Cole for making 1 C [*100*] of furse	00.02.00
For cartgrease	00.03.04
For mending a gunne	00.02.00
Aug: 1st to Goodwife Cobb and hir daughter for haymaking each	
6 dayes	00.05.00
To Goodwife Fenn 6 dayes haymaking	00.03.00
To Goodwife Woods 8 dayes haymaking	00.04.00
3rd to John Frank 6 dayes ½ 3s 3d	
To Eliz. Mileson 6 dayes ½ 3s 3d haymaking	00.12.00
To Jane Pightlin 6 dayes ½ 3s 3d	
To Mary Barten 2 dayes ½ 2s 3d	
For 2 sythes	00.05.00
For half a peck of turnep seed	00.06.00
To my mowers in full money all my meadowes except the Pound	
Meadowes	01.10.00
Given to them to drink	00.03.00
5th to John Cotton 6 dayes	00.06.00
To Tho: Bankes 6 dayes	00.06.00
To Tho: Woodes	00.04.00
To Tho: Bankes a weeke	00.06.00
To George Robinson 5 dayes	00.05.00

[*A15 August 1665*]

12th To John Cotton 6 dayes	00.06.00
To George Goddard <the like>	00.06.00
To Thomas Wood a week	00.04.00
To my harvest men a largesse	00.05.00
To Feakes for 6 hundred furres making	00.08.00
For 9 payre of harvest gloves	00.04.06
For 2 sedge collars	00.00.08
To Wm Winter 3 dayes haymaking	00.04.00
To Tho. Bankes 6 dayes harvestwork	00.10.00
To George Robinson the like	00.10.00
To Robert Cornwell the like	00.10.00
To John Fox and his youth 6 dayes harvest work	00.15.00
To 19 other Reapers 1 day at 1s 8d a peece	01.11.08
19th To George Goddard 6 dayes	00.06.00

	£ s d
To John Cotton 6 dayes	00.06.00
To Tho. Woods a weeke	00.04.00
To Tho. Bankes 6 dayes	00.10.00
To George Robinson 6 dayes	00.10.00
To Robert Cornell 6 dayes	00.10.00
To John Fox and his youth each 6 dayes	00.15.00
To two reapers each 2 dayes	00.06.00
To one reaper one day	00.01.06
To half a hundred of 8d nayles	00.00.04
26th to John Cotton 6 dayes	00.06.00
	09.08.06

[A16 August 1665]

To George Goddard 6 dayes	00.06.00
To Thomas Woodes a weeke	00.04.00
To Thomas Bankes 6 dayes	00.10.00
To George Robinson 6 dayes	00.10.00
To Robert Cornwall 6 dayes	00.10.00
To John Fox & his youth 6 dayes	00.15.00
To two helpers 1 day	00.01.08
To Jane Pightlin	00.03.00
To Goddards wife	00.01.00
To one man 5 dayes	00.04.02
Sept: 1st to John Cotton 6 dayes	00.06.00
To Thomas Woods a weeke	00.04.00
To Tho: Bankes 6 dayes	00.10.00
To Robert Cornwall 8 dayes	00.13.04
To George Robinson 6 dayes	00.10.00
To John Fox and his youth each 6 dayes	00.15.00
To John Fox 2 dayes more	00.03.04
To Raph Bee 2 dayes	00.01.00
To Mary Berton 6 dayes	00.03.00
To Jane Pightlin 6 dayes	00.03.00
To John Carre 2 dayes	00.02.00
To Sam: Bankes 1 day & ½	00.01.06
To Goddards wife 1 day	00.00.06
To Charles Stygell 10 dayes	00.05.00
To Wm Cotton 6 dayes	00.03.00
8th to John Cotton 6 dayes	00.06.00

£ s d

[*A17 September 1665*]

To George Goddard 6 dayes	00.06.00
To Thomas Woods a week	00.04.00
To Thomas Bankes 6 dayes	00.06.00
To George Robinson 6 dayes	00.06.00
To 6 haymakers in my Pound Meadowes	00.07.06
For loading 5 chaldirs of lyme	00.00.10
15th to John Cotton 6 dayes	00.05.00
To George Goddard 6 dayes	00.05.00
To Thomas Woods a week	00.04.00
16th to Tho: Bankes 6 dayes	00.06.00
To George Robinson 6 dayes	00.05.00
To Jane Pightlin 2 dayes haymaking	00.01.00
23rd to John Cotton 6 dayes	00.05.00
To George Goddard 6 dayes	00.05.00
To Thomas Woods a weeke	00.04.00
To Sayer the knacker his bill	01.08.00
For 8 pound of tallow 5d per li	00.03.04
To Thomas Bankes 6 dayes	00.06.00
To George Robinson 6 dayes	00.05.00
28th payd to Tho: Hopkins his quarters wages for this Michaelmas 1665	03.00.00
29th To George Goddard 6 dayes	00.05.00
To John Cotton 6 dayes	00.05.00
To Tho: Bankes 6 dayes	00.06.00
To George Robinson 6 dayes	<u>00.06.00</u>
	09.14.08

[*A18 September 1665*]

To Tho: Woods a weeke	00.04.00
To him that Edw: Turner had cheated him	00.04.00
For 24 lb. tarre to grease lambs	00.04.00
For half a peck of malt	00.00.04
To Sam: Bankes for drawing all my ditches above the fishouse. 90 rods	00.10.00
Oct. 6th for 10 bullocks at St Fayths fayre at £3 2s a peise	31.00.00
For toll 2d for tarre 2d	00.00.04
To George Goddard a weeke	00.05.00
To John Cotton a weeke	00.05.00
To Tho: Bankes a weeke	00.06.00
To George Robinson a weeke	00.06.00
To George Cockrell keeping bullocks	00.02.00

	£ s d
For a horshoe setting	00.00.04
9th to Tho: Hopkins for greasing 84 lambs 1d a lamb 6s 8d & for	
rings for the ramms couples 6d	00.07.06
For 20 Irish steeres at St Fayths fayre	37.00.00
For tarre & toll 8d Cullyers expenses	00.03.00
12th to Mrs Joanne Briggs hir half yeares rent due at Michaelmas	
for hir meadow	01.10.00
13th to John Cotton 6 dayes	00.05.00
To George Goddard 6 dayes	00.05.00
14th to Thomas Bankes 6 dayes	00.06.00
To George Robinson 6 dayes	00.06.00
To Richard Pightlin his quarters wages	04.10.00
	77.19.06

[A19 October 1665]

19th to Tho: Hopkins his bill layd out for tarre & oker	00.08.00
21st to John Cotton & Geo: Goddard each 6 dayes	00.10.00
To Thomas Bankes a weeke	00.06.00
To George Robinson a weeke	00.05.00
To George Cockrell a weeke	00.02.00
To John Frank formerly owing	00.02.00
28th to Cotton & Goddard each 6 dayes	00.10.00
To Tho: Bankes 6 dayes	00.06.00
To George Robinson 3 dayes	00.03.00
To George Cockrell a weeke	00.02.00
Nov. 4th to Cotton & Goddard each 6 dayes	00.10.00
To Tho: Bankes 6 dayes	00.06.00
To George Cockrell a weeke	00.02.00
For a skippett	00.01.06
To Edmund Turner his bill though part of it concerned Norwich	09.05.00
11th to Cotton & Goddard each a weeke	00.10.00
To Tho: Bankes 6 dayes	00.06.00
To George Cockerell a weeke	00.02.00
To [blank]	00.04.04
18th to Cotton & Goddard each a weeke	00.10.00
To Tho: Bankes 6 dayes	00.06.00
To George Cockerell a weeke	00.02.00
For 1lb of nayles	00.00.10
23rd to George Robinson for threshing of 47 coombs of barley	01.03.06
To Cole for 7 dayes	00.05.10
	16.09.06

	£ s d
[A20 November 1665]	
25th to Cotton & Goddard each a weeke	00.10.00
To Sam: Bankes for diking	00.07.00
To Tho. Bankes 6 dayes	00.06.00
To George Cockrell 6 dayes	00.02.00
Dec. 2nd to Cotton & Goddard each a weeke	00.10.00
To Tho. Bankes 6 dayes	00.06.00
To George Cockerell a weeke	00.02.00
For 2 sedge collars	00.00.08
5th to Pightlin for 2 cowes	04.10.00
9th to Cotton & Goddard each 6 dayes	00.10.00
For 1 month & ¼ of a months rate at £70000 *per mensem* to the militia	01.19.05
To Thomas Bankes a weeke	00.06.00
To George Cockerell a weeke	00.02.00
For a hedging hooke	00.01.02
16th to Cotton & Goddard each a weeke	00.10.00
To Tho: Bankes 6 dayes	00.06.00
To George Cockerell a weeke	00.02.00
23rd to Cotton & Goddard each a weeke	00.10.00
To George Robinson for threshing 47 coo.of barley	01.03.06
To George Cockerell a weeke	00.02.00
30th to Cotton & Goddard each a weeke	00.10.00
To Rich: Pightlin his quarters wages	04.10.00
To John Pightlin his quarters wages	03.15.00
To George Robinson for threshing 12 coo. barley	00.06.00
To George Cockerell a week	<u>00.02.00</u>
	21.08.09
[A21 December 1665]	
Jan. 6th To Tho: Bankes 5 dayes	00.05.00
To Cotton & Goddard each a week	00.10.00
To George Cockerell a weeke	00.02.00
To Eaton parish clerk	00.01.00
To Tho: Hopkins my shepherd his quarters wages due at Xtmas last	03.00.00
13th to Goddard & Cotton each a week	00.10.00
To Thomas Bankes a week	00.06.00
To George Cockerell a week	00.02.00
20th to Cotton & Goddard each a week	00.10.00
To Thomas Bankes a week	00.06.00
To George Cockerell a week	00.02.00
25th to George Robinson &c. for threshing 79 coo. 3 bs of barley whereof delivered to Mr John Ingram 74 coo. 2 bs sold	01.19.7½

	£ s d
27th to Cotton & Goddard each a week	00.10.00
To Sayer the knacker his bisydes the well rope therein of 13s 8d	02.03.00
<To 3 months rate ending 1st>	<04.06.00>
To Thomas Bankes a weeke	00.06.00
To George Cockerell a weeke	00.02.00
For mending the fannes	00.02.00
Feb. 2nd to Cotton & Goddard	00.10.00
To Tho Bankes a weeke	00.06.00
To George Cockerell a weeke	<u>00.02.00</u>
	11.14.07½

[A22 February 1666]

	£ s d
10th to Cotton & Goddard each a week	00.10.00
To Thomas Bankes a week	00.06.00
To George Cockerell a week	00.02.00
To George Robinson for threshing seven and twenty coombs 3 bs wheat	01.02.03
To Sam: Bankes in part of ditching	01.00.00
To Rich: Cole 3 dayes gathering layre	00.02.00
17th to Cotton & Goddard each a weeke	00.10.00
To Tho: Bankes a week	00.06.00
To George Cockerell a week	00.02.00
To George Robinson for threshing 16 coo. & 1 bs of oates	00.08.00
24th to Cotton & Goddard each a weeke	00.10.00
To Tho Banks a week	00.06.00
To George Cockerell a week	00.02.00
To John Browne 12 days stubbing of small furze before the plough	00.11.08
March 2nd to Cotton & Goddard each a week	00.10.00
3rd to Thomas Bankes 6 dayes	00.06.00
To George Cockerell a weeke	00.02.00
For 1 pound of nayles	00.00.05
For 6 bushels of fitches	00.15.04
To Samuel Bankes 19 dayes ½	00.16.03
10th to Cotton & Goddard each a weeke	00.10.00
To Tho: Bankes a week	00.06.00
To George Cockerell a week	00.02.00
To John Browne for stubbing 6 dayes	00.05.00
For two coombs of pease	01.00.00
For nayles 4d, for a porter 4d	<u>00.00.08</u>
	10.12.01

	£ s d

[A23 March 1666]

To George Robinson for threshing of 32 coombs 3 bushells of barley	00.16.04
17th to Cotton & Goddard each a week	00.10.00
Given to Goddard	00.00.00[*sic*]
To Sam. Banks 11 days fencing	00.09.02
To Thomas Banks 6 days	00.06.00
To George Cockerell a weeke	00.02.00
To Sam Browne for hay	04.00.00
24th to Cotton & Goddard each a week	00.10.00
To Samuel Banks 8 dayes ½	00.07.01
To Henry Feakes 6 dayes stubbing	00.05.00
To Thomas Bankes 2 dayes ½	00.02.06
To George Cockerell 6 dayes	00.02.00
For 1 ounce of aloes 6d for a pec of malt for mashes 3d for quarter of a pint of oyle 3d	00.01.05
30th to Ri: Pightlin his quarters wages	04.10.00
To his son John Pightlin his quarters wages	03.16.00
31st to George Robinson for threshing threescore & ten coombs of rye	03.16.00
To Cotton & Goddard each 6 dayes	00.10.00
To Thomas Bankes 6 dayes	00.06.00
To George Cockerell a weeke	00.02.00
To John Browne for stubbing	00.04.02
To Tho: Hopkins in part of his quarters wages	01.00.00
	21.17.08

[A24 April 1666]

April 5th 1666 to Sam Bankes in full for ditching 56 rodds being at the west end of the two closes now letten to Roger Basey at 7d per rodd formerly paid £1	00.12.08
To him for felling 7 loads of bushes	00.07.00
7th to Cotton & Goddard each a week	00.10.00
To Tho: Banks 6 dayes	00.06.00
For 6 bushels of syde oates	00.12.00
To a porter for bringing them	00.00.02
To Richard Coke for howing & making of 300 wood	00.10.04
For 12 pound of clover seed	00.12.00
To a porter for loading a chalder of coal	00.00.02
To Henry Feakes for stubbing	00.05.00
To Wm Winter for howing 20 acres of turneps at 6s 8d per acre twice howed	06.13.04

	£	s	d

13th to George Robinson for threshing & putting up 41 coombs
    of barley — 01.00.06

14th to Cotton & Goddard each a week — 00.10.00

To Richard Feakes for stubbing — 00.11.00

To John Browne for stubbing — 00.03.04

To Tho: Bankes a weeke — 00.06.00

To George Cockerell a week — 00.02.00

To George Robinson 4 dayes — 00.04.00

To George Young 4 dayes ½ — 00.04.06

16th to porters for carrying 6 lasts of rye for the granary in Dukes
    Place into the wherryes at 10d per last — 00.05.00

To Mr Salters maltster who measured it — <u>00.01.02</u>

                            13.18.02

[A25 April-May 1666]

To the porter at the Dukes Place — 00.01.00

20th to Cotton & Goddard each a week — 00.10.00

To Tho: Bankes 6d to Geo. Cockerell 2d — 00.00.08

24th to Tho: Hopkins in full of his wages for the quarter
  ending at Our Lady past — 02.00.00

<Sold to [*blank*] Love 5 coombs of barley> — [*illegible*]

<Sold to Tho. Greene 5 coombs of barley> — [*illegible*]

28th to Cotton & Goddard each a weeke — 00.12.00

To Tho. Bankes for a fortnight — 00.12.00

To George Cockerell a fortnight — 00.04.00

To George Robinson 10 dayes — 00.10.00

To John Young 7 dayes — 00.07.00

For mending 3 ploughes — 00.06.00

For [?6] coombs s[?....] of [?double] T[.....?] — 00.15.00

May 5th to Cotton & Goddard each 6 days — 00.12.00

For gelding of a colt 1s, of shotts 10d — 00.01.10

For grease — 00.00.04

To Tho. Bankes a weeke — 00.06.00

To George Cockerell 2 dayes — 00.00.08

To John Young 5 dayes — 00.05.00

To George Robinson 4 dayes — 00.04.00

12th to Cotton & Goddard each 6 dayes — 00.12.00

To Thomas Bankes 6 dayes — 00.06.00

To George Robinson — 00.04.00

To John Young 6 dayes — 00.06.00

18th to Sam. Bankes for drawing all my ditches in Westfield &
    the Poundmeadows — 01.05.00

	£ s d
More to him for scowring my partof the partable ditch between Mr Walls & me	00.03.06
	08.11.04
[*A26 May 1666*]	
18th To Cotton & Goddard each a weeke	00.12.00
To Tho. Bankes for 6 dayes	00.06.00
To George Robinson 5 dayes	00.05.00
To John Young 4 dayes	00.04.00
26th To Cotton & Goddard each a week	00.12.00
To Tho: Bankes a weeke	00.06.00
To Sam: Browne a constables rate	00.12.06
To George Robinson 6 dayes	00.06.00
To John Young 6 dayes	00.06.00
For a rubb	00.00.01
For 4 dosen of hurdles	00.18.00
June 1st to Cotton & Goddard each a week	00.12.00
To Tho Bankes 6 dayes	00.06.00
To George Robinson 3 dayes	00.03.00
To John Young 5 dayes ½	00.05.06
To George Cockerell a weeke	00.02.04
To weeders of my wheat	01.05.09
For 20 Cumberland & Irish steers at Magdalen fayre	37.00.00
9th to Cotton & Goddard each a week	00.12.00
To Tho. Bankes a weeke	00.06.00
To Geo: Robinson 2 dayes	00.02.00
To John Young 2 dayes ½	00.02.06
To George Cockerell a weeke	00.02.04
For 2 pare of plough wheeles	03.04.00
To weeders	00.04.09
	45.15.06
[*A27 June 1666*]	
16th to Cotton & Goddard each a week	00.12.00
To Tho: Bankes & Young each 6 dayes Robinson 6 dayes ½	00.18.06
To George Cockerell a week	00.02.04
To weeders	01.00.01
23rd to Cotton & Goddard each a week	00.12.00
For 29 [?li.] of pitch & tarre	00.06.00
For beare and bread for the sheepwashers	00.20.00
To Sam: Bankes for fencing	00.03.00
To Tho: Bankes a week	00.06.00
To George Robinson 3 dayes	00.03.00

	£ s d
To John Young 4 dayes	00.04.00
To George Cockerell	00.01.02
25th to Tho: Budd & his partners for washing and clipping 334	
sheep at six shilling per 100	01.00.00
To Ri: Cole & to other helpers	00.03.00
28th to Rich: Pightlin his quarters wages	04.10.00
29th to Cotton & Goddard each a week	00.12.00
For beere to the sheepshearers	00.02.06
For milk & eggs for their puddings	00.00.05
To Mr Salters porters for loading of 9 chalders of sea coales	00.02.03
To Tho: Bankes a weeke	00.06.00
To George Robinson 5 dayes	00.05.00
For a years rate for Kings Bench Marshalls Sea Maymed Soldiers	
&c. for Eaton	00.16.06

[*A28 July 1666*]

July 6 To Cotton & Goddard each a week	00.12.00
For draynes for the swine	00.00.06
To Wm. Budd for making 500 furrze	00.10.00
To John Young for the like	00.10.00
To Thomas Bankes 6 dayes	00.06.00
To George Robinson 5 dayes	00.05.00
To John Browne 2 dayes	00.02.00
To women haymakers 6d a day	00.04.00
14th to Cotton & Goddard each a weeke	00.12.00
For fleaing a bullock that dyed	00.00.06
For 200 of nayles	00.01.08
For 2 hayrakes	00.01.00
To John Browne 2 dayes ½	00.02.06
To George Cockerell 5 dayes	00.01.08
To George Robinson 2 dayes	00.02.00
To Thomas Bankes 6 dayes	00.06.00
To haymakers	00.13.00
21st to Cotton & Goddard each a week	00.12.00
For 100 of nayles	00.00.10
For draynes for the swynne	00.00.06
To Bawd shepheard part of wages	00.10.00
To Tho: Bankes a week	00.06.00
To haymakers	00.15.06
26th to mowers in part of £3 18s for mowing all my medows &	
a hardland close of 9 acres	02.00.00
To haymakers	00.02.06

	£ s d
[A29 July 1666]	
28th to Cotton & Goddard each a weeke	00.12.00
For a pare of cart wheeles	01.13.04
To haymakers	00.09.06
To Thomas Bankes a week harvest work	00.10.00
To John Fox & his youth 6 dayes	00.15.00
To George Robinson 4 dayes ½	00.07.06
To Matthew Reyney a week	00.10.06
To Henry Feakes 2 dayes	00.03.04
Aug. 3rd to Cotton & Goddard a week	00.12.00
For the pare of harvest gloves	00.04.06
For the draines for the swine	00.00.06
To Thomas Bankes a week	00.10.00
To Fox & his youth a week	00.15.00
To George Robinson a week	00.10.00
To Henry Feakes a weeke	00.10.00
To Matthew Renny a week	00.10.00
To Wm. Mann 3 dayes	00.05.00
To George Cockerell a week	00.02.06
To John Fox & his youth three dayes planchering & mending carts	00.07.06
10th to Cotton & Goddard each a weeke	00.12.00
11th to [blank] Baird in further part	00.10.00
To Thomas Bankes a weeke	00.10.00
To John Fox & his youth a week	00.15.00
To Matthew Renny a week	00.10.00
To George Robinson & Henry Feakes a week	01.00.00
[A30 August 1666]	
To George Cockerell a week	00.02.06
To women &c. heaping barley	00.10.01
14th to a rate upon Eaton for the releife of the infected poore	
in Norwich	02.18.00
18th to Cotton & Goddard each a weeke	00.12.00
To John Kerk	00.04.02
To Tho: Bankes a weeke	00.10.00
To George Robinson a weeke	00.10.00
To John Fox & his youth a weeke	00.15.00
To Matthew Renny a weeke	00.10.00
To Henry Feakes a weeke	00.10.00
To George Cockerell a weeke	00.02.06
25th to Cotton & Goddard each a weeke	00.12.00
To [blank] Bawd in part of his wages	00.10.00

	£ s d
To Tho: Bankes a weeke	00.10.00
To George Robinson a weeke	00.10.00
To John Fox & his youth a weeke	00.15.00
To Matthew Renny a weeke	00.10.00
To John Kerk a weeke	00.10.00
To Henry Feakes	00.07.00
To George Cockerell a weeke	00.02.06
To rakers & heapers of barley	00.14.04
Sept. 1st to Cotton & Goddard each a week	00.12.00
To John Fox for a pare of syth hookes	00.01.00
To Thomas Bankes a weeke	00.06.00
To George Cockerell a weeke	00.02.06

[*A31 September 1666*]

	£ s d
To John Kerk for half a dayes work	00.00.10
To John Young & his partners in full of mowing as before	
26th July last	01.00.00
To haymakers	00.02.02
To the sixth quarterly payment of the royall ayde Sam:	
Browne collector	04.06.00
Further present supply *idem* collector	03.04.08
Sept. 8th to Cotton & Goddard each a week	00.10.00
To Thomas Bankes a weeke	00.06.00
To George Cockerell a weeke	00.02.06
To Elizabeth Pightlin a day	00.00.06
To William Bawd shepheard in part	00.10.00
15th to Cotton & Goddard each a week	00.10.00
To Tho: Bankes 5 dayes	00.05.00
To George Robinson	00.06.00
To George Cockerell a weeke	00.02.06
For grease for the cart	00.00.08
22nd to Cotton & Goddard each a week	00.10.00
To Tho: Bankes a weeke	00.06.00
To George Robinson 5 dayes ½	00.05.06
To Richard Barford 3 dayes	00.03.00
To George Cockerell	00.01.06
To Renny for making of 200 furres	00.04.00
To a thatcher & his server 4 dayes	00.10.00
For tarre	00.00.08
To Wm Bawd which he defalted out of £1 2s for 9 lambes which	
he sold	00.10.00

	£ s d
[A32 September 1666]	
Sept. 29 to Cotton & Goddard each a week	00.10.00
To Thomas Bankes 6 dayes	00.06.00
To George Robinson 2 dayes ½	00.02.06
To Richard Barford 4 dayes	00.04.00
To the thatcher & his labourer 4 dayes	00.10.00
To William Bawd in full of this quarter	00.10.00
To Richard Pightlin his quarters wages	04.10.00
To John Pightlin his quarters wages	03.15.00
Oct. 6th to Cotton & Goddard each a week	00.10.00
To Thomas Bankes a weeke	00.06.00
To Richard Barford a weeke	00.06.00
To Matthew Renny for making 150 of furse 3s for 6 dayes work 6s	00.09.00
8th for 10 bullocks for turneps	26.00.00
For 30 steeres for winterstalls	60.00.00
For tarre 8 for toll 8d	00.01.04
Given to the drovers man 6d to a boy 2d	00.00.08
13th to Cotton & Goddard each a week	00.10.00
To Thomas Bankes a weeke	00.06.00
To Conley for sawing	00.04.04
To Wm Bawd in part	00.10.00
To Richard Barford 4 dayes	00.04.00
To George Robinson for threshing & tying up 11 coombs of rye	00.08.09
To John Chamberlayne	00.02.04
20 to Cotton & Goddard each a week	00.10.00
To Thomas Bankes a weeke	00.06.00
To George Robinson for threshing & tying fyve coombs of wheat	00.04.00
[A33 October 1666]	
To Richard Barford 1 day & ½	00.01.06
To Mathew Denny 2 dayes	00.02.00
To Joseph Chamberlayne a weeke	00.02.04
For one [*sic*]	00.00.04
27th to Cotton & Goddard each a week	00.10.00
To Thomas Bankes a weeke	00.06.00
To Joseph Chamberlayne a week	00.02.04
To the thatcher & his server for 7 dayes work	00.17.06
To Wm Bawd in part of his wages	00.10.00
For tobacco stalks	00.00.06
Nov. 3rd to Cotton & Goddard each a week	00.10.00
To Thomas Bankes a week	00.06.00
To Math: Renny 4 day	00.04.00

	£ s d
To Joseph Chamberlayne	00.02.04
To George Robinson for threshing & tying 9 coombes rye	00.09.06
10th to Cotton & Goddard each a weeke	00.10.00
To Tho Bankes a week	00.06.00
To Wm. Bawd in part of his wages	00.10.00
To Joseph Chamerlayne a weeke	00.02.04
To a thatcher and his server 5 dayes	00.12.06
For 16 lb broaches & 2 lb. bindings	00.08.00
17th to Cotton & Goddard each a week	00.10.00
To Thomas Bankes a week	00.06.00
To Joseph Chamberlaine a week	00.02.04
For a scuppet	00.01.00

[*A34 November 1666*]

To Mathew Renny for making ½ C [*500*] of furze	00.01.00
To George Robinson for threshing & tying 31coo. 2 bs of oats	00.15.09
For 8lb of tarre at 3d per lb.	00.24.00
To [*blank*] for 2 days threshing peas	00.02.00
22nd to Sam Browne churchwarden of Eaton for a rate to the	
poore 6 months	01.05.00
24th to Cotton & Goddard each a weeke	00.10.00
To Thomas Bankes a weeke	00.06.00
To Joseph Chamberlayne a weeke	00.02.04
To George Robinson for threshing & tying 21 coombs of barley	00.10.06
To Wm Bawd in part of his wages	00.10.00
Dec. 1st to Thomas Bankes 6 dayes	00.06.00
To Cotton & Goddard each a weeke	00.10.00
To Joseph Chamberlayne a weeke	00.02.04
For grease for the carts	00.00.09
To Cotton & Goddard each a weeke	00.10.00
To Thomas Bankes a weeke	00.06.00
To Joseph Chamerlaine a weeke	00.02.04
To Math: Renny & Rich: Coke for making 250 of wood at	
2s 8d per 100	00.06.08
To Wm Bawd in part of his wages	00.10.00
To George Robinson for threshing & tying up 21 coombs of barley	00.10.06
15th to Cotton & Goddard each a weeke	00.10.00
To Thomas Bankes a weeke	00.06.00

[*A35 December 1666*]

To Joseph Chamberlayne a week	00.02.04
To George Robinson for threshing & tying 21 coombs of barley	00.10.06

	£ s d
For 2 pare of plough wheeles	00.04.00
22nd to Cotton & Goddard each a weeke	00.10.00
To Thomas Bankes a weeke	00.06.00
To Joseph Chamberlain a week	00.02.04
To George Robinson for threshing & tying up 22 coombs of barley	00.11.00
To William Bawd in full of his quartridge	00.10.00
26th to Fox the carpenter 10 dayes & a halfe himselfe	
& 12 dayes & a halfe his youth	01.08.00
29th To Cotton & Goddard each a weeke	00.10.00
To Thomas Bankes a weeke	00.06.00
To Joseph Chamberlaine a week	00.02.04
To Richard Pightlin his quarters	4.10.00
To John Pightlin his quarters wages	3.15.00
Jan. 5th to Tho. Bankes a week	00.06.00
To Cotton & Goddard each a weeke	00.10.00
To Joseph Chamberlaine a week	00.02.04
To Wm Bawd in part of his wages	00.10.00
To George Robinson for threshing & putting up 12 coombs of oates	00.06.00
To him for threshing &c. 2 coo. 3 bs of barley	00.04.00
12th To Cotton & Goddard each a weeke	00.10.00
To Tho: Banks & Joseph Chamberlayne	00.08.04
To Wm Bawd in part 5s for 2 [blank] shotts	00.05.05

[A36 January 1667]

	£ s d
19th to Cotton & Goddard each a weeke	00.10.00
To George Robinson for threshing & tying eighteen coombs of wheat	00.13.06
To Richard Barford for threshing & tying two and twenty coombs	
of barley & 3 bushels	00.11.04
To Wm Bawd in part of his wages	00.05.00
To Thomas Banks a week	00.06.00
To Joseph Chamberlayne a week	00.02.04
26th to Cotton & Goddard each a weeke	00.10.00
To Thomas Bankes a weeke	00.06.00
To Joseph Chamberlayne a weeke	00.02.04
To Wm Bawd in part of his wages	00.05.00
For black sope	00.00.04
Feb. 2nd to Cotton & Goddard each	00.10.00
To George Robinson for threshing & tying 18 coombs of wheat	00.15.02
To Richard Barford for 1 dayes work	00.01.00
To Sam: Bankes for 1 dayes work	00.01.00
To Math. Reny for 1 dayes work	00.01.00
To Wm Bawd in part of his wages	00.05.00

	£ s d
To Thomas Bankes a week	00.06.00
To Joseph Chamberlayne a week	00.02.04
9th to Cotton & Goddard each a weeke	00.10.00
To Math Renny for making 325 of wood at 2s 8d per 100	00.08.00
More for ryveing 2 loads of blocks	00.04.04
To Wm Bawd in part of his wages	00.05.00

[A37 February 1667]

To Thomas Bankes a weeke	00.06.00
To Joseph Chamberlayne a weeke	00.02.08
16th to Cotton & Goddard each a weeke	00.10.00
To Thomas Bankes a weeke	00.06.00
To Joseph Chamberlayne a weeke	00.02.04
To Wm Bawd in part of his wages	00.05.00
To George Robinson for threshing & tying 33 coombs of barley	00.16.06
23rd to Cotton a week 5s Goddard 4s 2d	00.09.02
To Sam: Bankes & Mathew Renny for 4 dayes work a peice stubbing	00.08.00
For mending 8 skepps	00.01.06
For 3 hundred of spring layer	00.01.00
To Wm Bawd part of his wages	00.05.00
To Thomas Bankes a weeke	00.06.00
To Joseph Chamberlaine a week	00.02.04
March 2nd to Cotton Goddard each a week	00.10.00
To George Robinson for threshing tying & putting up 42 coombs of barley	01.01.00
To Samuel Bankes for ditching	00.10.00
To Wm Bawd in part of his wages	00.05.00
To Thomas Bankes for 6 dayes	00.06.00
To Joseph Chamberlayne a weeke	00.02.04
9th to Cotton & Goddard each a weeke	00.10.00
To Edmund Mane churchwarden for rate for reper of Eaton Church	07.02.11
To Thomas Bankes a weeke	00.06.00
To Joseph Chamberlayne a weeke	00.02.04
To Wm Bawd in part of his wages	00.05.00

[A38 March 1667]

For 4 C [400] of spring layer	00.01.04
For 6 bushelles of fitches	00.08.00
16th to Cotton & Goddard each a weeke	00.10.00
To Thomas Bankes a week	00.06.00
To Joseph Chamberlayne a week	00.02.04

	£ s d
To Wm Bawd in <full of his quarters>part of his wages due at Our Lady [25th March] 1667	00.05.00
For 3 lockes & keyes	00.03.00
To John Fox a day	00.01.06
To George Robinson for threshing & tying & putting up 16 coom rye	00.12.10
23rd to Cotton & Goddard each a week	00.10.00
To Joseph Chamberlayne a week	00.02.04
To Wm Bawd in full of his quarters wages due at Our Lady 1667	00.05.00
To George Robinson for threshing & putting up of 36 coo. 2 bs of barley	00.18.03
For 4 C [400] of spring layre	00.01.04
1667 30th to Cotton & Goddard each a week	00.10.00
To Thomas Bankes a week	00.06.00
To Wm Bawd in part of his wages	00.05.00
To Joseph Chamberlayne a week	00.02.04
For 5 skepps for turneps	00.02.06
To Rich Pightlin his quarters wages	04.10.00
To John Pightlin his quarters wages	03.15.00
To Mrs Joane Briggs for 1 year & ½ rent for her meddow ending at Our Lady past	04.10.00

[A39 April 1667]

6th April to Cotton & Goddard each a week	00.10.00
For tarre & a pott	00.01.05
To George Robinson for threshing & putting up 54 coomb of barley	01.07.00
To George Robinson a day	00.01.00
To Richard Barford a day	00.01.00
To Mathew Renny a day	00.01.00
For carting 2 load of clay	00.01.00
For 61 rodd of new ditching in the West Feild at 7d per rodd	01.15.07
For 3 C [300] spring layer	00.01.00
For 12 C [1,200] furrze layer	00.01.06
To Wm Bawd in part of his wages	00.05.00
To Thomas Bankes a weeke	00.06.00
To Joseph Chamberlayne a weeke	00.02.04
9th to William Winter for the 7th 9th [blank] payment for the royall ayd	04.06.00
To him for the 3 quarterly payment to his Majesties further supply	03.04.08
10th to Wm Winter for 20 weeke rate to the poore of Eaton	01.09.00
To Cotton & Goddard each a week	00.10.00
To Thomas Bankes a weeke	00.05.00

	£ s d
To Wm Bawd in part of his wages	00.05.00
For cartgrease	00.02.00
To Joseph Chamberlayne a week	00.02.04
For riving a load of wood	00.01.00
To George Robinson for threshing & putting up 24 coombs of barley	00.12.00

[*A40 April 1667*]

20th to Cotton & Goddard each a week	00.10.00
To Thomas Bankes a weeke	00.06.00
To Wm Bawd in part of his wages	00.05.00
To Joseph Chamberlayne a weeke	00.02.04
For 6 dayes to a man raking up ofts [*sic*]	00.03.00
27th to Cotton & Goddard each a week	00.10.00
To Thomas Bankes a weeke	00.06.00
To Wm Bawd in part of his wages	00.05.00
To Joseph Chamberlaine a weeke	00.02.04
May 3rd to Cotton & Goddard each a week	00.12.00
4th for 3 bushells of nonesuch seed	00.12.00
To George Robinson for threshing & putting up 4 coombs 1 bushell of barley	01.02.07½
To John Kerk for clearing 4 acres in the wood	01.00.00
To Thomas Bankes a weeke	00.06.00
To Wm Bawd in part of his wages	00.05.00
To Joseph Chamberlayne a weeke	00.02.04
To John Carre for 5 dayes ½	00.05.06
11th to John Cotton a week	00.06.00
To Goodwife Chamberlayne for 3 dayes & ½ pulling turneps	00.01.06
For a horse lock	00.00.08
For impounding crying booking and keeping of a stray sowe	00.01.08
To Thomas Bankes for 6 dayes	00.06.00
To Wm Bawd in part of his wages	00.05.00
To John Carre for 5 dayes worke	00.05.00
To Joseph Chamberlayne a weeke	00.02.04
For 30 C of clover grasse at 4d per 100	00.10.00

[*A41 May 1667*]

18th to John Cotton 6 dayes	00.06.00
For 4 dosen of hurdles	00.10.00
To Thomas Bankes 6 dayes	00.06.00
To Wm Bawd in part of his wages	00.05.00
To Joseph Chamberlayne a weeke	00.02.04
To John Carre 5 dayes ½	00.05.06

	£ s d
To George Robinson 6 dayes	00.06.00
25th to Sam Bankes for drawing all the meddowes in the Westfield & Pound Meadows	01.05.00
To Cotton & Tho: Bankes each a week	00.12.00
To Fox & his man a dayes worke	00.02.08
To a cooper for hooping 3 tubbs	00.02.08
Spent upon carters in read cheese butter & beere in 3 dayes carting	00.04.04
To Wm Bawd in part of his wages	00.05.00
To Robinson & Carre each 5 dayes	00.10.00
To Joseph Chamberlayne a week	00.02.04

[RECEIPT ACCOUNT]

[B1 October 1663]

Sold to Edmund Hubbert of Hingham forty seven stone of wooll at 6s per stone rec'd 27th March 1664	13.10.00
23rd sold to Tho: Murrell of Arminghall 60 weather lambs	15.00.00
Sold to Robert Gedge of Shottisham twenty small ewe lambs	34.00.00
28th sold Rich. Waight of Lakenham foure coombs 3 bs of seed rye	03.11.03
Nov. 25 sold to Mr George Gipps 15 coo. 3bs at 10s per coomb	07.10.00
Sold killd for my house the least of the 4 shotts bought of John Moore	00.13.04
Sold to myself 19 coom: 3 bs of seed rye	14.16.03
Sold to myself 15 coombs of wheat	15.00.00
Sold to Mr George Gipps 21 coom of barley	10.06.08
Dec. 6th.	
Memo Mr Gipps payed me £20 upon the 10th Dec. 1663 which was £2 3s 4d more than was due	
Sold delivered to Mr George Gipps 33 coo. 2bs of barley	15.10.00
Sold delivered to him more 10 coo. 2bs	05.03.04
Jan 7th sold to Tho Murrell fourscore ewe lambs for	12.00.00
	110.10.10

[B2 January 1664]

Sold delivered 12th Jan. 1663 to Mr George Gipps 31 coo. 2 bs of barly pd £26 recd £10 27th Feb.	15.00.00
Memorandum there is still due to me from Mr Gypps 12th Jan.1663 £7 10s	
Sold delivered 13th Jan. 1663 to Mr George Gypps 15 coo. 3 bs of barley	07.10.00
Feb. 8th sold to Richard Rose of Kirby the steeres bought at Harlston fayre upon the 29th of August last (which cost £29) & two of my stotts bought of John Moore	72.10.00

	£ s d

He is to pay 40s next Saturday, to draw one at Shrovetyde,
   2 at Easter, from thence 2 every weeke, the last 8th May
   19th sold delivered to Mr George Gipps 31coo 2 bs of barley   15.00.00
Sold to Richard Meere junior my twenty Scottish steeres bought at
   Magdalen fayre for £39 & my twenty Scottish steeres bought at
   St Fayths for £37 now together for   115.00.00
   to be drawne before May day next.
He payed £10 in earnest the rest when he drawes.
   April 1st 1664 sold to Tho & Wm Low the ten steeres bought
   at St Fayths fayre 6th of Oct. which cost £36, he is to draw   75.00.00
   two of them 7th, 2 more 14th, 2 more the 21st, 2 more 28th of
   this instant & the 2 last the 5th of May 1664

   300.00.00

[B3 April 1664]
13th Sold to Mr George Gipps 63 coo. of barley at 9s 8d per coomb   29.00.00
Sold to Tho: & Wm Low [blank] shotts   06.00.00
Sold to Mr George Gipps 52 coo of barley at 9s 6d per coomb   25.14.00
Sold 2 load of hay to [blank]   03.00.00
Sold to Rich. Rose a shott for   00.18.00

   64.12.00
   300. 0. 0
   116.10. 0
8 July 1664   481. 2.00
Remayning in rye 70 coombs
Scottish steeres 20
From Richard Key £26 10s 0d & charges
White pease 6 coombs

July 27 1664
Sold to my brother Tho. Aldrich 60 of my head weather lambes.
He paid me 30th July.   15.00.00
Aug. 10th sold to Mr Wild of Wimondham half a hundred
   crones for   15.00.00
More sold to him 2 ramms very old   00.10.00
22nd sold to Mr Mileham a milch shee asse & hir foale late Pettus   10.00.00
29th sold to my Cosine Hobart of Mendham tenn of my best crones   03.00.00
Oct . 6th sold to myselfe seed rye 11 coomb   06.00.00
29th sold to myself seed wheat 5 coomb   05.00.00
Sold to myselfe 80 store ewe lambs   18.00.00

	£ s d

[B4 *October 1664*]

Sold more to my self delivered at Norwich 20 coo. wheat	18.00.00
Nov. 5th sold to my cosine James Hobart of Mendham a she asse	
without the foal	08.00.00
Kill'd a shott of my breeding part sold	01.00.00
Sold 5 pigs for	00.13.02
Sold to Mr Tho: Cock of Ringland 122 lambs to be payd	
at Xmas rec'd 10	21.10.00
Dec. 3rd sold to Mr George Gipps 21 coo. barley (rec'd 10 coo.)	08.10.00
Sold more to myself delivered at Norwich 30 coo. mixlin	05.00.00
Sold more to myself delivered at Norwich 30 coo. rye	11.00.00
Dec. 22nd sold delivered to Mr George Gipps 43 coo. barley	17.00.00
Kill'd one the 15 shotts bought 16th Sept.	00.12.00
Sold 6 more of those shotts	03.12.00
Sold 2 shotts of my owne breeding	02.00.00
Kill'd a boare for my owne spending	02.00.00
Killed one of the 15 shotts aforesayd	00.12.00
Jan.19th sold delivered to my selfe at Norwich fifteen coombs	
3 bushells of oates & at Sam Brownes house 32 coo. 31 bs	
toto 48 coo. 2	14.00.00
Feb. 6th sold to Watts one of the tenn Cumberland steeres bought	
at Harlston fayre	06.00.00
17th sold 7 of the remayning 15 shotts	04.04.00
Kill'd one of the 13 shotts	00.14.00
Sold delivered to my selfe at Norwich 45 coo. of rye	
Sold delivered to my selfe at Eaton 23 coo. 3 bs of rye	
20th sold my 20 Scottish steeres bought at St Fayths fayre	
6th Oct 1663	48.00.00
March 7th sold 6 of the 13 shotts	04.04.00
Kill'd one other of the 13 shotts	00.14.00
17th sold to Robert & John Leesing two of the least to the 10	
Cumberland steeres	10.10.00
Sold to Wm Low 1 Cumberland steere	04.13.08

[B5 *March 1665*]

Sold 5 more of the turnep bullocks to Robert & John Leesing for	20.10.00
Sold one other of those bullocks to the Leesings	05.00.00
Kill'd one of the 11 shotts bought 25th Feb.	00.15.00
Sold the other 10 to [*blank*] for	07.10.00
April 21st sold to Mr Schollar forty of the 44 winter stalls bought	
at Magdalen & St Fayth fayre	114.10.00
rec 60 rec 40	

	£ s d
26th sold to Mr Turner 52 coo. 2 bs of barley at 7s 8d per coomb	19.03.04
28th sold to Dey a bullock for	06.00.00

May 11th sold to Mr Turner 38 coo. 2 bs of barley at 7s 8d
   per coomb   19.03.04

Rec'd of Mr Turner £7. Edw. Turner must accompt for the rest
   <July 3rd sold to Manns wife the miller of Cringleford a stone
   of wooll for>   <00.16.00>

June 30th sold to Wm. Coddenham 2 bullocks remayning of my
   turnep bullocks for   11.15.00

Whereof he payd with the earnest 8th July £3, payd more 1st July £3,
   remaynes £5 15s, payd more 19th Aug. 1665 £2, remaynes £3 15s,
   payd more 4th Nov: 1665 £3 10s, pd 27 Oct 1666 5s

[*B6 July 1665*]

July 3rd 1665 sold to Mathew Man his wife 2 stone of choyce wooll	00.16.00
Sold to myselfe 60 store ewe lambs	13.10.00
Sold more to my selfe 6 ewe lambs & six ramme lambs all for store	02.10.00
Aug. 31st sold to Mr Peter Brereton of Trowse 60 weather lambs for	15.00.00
Sept. 5th sold 40 crones for 4s 8d	09.06.08
11th sold 60 second weather lambs to Edmund Miles of Carlton for	10.00.00

Oct 2nd sold to Mr Babston foure & thirty refuse lambs at 2s 10d
   a peice & a refuse crone for 2s   01.10.04

5th sold to William Young of Trowse my last year wooll at 6s 2d
   per stone to pay halfe at Xtmas halfe at Our Lady [*25th March*]   12.16.00

<Sold to Mr Peter Brereton 8 loads of brakes standing at 1s per load>

Sold to Mr Smiler 5 loads of brakes	00.07.08
9th sold to myselfe 15 coombs 2 bs oates	05.00.00
Oct. 28th rec'd of Mr Peter Brereton for 30 loads of brakes standing	02.05.00
Nov:11 rec'd for [*blank*] mort sheepskins	00.03.02
23rd sold to Mr John Ingram 45 coo. barly	15.01.00
Dec. 2nd sold 2 shotts of my owne breed	01.16.00
5th rec'd of Pightling for keeping 2 cowes	02.10.00
	96.09.08

[*B7 December 1665*]

15th sold to Tho: Godbold of Harlston the two cows I bought of
   Pightlin to be drawne with him a month of Xtmas day   06.00.00

19th sold to Mr John Ingram 42 coo. barley	14.13.00
26th sold to Mr John Ingram 10 coo. 2 bs barley	03.13.04

Jan.13th sold my 3 of the 4 smaller steeres bought 7th Oct.1664 to
   Wm Watts for   12.00.00

	£ s d

He is to draw one next Thursday one other 25th instant & the last
   8th Feb.   rec. 4.10

   He gave me 5s in earnest and is to pay £4 10s at the drawing   & 4.10
   & 3s 0d of each of the 2 first & £3 at the drawing of the last

22nd sold delivered to Mr John Ingram 74 coombs of barley
   at 7s 6d   26.12.06

29th sold 4 shotts more & spent that were of my owne breeding   03.05.00

Sold 3 smaller shotts & spent of my breed   01.15.00

Feb. 2nd sold to Goddard 1 bushell of rye   00.02.00

24th sold to Thomas Corbold of Harlston the 10 bullocks I bought
   at St Fayths fayre past at £3 2s 0d a peice & 2 of the 26 steeres
   bought at Magdalen fayre at £1 10s a peice to draw & pay as   71.00.00
by his note. Rec'd £5 in part of payment   rec'd 48

Sold a sow & piggs for   01.04.06
                                             152.00.04

[B8 February 1666]

Sold two pounds of hemp   00.01.02

March 14 sold 31 coo. 2 bs of barley to Mr Bawd for 7s 8d
   per coomb   11.10.00

23rd sold killed a shott   00.16.00

30th sold to Wm Barker & Peter Watts two of my steeres bought at
   Magdalen fayre at £1 9s 6d a peice he is to draw them both 6th
   Aprill next & gave me in earnest   07.02.06

11th sold to Mr Bawd 21 coo. barley at 7s 10d per coomb   07.16.08

16th sold delivered to Captayne Lullman 12 lasts or two
   hundred or 240 coo. of rye at 8s 6d per coomb. full payd   102.00.00

23rd sold delivered to Mr Robins of Yarmouth 21 coombs of rye   09.00.00

25th sold to Love 5 coombs of barley   02.00.00

Sold to Tho Greene 5 coombs of barley   02.00.00

28th sold to Mr Schollar the remayning two & twenty of the six
   & twenty steeres bought at Magdalen fayre last 22nd July   59.00.00

Sold sow   00.15.00

Sold 12 bushells ½ of old wheat   00.08.09

Sold to myselfe 40 coombe of seed barley   15.00.00

May 14th sold to Mr Wm Tooke 20 steeres bought att St Fayths
   fayre 6th Oct. last   49.00.00

Sold a coombe of wheat for   00.13.00
                                           267.03.01

[B9 May 1666]

19th sold a coomb & 1 bushell of wheat   00.16.04

26th sold a coomb of wheat   00.13.00

June 9th sold 2 bushells of wheat   00.06.06

	£ s d
Sold 2 bushells of mixlin	00.04.06
16th sold 3 bushells of mixlin	00.06.09
23rd sold 2 bs of wheat	00.06.06
Sold 3 bs & 2 pecks of mixlin	00.07.11
Sold 1 coomb of mixlin	00.09.00
26th sold a coomb of mixlin	00.09.00
30th sold 2 bushells of wheat for	00.06.04
Sold 1 bushell of mixlin	00.02.03
July 14th sold 2 bs of wheat	00.06.00
21st sold 6 bs of wheat	00.08.00
Sold 1 bs ½ of mixlin	00.03.01
Aug: 9th sold to my Sister Aldrich fourscore wether lambes	19.00.00
11th sold six bushells of wheat	01.04.00
24th sold to Mr Ward of Stoke 60 second sorted ewe lambs	09.00.00
Sept:14 sold to [blank] of Carlton eight & thirty rixyes & foule lambs	05.18.00
21st sold 9 lambs to my shepheard	01.02.06

24th sold to Thomas Cockerell my wooll at 6s 6d per stone he is to
weight it at All Hollontide [*All Hallows, 1st November*] next & then
to pay for it & gave 5s in earnest

| 29th sold 2 small lambs to Wm Bawd for | 00.03.00 |
| | 42.04.08 |

[B10 October 1666]

Oct. 5th sold shipskins for	00.14.00
15th sold a score of flighty barley to Mr Bawd at 5s 10d per coom	05.06.08
Nov: 5th sold 40 crones & 1 old ramme to Mr Bythel of Caistor	10.00.00
Sold 21 coo. barley to Mr Bawd	06.06.08
Sold 21 coo. barley to Mr Bawd	06.06.08

Dec. 5th sold to Thomas Godbold of Harlston the remayning
   19 steeres of the 20 I bought at Magdalen fayre 2nd of June last
   (one of them dying) for £3 10s a peice   rec £60
   he is to draw [?9] of them befor Twelfth Day [*6th Jan.*] & to pay me
   half the money the first weeke in February next & to have the tyme
   of the turneps for the rest but if my seervant thinketh that my
   turneps will not hold out he is to draw 3 or 4 before Shrove tyde
   next [*19th Feb*] and to pay the remaynder of the money at
   midd Aprill next
rec 16th Feb. 1666 23 [*word illegible*]

13th sold 21 coom: barley to Mr Bawd	06.04.08
19th sold 21 coom: barley to Mr Bawd	06.04.08
January 4 sold 26 coomb barley to Mr Bawd	08.04.08

	£ s d
14th sold 21 coo. 6 bs barley to Mr Bawd	06.16.00

Febr. 2 sold to Loy Smyth of Wimondham my wooll being 44 stone
   at 6s per stone he is to fetch the one halfe upon Tuesday the
   19th instant

Sold a shott of my owne breed for	01.03.00
13th sold 31 coo: 2bs of barley to Wm Bawd	09.00.00
	146.15.02

[*B11 February 1667*]

18th recd of Wm Tooke junior for 6 loads of brakes	00.08.00
March 1st sold to Mr Bawd 38 coo. barley	11.08.00
9th sold porke for	00.17.00

22nd sold my 30 steeres which I bought at St Fayths fayre to
   Thomas Thurston of Yarmouth he is to draw them at or before
   May Day next

rec firstly in part	81.00.00
April 9th 1667 sold to Mr Bawd 21 coombs barley for	06.00.00
13th sold to Mr Bawd 21 coombs barley	05.19.00

May 10 sold to Thomas Godbold my tenn bullocks bought at

St Fayths fayre 6th Oct. last	48.00.00
Sold to Wm Bawd 41 coombs of barley at 5s 8d per coomb	11.12.04
Sold more to him 28 coombs barley at 6s per coomb	08.08.00
16th sold 2 hoggs for	02.01.00
22nd sold 2 bushels of mixling	00.04.08

GLOSSARY

J.Bristow, *The Local Historian's Glossary and Vade Mecum* (Nottingham 1997)
The Shorter Oxford English Dictionary (1978 reissue)
D.C.Yaxley, *A Researcher's Glossary of Words found in Historical Documents of East Anglia* (Larks Press, Guist, Norfolk, 2003)

brakes bracken
bs bushels. A bushel was a measure of capacity of eight gallons, but locally variable
chaldir, chaldron measure of capacity of 32 bushels
co., coo. coomb, measure of capacity of four bushels
crone old ewe
drawing cleaning ditches
fann, fanne shallow basket for winnowing grain by tossing in a breeze
fishouse a smokehouse or a fishing station ?
fitches vetches
fleaing flaying, skinning
flighty husky
furs, furrs furze
hogg ewes yearling ewes
idem (Latin) the same
King's Bench, Marshalsea and Maimed Soldiers taxes levied under Elizabethan Acts for the relief of prisoners and for pensions for soldiers and mariners injured in war
knacker ropemaker
largesse gift money demanded by harvest workers
last measure of capacity. Aldrich calculated 20 coomb per last of rye (see p. 240)
layre, layer live hedging material, rooted slips
li pound in weight, from Latin *libra*
mixlin mixed grain, often wheat and rye
mort sheepskins pelts of dead sheep
nonesuch a species of lucerne grown as fodder
ofts perhaps orts, refuse of cattle fodder
pec, peck a peck, quarter of a bushel
per mensem (Latin) per month
planchering flooring, laying a wooden floor
quartridge wage paid quarterly
refuse lambs worthless lambs
rixyes (from context) weakly or perhaps malformed lambs

scuppet, skippett narrow shovel with turned-up edges used for corn

shotts young weaned pigs

skepp large, deep basket

steeres bullocks

stotts draught horses

syde oats perhaps poor-quality oats

toto (Latin) in all

weather lambs wethers, gelded male lambs

winterstalls over-wintering cattle

Index

Persons referred to by surname only are placed at the beginning of their section.

Abbot, George, archbishop 140
accounting system 3–5, 11
Acton, George 64
Agas, Edward, vicar 11, 13, Loy 30, 34, 38, 41, 45, 49–51, 53, 57, 61, 63, 67, 70, 72, 75, 78, 82, 88, 93, 98, 103, 109, 115, 121, 127, Robert 88, 94, 98, 104, 109, 115, 121, 127, 133, 138, 142, 148–53, 158, 162, 165, 167, Stephen 10, 127, 130, 132, 135, 138, 142, 148, 150, 153, 155, 158, 160, 164–5, Thomas 10–11, 23, 33–4, 37, 40, 45, 49, 69, 70, 86
agriculture, innovation 206–8, wages 207, yield 207
aldercarr 207
Aldrich, John *passim* 205–42, Sister 214, 241, Thomas 237
alehouses and inns 17, 31
ale tasters 12
Allen, Allaine, Father 62, Mother 65, Thomas 75, 79, 82, 89, 94, 99, 104, 110, 116, 121, 128, 133, 138
almshouses 22, 158, 161–2
Amyas, Thomas 29
Andrewes 42–3, 59
Appleton, John 72, 91–2, 117, 122–3, 136
Appleyard, Henry 39
apprentices *see* carpenters; poor
archery butts 23, 25, 69, 95
armaments, parish 25–6, 39, 45, 51, 55, 58–9, 62, 69, 73, 80, 84, 95–6, 107, 113–14, 119, 125–6, 130–1, 134, 140, 146, 149, 152, 156, 160, 163
Armes, Thomas 59
Arminghall, Norf. 236
arson 21
Arundel, Thomas, Earl of, 163
Ashemor, Asheman, 62, 90
Ashwellthorpe, Norf. 6
asses 237–8
Austen, Thomas 32
Aylsham, Norf. 117, 119

Babster, Mr 239
Bacon, Nathaniel 8
Bale, Robert 54, 86, Thomas 86
Ballyston, John 8
Banks, Samuel 212, 214–15, 219–20, 223, 235–6, Thomas 211–36
Barford, Richard 229–30, 232, 234
Barker 54–5, 58, Henry 55, William 240
Barten, Berten, Mary 217–19
Barnard, Edmund 70, 86, John 46
Basey, Roger 224
bath, medicinal 16, 101
Bawd 227–8, Mr 240–2, William 229–36, 241–2
Baxter, Mr 9, 70, Nicholas 35, 39, Robert 167
Beart, Berte, Katherine 72, Mother 75, 79, Widow 110, 116, 121, 128, William 32
Bedingfield, Mr 47
Bee, Ralph 219
Bell, Thomas 50

Benton 59
Besthorpe, Norf. 6, 156
Bettes 55, 119, 124,164, Adam 155,
    James 51, Robert 30–1, 35–6, 38,
    62, 110, 116, 121, 128, 133,
    137–9, 141, 143, William 41, 145
Bird, Burd, John 52, 56, 67, 71, 74,
    78, 81
bishop *see* Norwich
Blackborne, Henry 86, Mr 107, 111,
    118, 125, 140
Blake, Henry 55
Blickling, Norf. 6–7, 149; Hall 1
blind preacher 140
Blodde, Bartylmew 80
Blys, Thomas 35
books purchased 126, 135, 169
Booth, Bothe 65, 144, Bartylmew 69,
    141, Simon 53
Bootie, Botye, Benet 50, John 78, 81,
    87, 93, 102
Borell, Robert 54
bounds, parish *see* Rogationtide
brakes (bracken) 239, 241–2
Breese, Agnes 75, Widow 133, 139,
    143
Brereton, Peter 239
brewing industry 208
brick and tile 19, 43, 80, 90–1, 95,
    100–1, 106–7, 118, 123–4, 130,
    134–5
brick kiln, brickmaking 19, 90, 123,
    212, 216
bridges 22–4, repair 23–4, 50, 58, 90,
    146, 152, 156, 164, suits
    concerning 80, 100, 140, 149
Briggs, Joan 215, 221, 234
Brown, Broune 62, 77, 107,
    Christopher 73, 75, 101, 111,
    113, 117, 124–5, 134, 144–5,
    John 223–5, 227, Samuel 224,
    226, 229, 231, 238, Thomas 51,
    70, 91

Browne schoolmaster 149
Buck 80, Edmund 78, 82, 88, 93, 98,
    103 109, 115, 120, 127, 132,
    138, 141, Mr 65
Buckenham, New, Norf. 6
Buckenham 51, 76, Widow 69–70,
    73, William 32, 145
Budd 216, Thomas 212–14, 227,
    William 227
building and repair 6, 18–21, 31–3,
    42–4, 50–1, 53–4, 65, 69–70, 73,
    86, 90–1, 100–1, 106, 110–13,
    118–19, 123–5, 130–1, 135,
    144–6, 166–7
Bullocke, Joseph 51
bullocks 211, 220, 227, 229, 238–40,
    242, wintering 215, 229, 238
Bunn 112, John 65, Richard 135–6,
    142, 152, 162, 165
Burdye, John 60, 63
Burley, Katherine 85–6
Burrell, Stephen 84, William 98, 104,
    110, 116, 121, 128, 133, 138,
    143, 148–9, 151, 154–5, 159,
    162, 166
Bushe 67, 72, 75, 79, 82, 85–6, John
    30, 35, 38, 41, 45, 49, 51, 53, 57,
    61, 64, Thomas 45, 49, 53, 56
Bysshop, Thomas 152
Bythel, Mr 241

Caddywold, Cadaworld, 163, 165–6,
    John 154, 158, 164, Richard
    135, 144, 148, 150, 153, 155,
    158–9, 161–2
Caistor, Norf. 241
Cambridge, Corpus Christi College
    12, 14, Trinity College 84,
    University 119. Corpus Christi
    see also preachers
Canterbury, archbishop 24, 51, 140,
    159–60. *See also* Parker,
    Matthew

'Carlton', perhaps East Carleton, Norf. 241

Carleton Rode, Norf. 25

Carpenters' Company or guild, apprenticeship 183, 186–7, 192, 194, 199–200, byelaws 179, decline 187–8, duties and privileges 181–3, 185–6, 189–91, 201, history and organisation 179–85, 191, 196–8, officers 181–2, 185, oaths 183–4, penalties 182, 185, 189–91, 203–4, quality control by 180, 182–5, 190–2, 196, 199, 202, restrictive practices 183, 186, 192, 196, 199, 201, training 183, 185, working practices 187

Carre, John 216, 219, 235–6, Robert 39, 112, 146, Thomas 52, 56, Widow 54

Carver 129, Roger 146

Caryngton, Anthony, vicar 35, 38, 41

Castle Rising, Norf. 6

Castleton, John 34, 37, 40, 44, 48, 69, Mr 66, schoolmaster 118

Catchpoll 113, 134, 140,145

cattle 2, 207–8, 239, sold as 'futures' 207–8. *See also* bullocks; steers. Drovers *see* Cumberland; Ireland; Scotland

Cecil, Robert, Earl of Salisbury 149

cereals 2, barley 208, 212–13, 221–2, 224–5, 228–9, 231–42; mixtlin 208, 238, 241–2; oats 208, 212, 214, 223–4, 232, 238–9; rye 208, 224–5, 230–1, 234, 236–8, 240; wheat 208, 212–13, 223, 230, 232, 236–7, 240–1

Chamberlaine 16, 47, Goodwife 235, John 230, Joseph 230–5, William 133, 137–8, 141, 143, 147

Churchman 212

Clare, Clere, John, glazier 14, 20, 44, 46, 49–50, 53, 55, 57, 59, 61–2, 64–5, 68, 70, 72–3, 75–7, 79–80, 82, 84, 89–90, 94–5, 98–9, 104–5, 110, 112, 116, 118, 121–2, 125–6, 128–30, 133–4, 138–40, 143–4

Clarke, 65, 99–100, Richard 118–19, William 32, 42–3, 118–19

Clayborne 14, 59, 113, 125

claypits 38 and *passim* as an abuttal

Clere, Sir Edward 33, 47, 149, family 6, Lady 160, Mr 51

clover 206, 224, 235

coal purchase 224, 227

Cobbe, 62, George 216–17, Goodwife 217–18

Cocke, Coke, Cooke 146, Richard 212–13, 224, 231, Thomas 238, Widow 99, 104, 110, 116, 121, 128, 133, 138, 143, 154, 158, 161, 165, William 30, 35, 38, 41, 46, 49, 53, 57, 61, 64, 68, 72, 75, 79, 82, 89, 94

Cockrell, George 220–9, Thomas 241

Coddenham, William 239

Coke, Sir Edward (*see* Cooke)

Cole, John 152–3, 158, 162, 165, Richard 212, 216, 218, 223, 227, Thomas 56, 61, 64, 67–8, 71, 74, 78, 82, 83, 93, 98, 103–4, 109, 115, 120, 127, 132, 138, 142, 148, 150

Colman, Coleman, Edward 86, 102, James 9, Robert 36, 65, 70, 76–7, 80, 90–1, William 167

Combes, Thomas 32

Conley 230, Richard 213

constables, chief 25, parish 16, 23, 25–6, 55, 95, 164

Cooke, Mr, lawyer (Sir Edward Coke) 36

Cooke *see* Cocke

Coolye, Richard 33

Cooper, Cowper 112–13, John 9,
   Thomas 9
Corbald, Thomas 240
Corball, Thomas, schoolmaster 46, 50
Cornwell, Cornell, Robert 218–19,
   Thomas 75
Cossey 130, Arthur 31
Cotton, Jane 55, 57, 68, 72, 75, 79,
   83, 89, 94, 99, 104, 116, 121,
   128, John 211–13, 216–36,
   George 216, Richard 31, 35, 38,
   42, 46, 49, William 219
Crane, Edward 29, 33, 35, 37, 39–40,
   44, 48, 52, 55, 60–1, 63, 66,
   Goodwife 77, Robert 68, 70, 83,
   106, 112, 125, 151, 155, 163,
   Thomas 56, 61–2, 64
Cringleford, Norf. 239, bridge 214
Crismas, Robert 48, 52, 56, 63, 66,
   71,74
Cromewell, Mr, preacher 76
Crosse 80, Em 82, 89, 94, 99, 104,
   110, 116, 121, 128, Widow 75,
   143
Crownthorpe ('Crownshaugh'), Norf.
   35, 41, 57, 67, 78, 154, 159
Cudworth, Mr, schoolmaster 164
Cullender, Anthony 119, 125, 133
Cullyer 221, Edmund 29, 34, 37, 40,
   44, 48, 52, 55, 58, 60, 62–3, 66,
   68, 71, 73–4, 76–7, 79, 81, 83,
   Gregory 145, 152, Philip 8, 10,
   11, 20–1, 24, 61, 86–7, 122, 154,
   158, 161–3, Robert 58–9, 86,
   99, 101, 104, 116, 122, 128, 154,
   159, 163, 166, William 70, 117
Cumberland, cattle from 215
Cusyng, Francis 49

d'Albini family 6
Danny, John 54
Davy, Henry 20, 32
Daynes, William 5, 30, 33, 35, 38–9,
   41–2, 45, 49, 52, 57, 61, 64,
   67–8
Daynne, Francis 89
Debney, Mr 55
Denny, Mathew 30
Dey 239, John 129, 134, 140, Robert
   87, Stephen 123, 125, 134,
   146–7
Dickerson, Nicholas 52, 55, 60, 62,
   66, 71, 73–4, 77, 81, 84, 86–7,
   William 35
Dillan, Dilham 146, 154, Richard 79,
   86, 133, 138, 141, 143, 148, 151,
   159, 162, 165
disease and treatment 36, 65, 70, 160.
   See also bath; epidemic; epilepsy;
   plague
Diss, Norf. 59
ditch making 234
Dixon 135, Robert 117, 129–30
Dorant, John 32, 35
Dowe 59, 62, 64–5, 68, 72, 75
Downyng, Randolf 38, 41, 45, 49, 53,
   57, 61, 64, 67–8, 72, 75, 79, 82,
   89, 94, 98, 104, 109, 116, 121,
   128, 133, 138
Dowsing 64, 138–9, 143
drovers *see* cattle
Drury family 6
Duffylde, Mr 51
Dunn, Margaret 91, 107
Durrant 65, John 130
Dye, Stephen 145
Dymer, Thomas 166
Dynn, John 123

Earle, Arthur 11, 22, 88, 93, 97, 103,
   109, 115, 120, 127, 132, 138,
   142, 147–8, 150, 153, 156,
   158–9, 161–2, 164–5
Easton, Nicholas, schoolmaster 119,
   122, 124–6, 128, 131, 134–6,
   140–1, 145–6

Eaton, Norf. 205–6, church repair 223, Hall, Hall Farm 206, 217, landscape 206–7, parish clerk 213, Pound Meadows 215, 218, 225, 236, rates and taxes 213–14, 222, 226–7, 231, 233–4, 243, West Field 206, 215, 217, 225, 234

Ebbes, William, mason 13, 32–3

Edwardes 143, 152, William 36, 98, 104, 109, 115, 121, 127, 133

Elder, Richard, 30, 39

enclosure 206, 224

Englyshe *see* Inglishe

epidemic 228. *See also* plague

epilepsy 6, 155

fairs, cattle *see* Harleston; Horsham; Sprowston

farming regions and practices 2, 205–8

Farrar 112, 135

Farrowe, Richard 91

Feakes 218, Henry 216–17, 224, 228–9

Fedymont 31, 59, 62, 72, 75, 79, 82, 89, Edmund 30, 37–8, 41, 46, 53, 57, 61, 64, 68

Fenn, Goodwife 217–18

Ferme, Farme, John 22–3, 96, Mother 38, 49, Widow 31, 35, 41, 46, 54, 57, 61

firewood 15, 32, 50, 58, 70, 79, 91–2, 111, 117, 134, 136, 161. *See also* poor

Firmurie, usher 160

fish-house 214, 220

Fitling, Ralph 44, 73, 129, 131, 134, 136, 140

flax 208

Flemyng, Thomas 58

Fletcher, Laurence 88, 93, 102–3, 109, 115, 120, 127, 132, 138, 142, 148, 151, 154, 159, 163, 166

flint, flintsone 19, gathering 146, digging 150

Flowerdew, Anne 148, 150, Agnes 71, 74, 77–8, 81, 85, 87, 93, 97, 103, 108, 111, 114, 120, 127, 132, 137, 142, John 9, 52, 56, 60–1, 63, 66

foldcourse 206

food and drink 5–6, 14, 22, 26, 31–3, 36, 43–4, 46–7, 50, 58, 65, 70, 84, 95, 100, 105–6, 110, 112, 116, 122, 125, 127, 129–30, 134, 139–40, 149, 151–2, 155, 159–60, 163, 166–7, 227, 236, quality control 12

Foster 55, 65, 73, 118, John 9, Robert 43, 46, 58–9, 128, 136, 137, 139, 143, 147

Foulsham, Folesame 105, 124–5, 130, 136, 149, Alexander 6, 72, 75, 77, 79–80, 82, 85–6, 89–90, 94–5, 100–2, 104, 108–9, 112, 116–17, 121–2, 127–8, 133–5, 138–40, 143–4

Fox 11, 228, 232, 236, Christopher 30, 35, 38, 41, John 213, 218–19, 229, R. 213, Ralph 88, 93, 98, 103, 109, 115, 121, 127, 133, 138

Francis, John 16, 39, Robert 47

Frank, John 212–13, 216–18, 221

Freeman, Esau 59, 76, 83, 86, 90, 117, 127, 133, 138, 143, 148, 151, 154, 159, 162, 166, Mr 165, 123–4, 131, 135–6, 146

Frosdicke 68, Edmond 64

Frosten, Alice 29, 34, 37, 40, 44, 48, 52, 55, 58, 60, 62–3, 66, 68, 71, 73–4, 77, 79, 81, 83, 87, 89, 92, 94, 97, 99, 103, 105, 108, 110, 114, 116, 120, 125–6, 128, 132, 134, 137, 141, 144, 154

fruit trees 214

Fuller, Thomas 112

Funston, Mr 39, 47, 50–1, 54, 89,
    Thomas 24, 45, 48, 78, 81, 83,
    85–7

furniture making 19, 31, 36, 69,
    106–7, 112, 118, 124, 129, 146

furze cutting 216–18, 227, 229–31

Fynderne 117, 152

Garrarde 74, 105–6, 155, 164,
    Robert 51, 68, 72

Gary, Mr, schoolmaster 99, 105–7,
    111–13, 117

Gawdy, Thomas 25

Gay, Henry 24, 42, 86, 119, 122,
    125, John 68, 73–5, 78–9, 81,
    83, 89, 94, 99, Thomas 81

Gedge, Robert 236

Gedney, Agnes 31, 65, John 31, 36,
    46, 58, Widow 73, 76, 124–5,
    134, 144–5, 151

gelding 225

Gibbs 16, 65, 118, 129, Widow 133,
    William 142, 148, 150

Gipps, George 236–8

glazing 77, 126, agreement 14.
    Glaziers see Clare, John; Turnor,
    Henry

Goche, Henry 34, 37, 40, 45, 48

Godbold, Thomas 239, 241–2

Goddard, George 211–13, 216–35,
    240

Godfry 91, 102, Mr 51, Thomas 66,
    134

Goldsenye 100, 106

Goldyng 73, 117

Goodwin, Thomas, master mason 13,
    73

Goslinge, Margery 75, 83, 89, 94, 99,
    104

Gould 146, William 102, 108, 116,
    122, 128, 134, 139, 143

Green, Thomas 29, 34, 37, 40, 45,

48, 58, William 29, 34, 37, 40,
    44, 48, 52, 60, 62, 66, 71, 83,
    155, 158, 161, 165, 225, 240

Griggs, Mr 24, 32

guilds, guildhouse see Norwich,
    Carpenters' Company;
    Wymondham

Gyllyngforde, John 16, 47

Hadley, Handley, Charles 129, 140

Hall, Mrs 129

Hallywaye, Agnes 113

Hammond, Hamond 96, 101, 111,
    Edmund 89, George 128, 134,
    William 152

Hankins, Thomas 220

Harleston, 239, 241, cattle fair 207,
    211, 236, 238

Harman, Mr 154, 159, 162, 166

Harsnett, John, bishop 166

harvest 219, 228–9, largess 218, 243

Harvy, Peter 39, 44, 48

Haste, Thomas 52, 54, 60, 64, 68, 70

Hawes, Andrew 86, 96, John 102,
    William 146

hay 224, 251, haymaking 216–18,
    220, 227–8

Heard, John 211–14

hedge-planting ('layer') 206, 213, 223,
    233–4, 243

Hedgeman, Abraham 98, 103, 109,
    115, 121, 127

Helwys, William 195

hen rent 36, 65, 69, 73, 80, 83, 96,
    99, 113, 118, 125, 135, 146, 156

Herbert, John 154, 159

Herne, Mr 65

Hethersett, Norf. 9

Heveningham, Sir Arthur 47, 133

Heyward, Mr 167

highway repair 22–3

Hingham, Norf. 25, 145, 236

Hobart family 1, 7, Sir Henry 7, 21–2,

149, 163, 167, James 237–8, John 205–6

Hobbes 65, Robert 29, 34, 38, 41, 54, 53–4, 56, 58, 60, 62–3, 67, 73, 76, 79, 97, Thomas 56, 63, 67, 71, 74, 78, 82, 85–6, 88–9, 93–4, 97–8, 103, 109, 115, 120, 127, 132, 138, 142, 149, 151, 154, 159, 163, 166

hospitality *see* food and drink

Hopkins, Thomas 216–18, 222, 124–5

Horsenell, Mr 134

horses 208, 211, 213

Horsham St Faith cattle fair 207, 215, 220–1, 237–8, 240, 242

How, Thomas 213

Howell 80, 84, 90, 94, 99

Howse 80, Simon 90, 96, 101, Thomas 76

Hubbert, Edmund 236

Hunsdon, Henry, Lord 24

Hunson, preacher 50

Huntley, Margaret 68, 74, 85–6, Robert 99, 104, 110, 116, 121, 128, 133, 138, 143

hurdles 226

immigrant craftsmen 183, 186–7, 192–3, 199

Inglishe, Englyshe, 42, 111, 130–1, 145–6, Anthony 35, 38, 41, 45, 49, Edmund 30, John 18, 143, Richard 55, 60, 63, 71, 74, 78–9, 81, 83, 97, 103, Robert 81, 135

impounding 235

Ingram, John 222, 239–40

Intwood, Norf. 149

Ipswich 9

Ireland, cattle from 211, 214, 217, 221, 226

iron, use of in building 20, 31

Isbells 78, 82, Thomas 88, 93, 98

Jackson, Mother 136, Stephen 94, 98, 104

Jacob, Robert 146

Jafferye, Thomas 60

James I, coronation celebrations 26, 83–4

Jegon, John, bishop 91, 163

Jessopp, Ralph 25

Johnson, Simon 39

Johnsons, John 217

joiners 187

Jubbs, Mr 69, 119, Ralph 73, 77, 135

Justices of Peace 7, 15, 17, 25, 83, 167, Petty Sessions 83, Sessions 105, 149

Kecheham, Nicholas 80

Keene 113, Reynold 30, 35, 38, 41, 45, 49–50, 53, 57, 61, 64, 67, 72, 75, 79, 82, 89, 94, 98, 104, 109, 116, 121, 127, 133–4, 138, 143, 151

Kensey, John 30, 35, 38, 41, 45, 49, 69

Kerk, John 228–9, 235

Kett, Bartylmew 43, Henry 16, 53, 57, 61, 63, 67, 72, 75, 78, 82, 84–5, 88, 91, 93, 95, 98, 100, 102, 104–5, 109, 111, 115, 118–19, 121, 127, John 30, 32, 35, 38, 41, 45, 49, 53–5, 57, 61, 64, 67, 72, 75, 79, 82, 88, 91, 94, 149, Loye 65, Richard 153, 158, Robert 46–7, 51, 117, Stephen 130, 132, 142, 148–9, 164, Thomas 16, 62, 65, 129, William 29, 34, 36–7, 40, 45, 49

Kett *alias* Knight, Valentine 9

Ketteringham, Norf. 123

Key, Richard 237

Kimberley, Norf. 6

King 99, 136, David 167, John 117, Thomas 14–15, 56, 60, 63, Walter 54, 65

King's Lynn 119
Kirby, Norf. 236
Kitmer, Kytmey 106, 123, Elizabeth 65, John 59, 100
knacker (ropemaker) 212, 223
Knight see Kett
Knightes 14, 118, 129, 135, 140, 144, 146, Robert 112–13, 130
Knyvett family 6, Lady (Muriel) 96, 101, (Thomas the younger) 47, 50–1, Sir Thomas 8, 48

Lakenham, Norf. 236
law and order enforcement 25
Lawes, Edward 78, 81, 88
Lawrence, Habakkuk 30–1, 34, 38, 41, 47
lawsuits and legal matters 3–5, 23–4, 33, 36, 39, 47, 50–1, 58–9, 65, 69–70, 73, 80, 84, 100, 106, 111–12, 122, 131, 135, 140, 144–5, 149, 153, 156, 158, 167
lead supply 8–9, 20, 32, 36
leather searchers 12
Leech 58, 139, Elizabeth 54, 57, 64, 69, 72, 75, 79, 83, 89, 94, 99, 104 110, 116, 121, 128, Widow 143
Leesing, John 238, Robert 238
leet jurisdiction 3, 4, 7, 10, 12, 25, 149
Lemman, Lemonde 16, 89, 93, 160
Lenard, Joan 16, 39
Leverington, Thomas 9, 11, 31, 36, 39, 70, 86, 94, 99, 101, 104–5, 110, 116, 122, 128, Thomas junior, schoolmaster 84, 90, 95, 105
Lincoln 61, 118, 160, Robert 54, 57–8
Locke, John 152
Lombe, Thomas 211–13
London 77, bishop 36, craftsman 183, 186–7, Tower 51

Lovell, Mr 39
Low, Thomas 237, William 237–8
Lowe bookseller 179
Luce, William 29, 34, 37, 40, 44, 48
Lullman, Captain 240
Lynes, Robert 155

Machyn 160, John 149, 163–4, 166–7
Male, Richard 17, 151, 166
malt 220, 224
Mann, Mane, Edmund 233, Mathew 239, William 228
Mapes, William 133, 138
Marshall 64, Robert 36, 47, 50
Martyn 112, Widow 146
masons see Ebbes; Goodwin
Mayde, Mayden 111, Widow 152
Mayere, Marion 31, Widow 41, 46
Mayes, Martha 36, Widow 35, 38
Mayhew, Francis 154, 158, 161, 164, George 68, 71, 74, 77, 79, 81,83, 87, 89, 92,94, 97, 99, 103, 105, 108, 110, 114, 116, 120, 125–6, 128, 132, 134, 137, 139, 141, 146, Robert 34, 37, 40, 44, 48, 52, 55, 58, 60, 62–3, 66, 73
Mayston 111,118, 122–3, 134
meadows 206, 215, 218, 227, partable 153, 148, 150, 158, 162
Meane, Henry 88, 93, 98, 104, 109, 115, 127, 138
Mendham, Suff. 237–8
Meere, Richard 237
Methwold, Norf. 2
Middleton, John 142, 148, 150–1, 153, 158, 160, 162, 164–5
Mileham, Mr 237
Miles, Edmund 239
Milesom, Elizabeth 216–18
militia 25–6, 39, 51, 55, 58, 69, 80, 95–6, 107, 114, 119, 125, 130–1, 134, 140, 149, 152, 156, 164, 167

mill 67, 74–5, hill 162, 165, new 67, 74, pool 57, 75, 82, 88, 94, 116, 121, 127, 133, 138, wind 34, 153, 159

Mitchell, John 9

Moore, Christian 68, 72, 75, 82, 85–6, 89, 94, 99, 104, 110, 116, 121, 128, 147, Francis 102, John 8, 25, 70, 83–4, 86, 127, 132, 137, 142, 148, 150, 153, 158, 162, 165, 236, Robert 80, 83, Thomas 153, 158, 160, 162, 168

Motley, Mother 125

Murrell, Humphrey 153, 158, 162, Thomas 236

musters see militia

Neave, Neve, 59, 154, Francis 74, 76–7, 79, 81, 83, 87, 89, 92, 94, 97, 99, 103, 105, 108, 110, 114, 116, 120, 125–6, 128, 132, 134, 137, 139, 141, 144, Peter 29, 34, 37, 40, 44, 48, 52, 55, 58, 60, 63–4, 66, 68, 71, 74, 77, 79, 81, 83, 87, 89, 92, 94, 97, 99, 103, 105, 108, 110, 114, 116, 120, 126, 128, 132, 134, 137, 139, 141, 144, 154

Nelyng 59, 118

Nevell 105, 152, John 51, 55, Stephen 58, 62

Nixon 32–3, Thomas 55, 63, 68, 71, 73–4, 76–7, 79, 81, 83, 87, 89, 93–4, 97, 99, 103, 105, 108, 110, 114, 116, 120, 126, 128, 132, 134, 137, 139, 141,144

nonsuch 208, 235, 243

Norrys, Dr 84, 159

Norton 131, George 39, 61, 64, 67, 72, 75, 78, 82, 88, 93, 98, 104, 109, 115, 121, 127, 133, 135–6, 138, 143, 148–9, 151–3, 155, 159, 162, 165, Henry 30, 33–4,

38, 41, 45, 49, 53, 57, William 59

Norwich 20, 32–3, 36, 50, 59, 69, 100, 149, 154, 159, 206, 221, 238; Assembly and Council 118, 195; bishop 58–9, 166, jurisdiction 24, 31, 39, 100, 156, 159, 163, 166, visitation 91; bishops see also Jegon, Overall, Redman; Blackfriars (New) Hall 18, 189; Cathedral 205–6, 238; disease among poor 228; Duke's Palace 225; economy 228; freemen 181, 183–4, 186, 190, 197, 200; guild regulation 180, 184–7; Guildhall 195; lazar houses 16, 36, 47, 155; Magdalen Gates 155; St Benet's Gates 36; St Giles parish 205; St Stephen's Gates 47. Norwich see also Carpenter's Company

Olyett 118, 125, 140, Daniel 131, 135–6

Osborne 136, John 151, Richard 154, 159, 161–2, 165,

Otes, Mr (Samuel Oates), preacher 46

Overall, John, bishop 14, 166

overseers of poor 15

Ovington, Widow 144, William 31, 46, 52, 56, 60, 63, 66, 71, 74, 78, 81, 89, 93, 97, 103, 108, 111, 120, 127, 132, 137–8, 141–2, 148, 150, 160

Page 113, Nicholas 154, 158, 161, 164

Pagrave, Palgrave, Sir Austin 138, 143, John 46, 50, 65, 69,

Palmer, John 20, 31–3, 39

Parke, Edward 25

Parker, Matthew, archbishop 11–12, scholarship 14

Payne, William 52, 56, 60, 63, 67, 71, 74, 78, 81, 83, 85, 88, 93, 97, 103, 109, 115, 120, 123, 127, 132, 135–6, 138, 142, 148, 150, 153, 158, 162, 165

Payton, Sir John 47

Peacham, Henry, schoolmaster 163

peas 208, 214, 223, 231, 237

Peirson, Widow 135

Pells, Anne 113

Pert, Mark 12

Pettus 237

pewter, town 6, 30, 35, 38, 41, 45, 49, 53, 57, 67, 72, 174, 177, stamp 6, 59

Pightlin 239, Elizabeth 229, Jane 217–20, 222, 232, John 222, 224, 230, 234, Richard 211–14, 216, 221–2, 224, 227, 230, 232, 234

pigs 212, 214–15, 225, 227–8, 232, 235–42, pork 242

Pile Anthony 129

Pitcher, Peter 30, 34, 41, 45, 49

plague 13, 16, 26, 84–5, 91

planned towns 6

Playford, Mr 133, 139, 143, 148–9, 151–2

Pleasance, Mrs 146

Plomer, Plummer, Francis 23, 97, 103, 107–8, 112, 114, 119–20, 126, 132, 136–7, 140–1, 145, 147–8, 150–1, 161, Thomas 104, 143, 145–6, 148, 151–2

ploughs 213, 225, 232

Plowman, Arthur 25

Poker, Thomas 49, 53

Poll, John 35

poor 1, 12, 15–18, 21, 144, 149, 189, 204; accouchement 16, 167; apprentices and servants 16, 117–18, 129, 144–6, 160; burial 16, 84, 136, 141, 144–6, 152, 159; children 16, 31, 36, 39, 47, 50–1, 54, 58–9, 62, 65, 69–70, 73, 76, 80, 84, 90, 94, 99–100, 107, 134, 140, 146, 156, 159; clothing 16, 70, 80, 90–1, 117, 125, 129, 144–6, 160; disease and treatment 16, 65, 70, 85, 101,135, 141, 147, 155, 160, 228; relief 15, 17, 70; overseers 15; rent respited 4, 31, 35, 42, 46, 54, 57–8, 61–2, 68, 72–3, 76, 79, 83, 87, 98–90, 94, 99, 116, 128, 144, 150, 154, 159; subsidised firewood 4, 15, 95–6, 100–1, 107–8, 113–14, 119, 122, 131, 141, 147; starvation 17; work 15, 17, 150

Porter 117, 123–4, Robert 29, 122

Pratt, William 44, 46

preachers 31, 112; blind 140. See also Cromewell, Hunson, Otes, Scottowe, Woodes, Rogationtide

Prethero, Dr 24, 31

pumps 18, 156,163

Pyttes, Mr 101

Queyntrell 146,155, Francis 43, 50, 59, 111–13, 118, 124, 130, 134, 136, John 39, 42–4, 51, 76–7, 152, Thomas 46, 49, 53–4, Walter 47, Widow 139, 143, William 65

Randoll 147, William 137, 143, 163

rates and taxes 36, 55, 58, 65, 69–70, 72–3. See also Eaton

Raven, John 87

Rawling, Goodman 95, John 117, Richard 30, 34, 37, 40, 47–8, 52, 56, 58, 60, 63, 65–6, 71, 74, 78, 81, 85–7, 93, 97, 102–3, 108, 114, 120, 126, 132, 138, 143, Robert 44, 109, 115, 120, 127, 137, 142, 148, 150–1, 154, 159, 161–3, 165–6

Reade, Bartylmew 31, 39
Reder, Robert 42
Redman, William, bishop 58–9
Rednalle, William 33
refugees *see* immigrant
Renny, Reyney, Matthew 228–34,
    Thomas 229
Reynolds, John 11, 25, 75, 78, 80,
    85–8, 91, 97–8, 100, 102, 104–5,
    108, 114–15, 120–1, 126–7,
    131–2, 137, 141–2, 147–8,
    Richard 122–3
Richardson, Serjeant 20, 140, 151
Ringland, Norf. 238
Ringwood, Margaret 52, 54–6, 60,
    63, 66, 71, 73, Robert 29, 34,
    37, 40, 42, 44, 47–8
river and ditch clearance 212, 214,
    220, 222–6, 233, 236
Rix, Michael 111
Robins, Mr 240
Robinson, George 211–20, 222–36
Rogationtide ('Gan Monday') proces-
    sion and sermon 14, 31, 36, 46,
    50, 65, 70, 73, 76, 80, 83, 90,
    95, 100, 117, 124, 129, 134, 140,
    145–6, 149, 151, 155, 160, 163,
    167, 171
ropemaker *see* knacker
Rose, Richard 236–7
Rowse, William 86, 130, 153, 159,
    162, 165
royal arms 6, 19, 113
Rudland, John 70, 87, Thomas 46
Russells 62, 65, 73, 90, 107, Richard
    91, 105
Rydnall, Edward 146
Rye, Walter 179

Sadler 146, Robert 139, 143
St Faith's *see* Horsham
St Thomas Becket 6, 9, chapel 18, 21,
    30, guild 9

Salters, Mr 227
sawpit 19, 152, 177
Sayer 220, 223, John 30, 34, 38, 41,
    45, 49, 141
Schollar, Mr 238, 240
Scotland, cattle from 207, 211, 237–8
Scottowe, (Miles), preacher 140
Seaberne, Sebborne, Thomas 53,
    103, 109, 115, 121, 127
sermon 14. *See also* preachers
Setherton, Mr 47
sheep 2, 149, 208, 211, 215–16,
    220–1, 226–7, 229, 236–9, 241,
    243–4, skins 239, 241, shearing
    214–16, 227, shepherd 216–17,
    222, 227, 229, 241
Shene, Mr 91, 96
Shepperd, John 87
sheriff's tourn 149
Shoo, John 159
shops 22, town 18, 28, 30–1, 35, 38,
    40–1, 45, 49–51, 53, 57, 61, 64,
    67, 72, 75, 82, 89, 94, 98, 109,
    111, 121, 127–8, 133, 139, 141,
    143–6, 148, 151–2, 154, pentice
    96, windows 20, 145
Shore, John 156
Shotesham, Norf. 236
Skypp, Mr 91–3, 98, 104, 109, 115,
    121, 127, 133, 138, 143, 148,
    151, 154, 159, 162, 166
Smiler, Mr 239
Smyth, Christian 16, 57, 68, 72, 89,
    94, 99, 101, 104, 110, 116, 121,
    128, 133, 138, 143, John 35, 38,
    41, 46, 54, 56, 61, Thomas 35,
    38, 41, 45, 52, 56, 60, 63–4, 66,
    69, 71, 74, 78, 106, Widow 54,
    61, 64, 75; Smyth *alias* Brewer,
    Alice 68, 72, 79, 89, 94, 99, 104,
    110, 116, 121, 128. *See also*
    Brewer
Soame, Christopher 189

Sparham, William 29, 31, 34, 37, 40, 45, 48, 52, 56, 60, 63–4, 67, 71
sparrow catcher 107, 111, 113, 117–18, 122, 124–5
Spendlove Henry 53, 57, 61, 64, 72, 75, 78, 80, 82, 88, 93, 98, 104, 109, 115, 127
Spinke 80–1, Thomas 64, 87
Sporle, Thomas 16, 36
Sprowston, Norf. cattle fair 206, 214, 217, 238, 240–1
Stafforde, Peter 84
Starling, Thomas 145
steers 236, 239–41, Cumberland 215, 226, 238, Irish 217, 226, Scottish 237
Stewarde, Jeffery 29, 51
Stocton, Nicholas 35, William 54
Stookes, Mr 50
Stubbes, Thomas 32–3, 36
Sturman 73, 125, Jeffery 53, 56, 61, 63, 67, 72, 75, 77
Stygell, Charles 219
suicide 25
Sunday working 201
swanhook 212
Swayne, John 77, 79, 82, 85–6, 89, 94, 99, 104, 110, 116, 121, 128, Lawrence 112, Widow 66, 75, 133, 138, 143, 147, 164
Symondes, Joan 30, 35, 38, 41, John 34, 37, 54, 60–1, 63, 67, 79, 81–3, 86, 88, 106, 110, 120, 132, 138, 142, 150, 153, 158, John senior 30, 38, 41, 45, 49, 53, 57, 72, 75, 83, 89, 93–4, 98, 104, 127, 162, 165, John junior 29, 33, 37, 40, 44–5, 48, 52, 56, 71, 74, 78, 88, 93, 97, 102–3, John son of John junior 52, Robert 31, 39, 46, 64

Talbot, Mr 43, 76, Mrs 65, 76, Dr

Thomas 30, 35, 38, 41, 45, 49–50, 53–4, 57–8, 61–2, 64, 67–8, 72–3, 76, 79, 82–3, 88–9, 94, 98–9, 104–5, 109–10, 115–16, 121, 126–8, 133–4, 138–9, 143–4, 154–5, 158–9, 161, 163–5, 169
Taylor, George, schoolmaster 12, John 30
thatcher, thatching, 18, 37, 59, 69, 80, 84, 91, 100, 105, 107, 118, 131, 135–6, 140, 152, 229–31, reed 6, 18–20, 42, 119, 123, 125, 129–30
Thorne 80, 107, John 146, 163
Thornton, Mr 30, 41, 45, 53, 101, 148, 151, 154, 159, 163, 166, Robert 35, 38, 49, 57, 64, 67, 72, 75, 79, 82, 88, 93, 98, 104, 109, 115, 121, 127, 133, 138, 143
Thowelldell, Widow 117
threshing 213, 221–5, 230–5
Thurston 129, Thomas 242, William 30
Tiffey, River 2
timber, purchase 194, preparation 19, 21, 136, 152, 176–7, sale monopoly 183, 193, 200. *See also* woodland
timber-framing 19, assemblage 183, 193, 203
tobacco 230
Toly, Tooly 124, Elizabeth 57, Mother 64, Robert 58, 68, 72, 75, 80, 82, 84, 89–90, 94, 98–100, 110, 116 121, 128, 133, 138, 141, 143–4, Widow 20, 61, 99, 104, 107, 110–11, 116, 119, 122, 124, 128, 131, 133, 135–7, 139, 149, 151, 154, 159, 163, 166
Tooke, Alderman 212, William 240, 242

Towneley, John 179
Townesende, Mr 39
trenchers 113
Trowse, Norf. 239
Tungood, Tungwood, Robert 151, 154, 159, 162, 166
Turner 59, 211, Edmund 221, Edward 214–15, 220, Henry 68, 70, 72–3, 75, 77, Mr 239
turnip cultivation 206–7, 211, 214–15, 217–18, 234–5, 239, 241
Tyrrell, Terell, Thomas 47–8, 50–1

Ubanke, Bartholomew 91

Venyour, Vyniord 61, John 30, 34, 38, 41, 45, 56, 61, 67, 71, 75, 78, 85, Mr 63, 82
vetches 223
Vyncente, John 100

Waddesworth, Mr 212
Wade 90–1, 100–1, 113, 124, 131, 135, Henry 19, 95–6, 106–7, 117, 130, Stephen 30
Waight, Richard 236
Ward, Mr 241
Watts 238, Peter 240, William 239–40
Waxham, Norf. 23
weeding 216, 226
weights and measures 42, 46, 59, 65, 155
Weld, Mr 76, Thomas 8, 12, 24, 65, 76, 80, 86, 90, 95–6, 100, 106, 111, 131, 140, 144
Wells, John 100, Mr 76, 91, 95, 117, Simon, schoolmaster and vicar, 50, 58, 62, 65, 69, 77, 84, Thomas 91, 100, William 16, 60
wells 18, 36, 39, 65, 69–70, 85, 95, 99–101, 130, 134, 156

Wetherley 84, 90, 114, Richard 95, Robert 128, 133
Whelpsdale 129, Nicholas 100
wherries 225
White, Mother 144
Whitle, John 64
Wicklewood, Norf. 138, 143
Wild, Mr 237
Williams, Arthur 53, 57, 59, 64, 67–8, 71–3, 75, 79, 82, 86, 88, 94, 98, 104–5, 109, 116, 121, 127, 133, 138, 143, Mr 61–2, 64, 117
windows, repair agreement 14. See also Clare, John
Winter, William 216, 218, 224, 234
Wiseman, Agnes 29, 33, 44, 48, 52, 55, 58, 60–3, 66, 68, 71, 73, Charles 123, Mr 136, Robert 30, 34, 38, 41, 45, 49, 53, 56, 63, 67, 69, 72, 75–6, 78, 82, 85, 88, 93, 98, 109, 115, 120, 127, 133, 138, 142, 148, 150–1, Stephen 11, 23, 70, 87, 97, 102–3, 106, 108, 114, 127, 132, 137, 142, 148, 150, 153, 158, 162, 165
Wodehouse family 6, Lord John 1
Woodcock, John 111, Thomas 30, 34–5, 38, 41, 45, 49, 53, 57, 61, 72, 75, 78, 82, 85–6, 93, 98, 104, 109, 115, 121, 127, 133, 138, 143, 148, 151, 154, 159
wood turners 147
Woodes preacher 246
Woodfall, John, vicar 50
Woodhouse, Sir Henry 23, 70
woodland, management and clearance 2, 15, 75, 91, 125, 135–6, 213, 223–5, 233, 235, nursery 207. See also firewood; timber
Woods, Goodwife 216–18, Thomas 216–20
wool 2, 236, 239, 241–2
Wyllis 145, John 92

Wymondham *Minor place-names are included selectively.*

abbey church 6–10, 13, 15, 92, 129, 140, 159; bells 9, 13, 46, 117, 166, casting 102, 114, ringing 15, 135, 146; bier 14, 140; burials 31, 76; churchyard 20, 42, 139, 164; communion table 146; lectern 14, 118; organs 14, 113; porch 92, 96; repair 1, 9, 13, 18, 20, 31–2, 43, 69, 73, 76–7, 80, 91, 96, 100, 113, 122, 129–30, 140, 160, of windows 14, 44, 46, 53; sextons 14–15; vestry 140

accountants *see* collectors

Bartlett's bridge 23, 140

Beast bridge 44

bridewell 7, 17, 26, 30, 161, 165

bridge repair 23–4, 50, 58, 146, 152, 164

Browick 10, 25, 86–7

Cavick House 65

Chapelgate 25, 86

chapels, St Thomas Becket 6, 9, 21, 30, 174, Westwade 56, 58, 60, 63, 65–6, 81, 87, 149

church *see* abbey

churchwardens 8–10, 12–13, 15, 24, 35, 38–9, 46, 69, 76–7, 80, 105, 117, 155, 164, 167

collectors 3–5, 15, 102, 170, malpractices 10–11, 22, 147, 161

cuckstool 18, 25, 124–5, 134, 145

Damgate 25, 86, bridge 23, 156, 164

Downham 2, 25, 45, 82, 117, 132, 138, 148, 151, 153

Endless way 139,143

Fairland 35, 38, 41

fire and aftermath 3, 6–7, 13, 18, 21–2, 26, 147–8, 151, 154–6, 158, 161–2; fire buckets ('tanks') 84, 109, 164

gameplace 17, 30, 35, 38, 41, 45, 48, 53, 57, 61, 64, 67, 72, 79, 82, 88, 94, 104, 109, 115, 121, 127, 133, 138, 154, 158, 161, 165, 171

grammar school *see* school

Grishaugh leet 4, 25

guildhouse/guildhall 5–6, 9–10, 18, 21, 38, 45, 49, 55, 61, 67–8, 70, 73, 75, 139, 176, repair 6, 18, 47, 54, 69, 83, 91, 95, 99, 106, 112–13, 117, 123, 125, 129–31, 144, 150

guilds 1, 5, 7–9

Half Mile bridge 23

headboroughs, of leet 10, 171, of town *see* Seventeen

Hell lane 30, 34, 38, 41, 53, 57, 63, 67, 72, 75, 78

loans to parishioners 3, 54–5, 60, 66, 71, 73, 76–8, 87, 95, 102, 110, 122, 127, 134, 139, 143

manor courts 3, 6, 12, 26

manors, Cromwells 7, 69–70, 149, rents *passim*; Grishaugh 7, 10, 12, 149; Hethersett's *alias* Palgrave's 31, 36, 39, 42, 46, 50; Queen's *alias* King's *alias* Prince's 1–2, 8, 24, 51, 122, rents *passim*; Rusten's 7, 149

market, market place, marketstead, 7, 25, 59, 65, 86, 148, 151, clerk 42, 47, 50, 145, 150, 155, 163, 166, 169, court 77, cross 7, 18–19, 21–2, 62, 65, 155, 163, tolls exemption 22–3, 36, 39, 66, 76, 80, 83, 90, 95–6, 100, 111, 119, 124, 129, 134, 140, 144, 150, 155, 159,163, 166

Mile bridge 23

Norton 2, 25

parish chest 92, 106, 130

parish clerk 14–15, 39, 111–13,

117–19, 122, 124–5, 169
pillory 18, 25, 96, 101
Pople Street 169
school, schoolhouse 1, 3, 5, 9, 12,
     14–15, 18, 20–1, 24, 77, 90–1,
     118, 123–4, 126, 147, 151–2,
     156, 160, 164, 166, scholars 14,
     20–1, 50, 125, 151, steeple and
     cellar 94, 99, 104, 110, 116, 118,
     122, 128, 133, 139, 148, 151,
     154, 159–60
schoolmasters 9,12, 42, 50–1, 54,
     76, 80, 84, 127, 139, 143, 151–2,
     155–6, 163, 166–7. *See also*
     Browne, Castleton, Corball,
     Cudworth, Easton, Firmurie,
     Gary, Leverington, Peacham,
     Taylor, Wells
Seventeen, The 1, 3, 8, 10, 12–13,
     22, 86–7, 90, 101–2, 105–6,
     110–11, 116–17, 122, 129, 140,
     144, 147, 171, composition 5,
     10–11
Silfield 2, 15, 25, 29, 35, 87, 126.
     132, 137, 141, 148, 151
Spooner Row 87
Stanfield 25, 45, 86
stocks 25, 152, 167
Suton 2, 25, 34, 38, 86, 132, 137,
     142, 148

tithes 2, 50
tithings 10
Toly's cross 72, 82, 108
town, origins and governance 2, 6,
     8–12, litigiousness 7, 23, non-
     borough status 6, 26, population
     and area 1, wealth 7–8
Town Green 65, 86, 148, 156
townhouse *see* guildhouse
townlands *passim* in receipt
     accounts, feoffees 1, 3, 7, 9–10,
     12, surveys 105, 144
Tyfford bridge 23, 30, 80
vestry 1, 3, 5, 8–13, 26, income 10,
     meeting-place 5, membership 10
vicar/minister 13, 35, 47–8, 50, 69,
     84. *See also* Agas; Caryngton;
     Wells
Vicar Street 25, 148, 154, 159,
     162, 166
Wattlefield 2, 45, 48, 50, 87, 133,
     138, 143
Westwade bridge 23, 29, 50, 58,
     148–9, 165
workhouse 17–18, 26

Yarmouth, Great 240, 242
Young, John 211–12, 216, 225–7,
     229, William 239